TEST YOUR
CULTURAL
LITERACY
IQ

D1289977

TEST YOUR
CULTURAL
LITERACY
IQ

Previously published as
Test-Prep Your IQ with the
Essentials of Cultural Literacy

DIANE ZAHLER AND
KATHY A. ZAHLER

POCKET BOOKS
New York London Toronto Sydney Singapore

POCKET BOOKS, a division of Simon & Schuster, Inc.
1230 Avenue of the Americas, New York, NY 10020

Copyright © 2003 by Diane Zahler and Kathy A. Zahler

Published by arrangement with Peterson's

ISBN: 0-7434-7578-X

First Pocket Books printing July 2003

10 9 8 7 6 5 4 3 2 1

POCKET and colophon are registered trademarks of
Simon & Schuster, Inc.

Cover design by Tom McKeveny

Manufactured in the United States of America

For information regarding special discounts for bulk
purchases, please contact Simon & Schuster Special Sales
at 1-800-456-6798 or business@simonandschuster.com

ACKNOWLEDGMENTS

Our thanks to PZ, YY, ML, PS, JG, JZ, and SAZ for their expertise, suggestions, and/or support: special thanks to PS and PZ, who answered every question, many of them correctly.

CONTENTS

TEST YOUR
CULTURAL
LITERACY
IQ

INTRODUCTION

Test-Prep Your Cultural Literacy IQ has been written by test-prep experts with two goals in mind:

The first, and the most important, goal of this book is to help you score high on standardized tests. Our proven test-taking strategies will not only help you feel more confident about taking standardized tests but will also improve your performance. This book includes fourteen practice tests so you can practice with your new test-taking strategies. After all, practice makes perfect!

The second goal of this book is to have some fun! Really! And hey, after taking the tests in this book and reading the answers, you'll be more than ready to impress your friends and family. Go ahead—challenge someone to a game of Trivial Pursuit™ or play along with *Jeopardy!*™. And the next time you get stuck with a bunch of intellectual snobs at some party, be confident that you can keep up with the conversation.

Why You Need This Book

Like it or not, multiple-choice tests play a pretty large role in people's lives today—more so than ever before. In truth, high school teachers and college professors are actually *in love* with multiple-choice tests. Think of those pesky Advanced Placement tests and college entrance exams like the SAT and ACT Assessment that all use multiple-choice questions. Bottom line: You can't escape multiple-choice tests, so you might as well have fun while you learn to master them.

What Is Cultural Literacy?

There you are, sitting back in your favorite chair, scanning your favorite magazine, when you come across this phrase:

Here is a man who seemed to have the Midas touch . . .

What's the Midas touch? Do you know? Supposedly, if you're "culturally literate," you would know. Midas was a king who wished that everything he touched would turn to gold. He got his wish, turned his daughter into gold, and then realized that the touch was also a curse. How do we know that? Because we're culturally literate, and soon you will be too! But what exactly do we mean by cultural literacy? Read on . . .

A contemporary writer named E. D. Hirsch started a movement called the "Core Knowledge" movement. Basically, he believed that if students across the nation could learn a "core" of common knowledge, they would be certain to have a fair and solid elementary education. Hirsch wrote a book called *Cultural Literacy: What Every American Needs to Know,* and with this, the phrase "cultural literacy" was coined. You could read for hours about the Core Knowledge movement and cultural literacy on the Web, because there is so much information on it, but we're going to simplify cultural literacy in the following definition, which is all you need to know for this book:

> **Cultural literacy is stuff in the arts, humanities, and history that you (and everyone else) probably know.**

How To Know If You Are Culturally Literate

When you complete a test, use the explanatory answers that follow the test to check your responses. The answers give information for you to determine why your response was correct or incorrect, and you can learn a lot by reading the explanations!

Use the scoring key at the end of this introduction to grade yourself and see how culturally literate you are.

Scoring Key

Give yourself two points for each correct answer.

90–100   *Excellent.* You are culturally literate.

80–89   *Good.* You have more than a passing knowledge of this subject.

70–79 *Fair.* You have a competent grasp of many aspects of this subject.

60–69 *Poor.* You could use some improvement in this area.

Below 60 *Time for cultural literacy training.* See the Bibliography in the back of this book.

TEST-TAKING
STRATEGIES

The Multiple-Choice Test

Many people think that a multiple-choice test simply requires the test-taker to use recognition skills to pick out or recognize facts. Unfortunately, that isn't true—sorry! A multiple-choice test can be simple or very difficult. It can measure recognition skills or it can measure "higher order" thinking skills, such as *application, comprehension, analysis,* or *synthesis.* A well-written multiple-choice test will most likely contain questions that range from simple to difficult and will measure a number of different levels of thinking. So, to be a successful test-taker, you've got to know about the different kinds of multiple-choice questions and the best strategies for answering them. Let's begin with the questions, and then we'll talk briefly about some strategies to help you ace that exam!

A multiple-choice question has two elements:

1. The stem (or question)
2. The answer choices

The stem may be in the form of a question:

EXAMPLE: What painter is considered the "father of modern art"?

Or, the stem may be in the form of an incomplete statement:

EXAMPLE: The "father of modern art" is

In the first case, the correct answer will answer the question that is asked. In the second example, the answer will accurately complete the incomplete statement. For both questions, the answer would be the same: Cézanne. Occasionally, however, multiple-choice stems will contain words such as *except* or *not:*

EXAMPLE: All of the following are associated with ballet *except*

EXAMPLE: Which of the following is *not* associated with ballet?

In cases such as these, the multiple-choice question is essentially a true/false question. The correct answer choice is the one that is *not* true or is the exception to the statement. For example, if "Jon Bon Jovi" was given as an answer choice for either question above, you should choose it because Jon Bon Jovi is a rock star—and is *not* associated with ballet. This may seem overly simple, but these kind of questions often confuse test-takers. Strategies regarding these questions will be addressed later in the chapter.

Answer choices probably won't vary much from test to test as far as format, but there might be one or two small exceptions. First, the questions will usually have either four or five answer choices. Tests in high school or college often will vary and may have either fewer than four or more than five answer choices, depending on the personality of the instructor, the level of difficulty of the test, and the material that is being tested. However, most standardized tests will use either four or five answer choices. The second way tests might differ is how the answers are listed. Some exams will use lettered answer choices (A, B, C, D, and E), while others will use numbered choices (1, 2, 3, 4, and 5). Regardless of how the answers are listed, the strategies for answering the questions remain the same.

Strategies For Answering Multiple-Choice Questions

Unfortunately, there is no one strategy that will enable you to answer correctly *every* question on *every* test you take. And there is no substitute for a solid, working knowledge of the subject matter being tested. In other words, test-taking strategies are going to be most effective when you combine them with good study habits. So, if you're looking for a shortcut that relieves you of actually studying the material being tested, you've come to the wrong place. (And if you ever find that place where no studying is necessary, let us know; we'd love to go there!) That being said, let's look at some of the most effective strategies for taking multiple-choice tests.

1. Read the question carefully. This suggestion seems really obvious, but it is probably the *most important* and the most overlooked strategy. Realizing you answered a question incorrectly because you didn't read it carefully is pretty frustrating. So, read the question carefully, and make sure you know exactly what the question is asking. As you read the question, look for any key words within the stem that have significance. You may also find it helpful to circle the key words in the stem when you see them. This will reinforce the key words in your mind. For example, if the question includes a negative, circle the negative and treat the question as a true/false question. As mentioned earlier, some multiple-choice questions contain negatives like *except* or *not*. When you encounter a negative, circle it, underline it, or put a star by it. First, this will help you remember that there is a negative in the question. Second, this will help you remember that you are looking for a false statement in the answer choices.

EXAMPLE:

All of the following are types of paint (except)

(1) tempera.

(2) charcoal.

(3) oil.

(4) acrylic.

(5) watercolor.

When answering this question, make sure you circle the word *except* so you remember that you are looking for the answer that does not make the stem true. If you were to choose answer choice (2), you would be correct.

2. Try to answer the question in your mind before you look at the answer choices. As you read the question, try to figure out the answer. If you can answer the question in your head and then match that answer to one of the answer choices provided, you can be pretty sure that you have answered the question correctly.

3. Read every answer choice carefully before you make your selection. This is another suggestion that may seem obvious, but it is of the utmost importance. Read every answer choice, even if you think you know the answer. In other words, although you think you know the answer is (B), and (B) may be a *good* answer, (D) may be the *best* answer to the question.

4. Use the process of elimination. If you read all of the answer choices, and you still don't know the correct answer right away, use the process of elimination to narrow your choices. Usually, multiple-choice questions will have a set of answer choices that includes a very unlikely answer, one or two poor answers, a possible answer, and a best answer. You should read through the answer choices and cross out any that you are sure are incorrect. The more you can narrow down the choices, the better your odds if you have to guess. Most of the time, you will be able to narrow the choices to two or three possible answers. With these odds (1:2 or 1:3), guessing will usually produce a higher score than if you leave the question unanswered.

EXAMPLE:

Of the following, who is a writer?

(A) Chewbacca the Wookie

(B) Kermit the Frog

(C) Genghis Khan

(D) The Old Woman Who Lived in a Shoe

(E) Dave Barry

The correct answer is (E). Even if you've never heard of Dave Barry, we're hoping you were able to figure out that the other choices definitely are *not* writers!

5. Beware of answer choices that seem to mean the same thing. If, when you are reading through all of the answer choices, you find two choices that seem to say the same thing, only in different words, be careful about choosing either of the two as your answer. When two answer choices seem unusually similar or when two answer choices seem almost identical, both choices are probably incorrect.

EXAMPLE:

The term "politically correct" has come to mean

(1) repressive and reactionary.

(2) unusually sensitive to racism and sexism.

(3) belonging to the party in power.

(4) definitely left-wing.

(5) bowing to the opinion of the party in power.

If you read through this example carefully, you probably noticed that choices (3) and (5) say practically the same thing. Even if you aren't sure if these answers are correct, logically, only one answer can be correct. Therefore, if two choices say the same thing and you can't choose two answer choices, your correct answer is another answer choice. The correct answer is (2), for this example.

6. Watch for answer choices that are different by only one or two words yet have opposite meanings. One or two words can completely change the meaning of a phrase or sentence. When you find two answer choices that are similar in construction except for one or two words, the two answer choices are usually opposites. The one- or two-word difference will probably have a world of difference in meaning—so watch out!

EXAMPLE:

As of the end of the 2002 season, Barry Bonds holds which of the following major league records?

(A) The single season home run record

(B) The career home run record

(C) Most hits against Nolan Ryan

(D) Most teams played for in a career

(E) The longest home run ever at Dodger Stadium

If you read these answer choices carefully, you probably noticed that answer choices (1) and (2) vary only by the words *single season* and *career*. Choice (A) is correct; but if you did not read all of the choices carefully, you might have chosen choice (B), which only slightly varies from choice (A), but is incorrect.

7. Take the question at face value. Take each question at face value and don't try to read too much into it. Don't try to "read between the lines" or overanalyze what the question is asking. By overanalyzing, you run the risk of misinterpreting the question, thereby seriously decreasing your chances of choosing the correct answer. There are such things as trick questions. You can find them on all sorts of tests. You want to be on the lookout, but don't obsess by looking for a trick question around every corner.

8. Look for absolutes within the answer choices. As you read through all the answer choices, watch for absolutes such as *all, never, none,* and *always.* These are absolutes because these words leave no room for exceptions of any kind. Unless you specifically remember a major point of emphasis on whatever the subject of the question is, the answer choice or choices containing an absolute are probably not correct:

EXAMPLE:

Which of the following can be said of American colonists under British rule?

(1) All colonists wanted to be free of British rule.

(2) All colonists wanted to drink tea.

(3) Colonists were never forced to board British soldiers.

(4) Colonists who were unhappy with British rule organized to fight for freedom.

(5) Colonists were always very unhappy with British rule.

If you read the answer choices carefully, you probably noticed that choices (1), (2), (3), and (5) contain absolutes. Therefore, you can be fairly certain that these are incorrect. You probably already knew that (4) is the correct answer, but in case you didn't, you could have figured it out with the strategy in the paragraph above.

9. Don't spend too much time on any one question. Practically all standardized tests have a time limit. This means that you, as the test-taker, must manage your time wisely. It isn't uncommon for a test to require an average of less than one minute per answer. Therefore, if you encounter a question that really stumps you, put a star next to it and move on. If you have time to work on it after you answer all the other questions, go back to it. It is much more productive to spend your time answering other questions than spending precious time struggling with one.

EXAMPLE:

What was the first race horse to win 1 million dollars in his career?

(A) Man o' War

(B) Secretariat

(C) Citation

(D) Cigar

(E) Gallant Fox

Do you know the answer to this question? If so, kudos to you. If not, do you really think you'll figure it out by just staring at the answer choices? Probably not. Therefore, why spend precious time racking your brain on this question when you could be answering other questions? On this IQ test, you can guess as we don't penalize you for wrong answers.

10. **Don't change your answers.** The oldest test-taking strategy in the history of test-taking strategies is "go with your first choice." If you choose an answer and then feel an urge to change the answer later, the urge is probably just nerves. Don't second-guess yourself. There was probably a reason you chose the answer you did. Therefore, don't change an answer unless you are absolutely,

positively sure that the answer you chose is incorrect *and* you are positively sure you know which
answer is correct.

The Answer Sheet

On standardized tests that are used on a statewide
or nationwide level, computer-read answer sheets
are provided for you to mark your answers. When
you use answer sheets, much like the ones provided
in this book, there are a few important things to
remember. First, completely fill in the circle of your
choice with your pencil. The sheets are "read" and
graded by a computer, so it's important that your
mark is clear and complete. A check in the circle or
an X marked through it might not be readable by
the machine and possibly won't be counted, even if
your answer is correct. See below for an example of
an answer sheet and the correct way to fill in your
answers (you'll see some incorrect examples there,
too). Be sure to mark only one circle per question.
Do not skip lines by mistake, because one misplaced
mark can make every answer following it wrong.

1.Ⓐ●ⒸⒹ   2.ⒶⒷⒸ●   3.Ⓐ●ⒸⒹ   4.●ⒷⒸⒹ   5.ⒶⒷⒸⒹ
6.ⒶⒷⒸⒹ   7.ⒶⒷⒸⒹ   8.ⒶⒷⒸⒹ   9.ⒶⒷⒸⒹ   10.ⒶⒷ●Ⓓ
11.Ⓐ●ⒸⒹ   12.ⒶⒷ●Ⓓ   13.●ⒷⒸⒹ   14.ⒶⒷ●Ⓓ   15.ⒶⒷⒸⒹ

Numbers 1–4 are marked correctly. Numbers 10–14 are
marked incorrectly.

Good Luck!

TEST 1
CONCEIVED IN LIBERTY: AMERICAN HISTORY

A people without history is like the wind on the buffalo grass.

—SIOUX SAYING

1. Which three states were among those that seceded from the Union to form the Confederacy?
   (A) Kentucky, Mississippi, and West Virginia
   (B) South Carolina, Florida, and Ohio
   (C) Alabama, Tennessee, and Georgia
   (D) Virginia, Maryland, and Delaware

2. What happened at Pearl Harbor on December 7, 1941?
   (A) Japanese forces bombed a U.S. naval base.
   (B) The Atlantic Charter was signed by Winston S. Churchill and Franklin D. Roosevelt.
   (C) The first atomic bomb was completed.
   (D) The U.S. fleet set sail to recapture the Philippines from the Japanese.

3. The precursor of the U.S. Constitution was
   (A) the Declaration of Independence.
   (B) the Emancipation Proclamation.
   (C) the Mayflower Compact.
   (D) the Articles of Confederation.

4. The Missouri Compromise determined that Missouri could become a state if
   (A) slavery was prohibited throughout the rest of the Louisiana Purchase north of Missouri.
   (B) slavery was outlawed within the state.
   (C) the Indians of Missouri signed a peace treaty with the government.
   (D) the inhabitants renounced their alliance with France.

5. The Open Door policy required that
   (A) all nations must welcome immigrants from China.
   (B) no nation could claim exclusive trading rights in China.
   (C) reporters must be allowed to observe the effects of the Chinese Cultural Revolution.
   (D) the United States and the Soviet Union must conduct cultural exchanges.

6. The Bay of Pigs episode took place when
   (A) Cuban exiles from Florida landed in Cuba in an attempt to overthrow Fidel Castro.
   (B) U.S. troops invaded Mexico in pursuit of Pancho Villa.
   (C) UN forces undertook an amphibious landing behind enemy lines in Korea.
   (D) U.S. marines were sent by President Lyndon Johnson to the Dominican Republic.

7. The first Thanksgiving was celebrated to give thanks for
   (A) the rescue of Captain John Smith by Poca-hontas.
   (B) the establishment of the colony at Jamestown.
   (C) the survival of the Plymouth Pilgrims through their first year.
   (D) the unification of the thirteen American colonies.

8. U.S. forces fought in Europe in World War I during which of the following years?
   (A) 1914–1918
   (B) 1914–1921
   (C) 1917–1918
   (D) 1917–1921

9. The term "Seward's Folly" refers to
   (A) the purchase of Alaska negotiated by Secretary of State William Seward.
   (B) the impeachment of Andrew Johnson urged by Secretary of State William Seward.
   (C) the cornering of gold by financier George Seward, which led to the stock market crash of 1869.
   (D) the Great Fire of Chicago, which started in Seward's Tavern.

10. What happened on July 4, 1776?
   (A) The first shots of the American Revolution were fired.
   (B) The treaty ending the American Revolution was signed.
   (C) The Continental Congress adopted the Declaration of Independence.
   (D) The Continental Congress adopted the Constitution.

11. The Korean War was a conflict between
   (A) North Korea, supported by the United States, and South Korea, supported by China.
   (B) South Korea, supported by the United States, and North Korea, supported by China and the Soviet Union.
   (C) Korea, supported by the United States, and China.
   (D) South Korea, supported by the United States, and North Korea, supported by the Chinese Nationalists.

12. In the Dred Scott case, the Supreme Court ruled that
   (A) an escaped slave could be forcibly returned to his master.
   (B) segregated facilities in public places were legal.
   (C) no slave could claim U.S. citizenship.
   (D) public schools must be desegregated.

13. Why is the year 1492 important in American history?
    (A) In 1492, Henry Hudson sailed up the Hudson River to New York.
    (B) In 1492, the first English colony was established at Jamestown.
    (C) In 1492 the Spanish settled St. Augustine, the first colony in America.
    (D) In 1492, Christopher Columbus landed in the New World.

14. What event or events resulted in the scandal called Irangate?
    (A) The CIA made secret deals with Iran's Ayatollah Khomeini to obtain the release of U.S. hostages held in Tehran.
    (B) U.S. officials sold arms to Iran and funneled the profits to Nicaraguan *contra* guerrillas.
    (C) President Ronald Reagan authorized a break-in at Democratic Party National Headquarters.
    (D) U.S. forces attempted to rescue hostages in Iran but failed.

15. What was the final result of the political rivalry between Alexander Hamilton and Aaron Burr?
    (A) A duel in which Alexander Hamilton was shot and killed.
    (B) An election in which Aaron Burr became vice president.
    (C) A duel in which both men were wounded.
    (D) A feud that forced Alexander Hamilton to flee to Canada.

16. What was the initial purpose of the League of Nations?
    (A) It was intended to reduce Germany's power after World War II.
    (B) It was intended to found a Jewish homeland after World War II.
    (C) It was intended to combat the growing threat of Germany and Italy before World War I.
    (D) It was intended to preserve peace after World War I.

17. The United States acquired California, Nevada, Utah, and parts of Texas, Arizona, Colorado, New Mexico, and Wyoming as a result of
    (A) the Gadsden Purchase of 1853.
    (B) the Mexican War of the 1840s.
    (C) the Land Grant Act of 1862.
    (D) the Louisiana Purchase of 1803.

18. What happened at My Lai, Vietnam, in 1968?
    (A) Communist troops attacked the town, resulting in the Tet offensive.
    (B) Peace talks began among the Viet Cong, the South Vietnamese, the North Vietnamese, and the Americans.
    (C) Ngo Dinh Diem, president of South Vietnam, was assassinated.
    (D) Lieutenant William Calley, Jr. led an attack that resulted in the massacre of twenty-two South Vietnamese.

19. For what is Senator Joseph McCarthy best known?
    (A) Running unsuccessfully for president in 1972.
    (B) Playing a leading part in the settling of the Oregon Territory.
    (C) Leading investigations of numerous people suspected of being Communists in the 1950s.
    (D) Opposing American involvement in the Vietnam War in the 1960s.

20. The French and Indian War was a conflict between
    (A) France and India over control of the spice trade.
    (B) French Canadians and the Iroquois Nation.
    (C) England and France in the worldwide struggle for an empire.
    (D) French settlers and their Carib slaves.

21. Four presidents of the United States have been assassinated while in office. Who were they?
    (A) Abraham Lincoln, James A. Garfield, William McKinley, and John F. Kennedy
    (B) William McKinley, Andrew Johnson, John F. Kennedy, and Franklin Roosevelt
    (C) Abraham Lincoln, John F. Kennedy, James Madison, and Millard Fillmore
    (D) William Henry Harrison, Abraham Lincoln, Martin Van Buren, and James Buchanan

22. The "energy crisis" of the 1970s was primarily caused by
    (A) the embargo of Arab oil shipments to the United States.
    (B) the failure of the Alaska pipeline.
    (C) the explosion of the Three Mile Island nuclear power plant.
    (D) the massive increase in the number of automobiles owned by Americans.

23. What was the League of the Iroquois?
    (A) An Indian congress formed to oppose the resettlement of Indians on reservations
    (B) A group of Plains Indians who united to oppose white settlement
    (C) A group of five eastern Indian tribes that shared a common language
    (D) A community of pueblo-dwelling Indians who lived by farming

24. What was Custer's Last Stand?
    (A) A steel mill strike at Homestead, Pennsylvania, in which eighteen people were killed
    (B) The battle of Little Big Horn, in which 264 soldiers were killed
    (C) The siege of the Alamo by Mexicans under Santa Ana
    (D) The attack on Harper's Ferry by abolitionists

25. Theodore Roosevelt's "trustbusting" efforts were directed against
   (A) political opponents who tried to destroy the public's trust in elected officials.
   (B) stock market speculators who made investments without security to back them up.
   (C) huge corporations that prevented competition in business.
   (D) political machines that controlled power in major American cities.

26. Which one of these statements is true?
   (A) The United States gave Iraqi leader Saddam Hussein financial and military aid until just weeks before the Gulf War began.
   (B) Before its invasion by Iraq, Kuwait was a democracy.
   (C) On the eve of the Gulf War, more than 50 percent of Americans polled supported entering into a war with Iraq.
   (D) When the January 15, 1990, deadline for Iraq's withdrawal from Kuwait had passed, the Bush administration decided to strike militarily.

27. In U.S. history, *Prohibition* meant
   (A) the closing of U.S. borders to new immigrants.
   (B) the outlawing of slavery.
   (C) laws forbidding the manufacture and sale of alcoholic beverages.
   (D) state regulations against collective bargaining.

28. The War of 1812 was primarily caused by
    (A) Britain's interference with American commerce.
    (B) Napoleon's sale of the Louisiana Territory.
    (C) Jefferson's refusal to serve a third term.
    (D) the colonists' desire to be free of British rule.

29. The New Deal was the name given to
    (A) Theodore Roosevelt's foreign policy.
    (B) Harry S. Truman's domestic programs.
    (C) Franklin D. Roosevelt's social and economic reforms.
    (D) Lyndon B. Johnson's social programs.

30. In his Emancipation Proclamation, Abraham Lincoln
    (A) declared that the slaves in the Confederate States would henceforth be considered free.
    (B) announced the withdrawal of Union troops from the South.
    (C) dedicated a cemetery in Pennsylvania.
    (D) declared war on the Confederacy.

31. An immigrant arriving at Ellis Island in 1900 was most likely to be from which of the following places?
    (A) England or Ireland
    (B) Scandinavia
    (C) Latin America
    (D) Eastern Europe

32. Which of the following statements is *not* true of the Spanish-American War?
    (A) The United States asked Spain to withdraw from Cuba.
    (B) Theodore Roosevelt was involved in the fighting.
    (C) Guam and Puerto Rico became U.S. territories.
    (D) Germany aided the Nationalists.

33. The pony express was no longer needed after
    (A) coast-to-coast telegraph lines were completed.
    (B) cattle rustling became a federal offense.
    (C) wagon trains began to head west.
    (D) Texas was admitted to the Union.

34. The town of Salem, Massachussetts, is perhaps best known for which of the following?
    (A) Paul Revere's ride in 1775
    (B) The St. Valentine's Day Massacre of 1929
    (C) Witchcraft trials in 1692
    (D) The Triangle Shirtwaist Company fire of 1911

35. U.S. military involvement in Vietnam followed
    (A) the defeat of the French and partition of the country in 1954.
    (B) the Tet Offensive in 1968.
    (C) the death of Ho Chi Minh in 1969.
    (D) the invasion of Cambodia by Vietnamese forces in 1978.

36. Valley Forge was the site of an encampment by
    (A) Union troops under Grant during the winter of 1863.
    (B) federal troops under Lee preceding the Harper's Ferry raid.
    (C) British forces under Cornwallis in 1783.
    (D) the Continental army under Washington in 1777–1778.

37. The Monroe Doctrine and its "Roosevelt corollary" were used to
    (A) lower tariffs and make trade with Europe easier.
    (B) provide incentives for farmers to switch to ranching.
    (C) support policies of European exclusion and American domination in the Western Hemisphere.
    (D) allow the United States to abandon isolationism and form alliances.

38. An oil reserve called Teapot Dome gave its name to
    (A) a scandal involving bribery during the Harding administration.
    (B) a corrupt group of New York City Democrats under Boss Tweed.
    (C) an energy commission set up by Jimmy Carter.
    (D) an act of rebellion by Boston colonists.

39. The Watergate scandal began when
    (A) Richard Nixon resigned the presidency under pressure from Congress.
    (B) five men were arrested for breaking into an office.
    (C) a U.S. pilot was caught running guns to Nicaragua.
    (D) the House Un-American Activities Committee discovered Communist sympathizers in the Senate.

40. Aided by an Indian woman named Sacajawea, Meriwether Lewis and William Clark
    (A) led a party of explorers to the fountain of youth.
    (B) defeated Chief Sitting Bull at Little Bighorn.
    (C) charted a route from Missouri to the Pacific.
    (D) searched for the headwaters of the Hudson River.

41. Carpetbaggers, scalawags, and the Ku Klux Klan were groups that flourished during the Reconstruction period
    (A) between the World Wars.
    (B) after the Civil War.
    (C) in the post-Depression years.
    (D) following the American Revolution.

42. During the Boston Tea Party,
    (A) John Brown led an uprising in support of abo-
        litionism.
    (B) thousands protested the execution of Sacco
        and Vanzetti.
    (C) colonists protested taxation by the British.
    (D) Minutemen celebrated their siege of Boston.

43. Which of the following was *not* a result of the
    Homestead Act?
    (A) The Midwest experienced a great increase in
        population.
    (B) Steelworkers achieved the right to organize
        unions.
    (C) U.S. agricultural production increased dra-
        matically.
    (D) People with little money were able to own
        land.

44. What important event took place in Seneca Falls,
    New York, in 1848?
    (A) Women met to call for their rights as citizens.
    (B) The Johnstown Flood killed over two thou-
        sand people.
    (C) A revelation led Joseph Smith to create the
        Book of Mormon.
    (D) The Erie Canal was completed.

45. Which country has the United States occupied militarily?
    (A) Haiti
    (B) Grenada
    (C) Nicaragua
    (D) All of the above

46. The gold rush of 1848
    (A) justified the purchase of Alaska.
    (B) ensured the conversion of paper money to gold.
    (C) brought 100,000 settlers into a new territory.
    (D) made millionaires of Andrew Carnegie and John D. Rockefeller.

47. Which of the following was *not* an episode in the civil rights movement of the 1950s and 1960s?
    (A) The enactment of the Jim Crow laws
    (B) The March on Washington
    (C) The passage of the Voting Rights Act
    (D) The "freedom rides"

48. Harriet Tubman is primarily known for
    (A) founding the first college for black students.
    (B) spying for Confederate forces during the Civil War.
    (C) leading slaves north on the Underground Railroad.
    (D) her work with the suffragist movement.

49. Through the Marshall Plan, the United States
    (A) aided European economies after World War II.
    (B) supplied arms to developing nations in the 1970s.
    (C) allied with France and Great Britain in 1917.
    (D) developed plans for the League of Nations.

50. The term *isolationism* describes
    (A) American foreign policy during the 1970s and 1980s.
    (B) a military theory best paraphrased as "divide and conquer."
    (C) an ideal economic balance between nations.
    (D) a policy of nonintervention in other countries' affairs.

TEST 1:
Explanatory Answers

1. The correct answer is (C). The states that seceded from the Union in 1860–1861 to form the Confederacy were Mississippi, Florida, Alabama, Georgia, Louisiana, Texas, Virginia, Arkansas, Tennessee, North Carolina, and South Carolina. Parts of Kentucky and Missouri also seceded: their representatives were seated in the Confederate Congress.

2. The correct answer is (A). On December 7, 1941, Japanese bombers attacked the American naval base at Pearl Harbor, Hawaii, sinking or damaging nineteen ships and killing twenty-three hundred soldiers and civilians. On December 8, the United States declared war on Japan.

3. The correct answer is (D). By the Articles of Confederation, adopted at the second Continental Congress in 1777, the states united in a "firm league of friendship." A one-house congress was created in which each state had one vote; however, no provision was made for a president or a federal court system.

4. The correct answer is (A). When Missouri sought to become a state in 1820, the Union was equally divided between slave states and free states. To maintain the balance, legislators worked out a compromise by which Missouri slave owners could keep their slaves but slavery was outlawed through-

out the rest of the Louisiana Purchase north of Missouri.

5. The correct answer is (B). In 1899, the United States, concerned about being excluded by the European powers from trading with China, proposed the Open Door policy, under which all nations interested in trading with China would have equal trading rights. The policy was rarely honored by any of the nations involved.

6. The correct answer is (A). In 1961, U.S. President John F. Kennedy approved a plan prepared under the Eisenhower administration to land American-trained Cuban exiles in Cuba in an attempt to overthrow the government of Fidel Castro. The landing—at the Bay of Pigs—was a failure, and many of the invaders were killed or captured. Many Cuban exiles later blamed their loss on a lack of U.S. military air support.

7. The correct answer is (C). After their first year at Plymouth in 1620–1621, during which half of the colonists died, the Pilgrims celebrated in the fall with a feast from the crops the local Indians helped them grow.

8. The correct answer is (C). Although World War I began in Europe in 1914, the United States remained neutral until April 1917, when German submarine attacks at last led President Woodrow Wilson to seek a declaration of war. The fighting in Europe continued until November 11, 1918.

9. The correct answer is (A). In 1867, William Seward negotiated the purchase of Alaska from Russia for

$7.2 million; this was called "Seward's Folly" because, until the discovery of gold and oil in Alaska, Americans could not see any use for the distant, frozen territory.

10. The correct answer is (C). The Declaration of Independence, which declared the American colonies' independence from Great Britain, was adopted on July 4, 1776, a date that is now a national holiday—the Fourth of July (or Independence Day).

11. The correct answer is (B). After World War II, the Soviet Union occupied northern Korea, and the United States occupied southern Korea. Separate North Korean and South Korean states were established. In June 1950, the North Korean army invaded South Korea; UN and U.S. troops fought back. China later entered the war on the side of North Korea; the fighting continued until a ceasefire was reached in 1953.

12. The correct answer is (C). Dred Scott, a slave from Missouri, sued for his freedom in 1847 after having been taken to live in a free state. The case eventually went to the Supreme Court, which, in 1857, ruled that Scott and all other slaves were merely property and had no claim to the rights of citizenship. This decision encouraged Southern slaveholders. However, it infuriated many Northerners, who believed that slaves were not property but "persons held to service by state laws." These Northerners contended that, in the case of slaves, the government's duty was not to defend property but to protect liberty.

13. The correct answer is (D). In October 1492, three small ships commanded by Christopher Columbus reached the Bahamas, making Europe's first documented contact with the Americas.

14. The correct answer is (B). In 1979, the leftist Sandinista National Liberation Front took power in Nicaragua. Right-wing leaders soon organized the so-called *contra* guerrillas to fight the Sandinistas, often from base camps in neighboring countries. The U.S. Congress forbade the administration of President Ronald Reagan from providing the *contras* with U.S. government funding, but administration officials sought to circumvent the ban by raising money from private sources. Oliver North, a Marine colonel, was put in charge of the secret project. Meanwhile, in a seemingly unrelated development, officials of the U.S. National Security Council began selling arms clandestinely (in opposition to stated U.S. policy) to Iran in the hope that Iran would pressure guerrillas in Lebanon to release U.S. hostages. These secret sales produced profits, which North and others began funneling to the *contra* leaders. Late in 1986, news stories about these arrangements began to surface. In November, for the first time, congressional leaders were briefed about the arms sale. In December, President Reagan agreed to appoint an independent counsel to investigate the entire affair. A 23-count indictment was brought against North and other officials. North was eventually convicted, but his conviction was overturned on appeal. Indictments and

trials of other officials continued into the early 1990s.

15. The correct answer is (A). In 1804, Alexander Hamilton, a liberal who advocated a strong federal government, and Aaron Burr, who believed in states' rights, fought a duel in Weehawken, New Jersey, that ended in Hamilton's death. The duel took place because Burr blamed his loss of an election campaign on Hamilton's criticism of his character.

16. The correct answer is (D). President Woodrow Wilson proposed the creation of the League of Nations to preserve the hard-won post–World War I peace. Ironically, however, the United States never became a member because the U.S. Senate refused to ratify the Versailles Peace Treaty, which established the League.

17. The correct answer is (B). In 1845, the United States annexed most of what is now Texas; disputes over the remainder soon led to war, and in 1848, Mexico ceded claim to much of what is now the American West and Southwest.

18. The correct answer is (D). In March 1968, Lieutenant Calley led an attack on the village of My Lai that led to the murder of twenty-two Vietnamese civilians. Calley was convicted of premeditated murder in 1971 and sentenced to life in prison, a sentence that was later reduced to twenty years. The incident galvanized antiwar sentiment in the United States.

19. The correct answer is (C). During the mid-1950s, Senator Joseph R. McCarthy, a Wisconsin Republican, leveled charges of Communist sympathy or conspiracy against numerous officials, writers, journalists, teachers, and others. In 1953–1954, he headed the House Committee on Un-American Activities, which investigated many suspected Communists. McCarthy's accusations were frequently unsubstantiated, but many Americans lost their jobs or went to jail as a result of "McCarthyism."

20. The correct answer is (C). The French and Indian War (1754–1763) was a North American extension of a conflict that was then taking place in Europe between France and England, a conflict called the Seven Years' War. The French allied with local Indians and sought control of the Ohio Valley. However, the British were eventually victorious, and France lost its territory both in the Ohio Valley and in Canada.

21. The correct answer is (A). On April 14, 1865, Abraham Lincoln was shot in Washington, D.C.; he died on April 15. On July 2, 1881, James A. Garfield was shot in Washington, D.C.; he died on September 12. On September 6, 1901, William McKinley was shot in Buffalo, New York; he died on September 14. On November 22, 1963, John F. Kennedy was shot and killed in Dallas, Texas.

22. The correct answer is (A). After the Arab-Israeli War of 1973, Arab nations refused for a time to

ship oil to the United States, which had supported
Israel. This embargo sparked a shortage that raised
prices sharply and caused an economic recession.

23. The correct answer is (C). The League of the Iro-
    quois, which lasted for hundreds of years, included
    the Cayugas, the Mohawks, the Oneidas, the
    Onondagas, and the Senecas and was established
    to bring an end to destructive warfare among these
    tribes of the eastern seaboard.

24. The correct answer is (B). In June 1876, General
    George Custer and his Seventh Cavalry were killed
    to the last man in this Dakota Territory battle
    against the Sioux Indians.

25. The correct answer is (C). The formation of the
    U.S. Steel Corporation and of the Northern Securi-
    ties Company in 1901 alerted President Roosevelt
    to the fact that through great monopolies, or
    "trusts," control of the nation's economy was pass-
    ing into the hands of just a few individuals. Roo-
    sevelt's efforts against trusts later led to the Clayton
    Antitrust Act of 1914.

26. The correct answer is (A). The United States sup-
    ported Saddam Hussein in the Iran-Iraq War, and
    only withdrew financial and advisory support com-
    pletely when Iraq invaded Kuwait. Supporting
    Kuwait might have been embarrassing had anyone
    in the United States paid attention to that nation's
    antidemocratic policies, which culminated in the
    arrests of many pro-democracy leaders only weeks
    before the Iraqi invasion. In fact, fewer than 50

percent of Americans supported the war; most hoped to see a Mideast Peace Conference that would end the hostilities before the United States became involved. Even the Senate was deeply divided over the issue. This changed only when it became clear that the United States would win decisively. After a brief experiment with sanctions, the United States urged the United Nations to support setting a deadline for Iraq's withdrawal from Kuwait. The choice of Martin Luther King's birthday for this deadline incensed many African-Americans, who would prove to be the staunchest supporters of the peace movement. George Bush revealed months after the war, however, that he had decided to strike militarily and had, in fact, approved a timetable for such action much earlier, in October 1990.

27. The correct answer is (C). Temperance movements gained strength in the early 1900s, culminating after World War I in the Eighteenth Amendment and the Volstead Act. The Amendment stated that "the manufacture, sale, or transportation of intoxicating liquors . . . is hereby prohibited." In 1933, the Twenty-first Amendment repealed Prohibition.

28. The correct answer is (A). The United States asked for neutral shipping rights during hostilities between France and Great Britain, but the British confiscated U.S. ships and generally interfered with trade. In 1812, Congress declared war on Great Britain. The war was unpopular and costly for both sides. A peace treaty was signed in December

1814, but the real end of the war came with Andrew Jackson's defeat of British troops at the Battle of New Orleans in January 1815.

29. The correct answer is (C). The "New Deal" was designed in the early 1930s by the Roosevelt administration to enable the United States to recover from the Great Depression. It consisted of regulatory policies, emergency organizations, public work projects, and social and economic legislation.

30. The correct answer is (A). The Emancipation Proclamation in fact freed no one; it proclaimed the freeing of slaves in areas no longer loyal to the Union. Nevertheless, it guided the actions of the Union army, which liberated the slaves in each new territory that came under its control.

31. The correct answer is (D). Whereas the majority of earlier immigrants had arrived from northern and western Europe, ports of entry now saw a dramatic increase in people from eastern Europe, southern Europe, and Asia. These immigrants were considered undesirable by nativist groups, and lobbying by these groups led to strict quotas on immigrants in the 1920s.

32. The correct answer is (D). Nazi Germany aided the Nationalists in the Spanish Civil War (1936–1939), a war that involved volunteers from many countries. The Spanish-American War (1898) pitted the United States against Spain over Spain's harsh treatment of Cuban rebels. The sinking of the

U.S.S. *Maine* in the harbor of Havana set the stage for war. Theodore Roosevelt and his Rough Riders fought a major battle on San Juan Hill in Cuba in July. Eventual U.S. victory led to U.S. control of Cuba, Puerto Rico, Guam, and the Philippines.

33. The correct answer is (A). A horse-and-rider system of mail delivery sped mail from Missouri to the West Coast in a little over a week. After transcontinental telegraph service began in 1861, the pony express was phased out.

34. The correct answer is (C). In 1692, three girls in Salem claimed to be possessed by Satan. Their accusations of neighbors led to the execution of nineteen people for witchcraft.

35. The correct answer is (A). After French colonial forces in Indochina were defeated by Nationalists and Communists, France withdrew and the country was divided into South Vietnam and Communist-led North Vietnam. President Eisenhower sent American advisers to train the South Vietnamese army, thus initiating twenty years of American involvement in the region.

36. The correct answer is (D). Following a disastrous campaign in Philadelphia and Germantown, George Washington's troops wintered at Valley Forge, Pennsylvania, in 1777–1778.

37. The correct answer is (C). Under the Monroe Doctrine (1823), the United States regarded any European intervention or attempt at colonization of the Americas as an act of aggression. In 1904, Presi-

dent Theodore Roosevelt proclaimed a "corollary" asserting the right of the United States to act as an "international police power" in the Americas and to intervene militarily anywhere in the region whenever circumstances required it.

38. The correct answer is (A). The assignment of oil field leases to the highest briber by Secretary of the Interior Albert Fall led to one of the greatest scandals in American politics. Fall was convicted in 1929.

39. The correct answer is (B). On June 17, 1972, five men were found breaking into Democratic party headquarters in the Watergate apartment complex in Washington, D.C. Accusations of involvement of high officials in the Nixon administration led to Nixon's resignation in 1974.

40. The correct answer is (C). Meriwether Lewis and William Clark were commissioned by the U.S. government to map the lands between St. Louis and the Pacific. Their trip took two years (1804–1806). Sacajawea, a Shoshone, served as a guide and interpreter for much of the journey.

41. The correct answer is (B). After the end of the Civil War, economic and political power in the war-ravaged Southern states was wielded by Northern businessmen (carpetbaggers) who sought financial gain amid the ruined economy, and Southern white Republicans (scalawags), who supported the federal government. Other Southern whites organized the Ku Klux Klan, a racist terrorist group that aimed to prevent Southern blacks from voting.

42. The correct answer is (C). The Boston Tea Party of
    1773 was a protest by colonists against Britain's
    high tax on tea. Protestors stole aboard British
    ships in Boston harbor, seized their cargoes of tea,
    and threw the tea overboard. The British govern-
    ment's retaliatory measures led to the convening of
    the First Continental Congress.

43. The correct answer is (B). The Homestead Act of
    1862 granted 160 acres of land to any settler who
    would spend five years on the land. To take advan-
    tage of this offer, great numbers of people—many
    of them property-less immigrants—moved into the
    Midwest in the 1860s and 1870s. The new farms
    they established resulted in a huge increase in agri-
    cultural production.

44. The correct answer is (A). The Seneca Falls Con-
    vention was organized by the great women's rights
    advocate Elizabeth Cady Stanton. The convention
    produced a declaration of women's rights drafted
    by Stanton, Lucretia Mott, and other suffragists.

45. The correct answer is (D). From 1915 to 1934,
    Haiti was occupied by U.S. Marines. U.S. troops
    invaded Grenada in 1983. Nicaragua was occupied
    by U.S. forces from 1855 to 1857, and the United
    States maintained a military presence there from
    1912 to 1933, with increased forces added in 1926.

46. The correct answer is (C). The newly formed terri-
    tory of California was invaded by thousands of
    prospectors after gold was discovered at Sutter's
    Mill in 1848. Although few found gold, the new

population was enough to force the issue of state-hood for the new territory.

47. The correct answer is (A). The Jim Crow laws were passed by Southern states during the Reconstruction era. They were designed to segregate blacks from whites in public facilities. Civil rights activists worked to eliminate these laws in the 1950s and 1960s.

48. The correct answer is (C). Harriet Tubman, herself an escaped slave, led more than three hundred slaves to freedom on the Underground Railroad before working as a spy for Union forces during the Civil War.

49. The correct answer is (A). The Marshall Plan, also known as the European Recovery Program, was a program supported by Secretary of State George Marshall and designed to promote the economic recovery of Europe following World War II. More than $12 billion in economic aid was distributed between 1948 and 1952.

50. The correct answer is (D). Isolationism was the keystone of U.S. foreign policy in much of the nineteenth century and during the years immediately following World War I.

TEST 2
WHAT'S PAST IS PROLOGUE: WORLD HISTORY

History is the witness that testifies to the passing of time; it illumines reality, vitalizes memory, provides guidance in daily life, and brings us tidings of antiquity.

—Marcus Tullius Cicero

1. Simón Bolívar was a hero of the
   (A) American Revolution.
   (B) Spanish civil war.
   (C) South American wars of independence.
   (D) era of exploration during the Spanish Golden Age.

2. The major result of the Peloponnesian Wars was
   (A) Athens's loss of supremacy.
   (B) Julius Caesar's fall from power.
   (C) the rise of Islam in the Middle East and North Africa.
   (D) the establishment of the Ottoman Empire.

3. Which of the following was *not* a result of South Africa's policy of apartheid?
   (A) South Africa left the British Commonwealth.
   (B) Black Africans in South Africa were forbidden to own businesses.
   (C) Black Africans in South Africa were resettled in "homelands."
   (D) Asians and black Africans in South Africa were forced to live in separate areas.

4. The revolutions of 1848 took place in
   (A) France, Germany, Austria, and Italy.
   (B) England and Ireland.
   (C) Venezuela, Brazil, and Ecuador.
   (D) Lithuania and Latvia.

5. The World War II coalition known as the Axis consisted of which of the following?
   (A) The United States, Great Britain, and France
   (B) The Soviet Union and Germany
   (C) The neutral nations
   (D) Germany, Italy, and Japan

6. Where did "Operation Just Cause" take place?
   (A) Iraq
   (B) Panama
   (C) Grenada
   (D) Los Angeles

7. An important event during the reign of Henry VIII was
   (A) the English civil war.
   (B) the signing of the Magna Carta.
   (C) the Wars of the Roses.
   (D) the creation of the Church of England.

8. Which of the following was *not* a result of the Russian Revolution of 1917?
   (A) The Bolsheviks came to power under Lenin.
   (B) Czar Nicholas and his family were executed.
   (C) Karl Marx became head of the First International.
   (D) Russia signed a peace treaty with Germany and withdrew from World War I.

9. The term *Third World* is applied to
   (A) any area found after the discovery of the New World.
   (B) a cartel of Commonwealth nations and NATO nations.
   (C) any country in Africa or South America.
   (D) nations that are economically underdeveloped.

10. Mohandas (Mahatma) Gandhi is famous for
    (A) resisting British rule in India.
    (B) leading India at the turn of the century.
    (C) supervising the creation of Pakistan.
    (D) instructing American civil rights activists in "passive resistance."

11. Charlemagne ruled a large part of western and central Europe in the years
    (A) 30 B.C.E.—20 C.E.
    (B) 800–814.
    (C) 1050–1070.
    (D) 1400–1410.

12. In 1949, Mao Zedong
    (A) became chairman of the People's Republic of China.
    (B) led the Chinese Cultural Revolution.
    (C) overthrew the Ch'ing dynasty.
    (D) fled to Taiwan to establish a nationalist republic.

13. Which of the following countries were most involved in world exploration during the fifteenth, sixteenth, and seventeenth centuries?
    (A) Belgium, France, Austria, and Germany
    (B) Spain, France, England, Portugal, and the Netherlands
    (C) England, Scotland, Norway, Denmark, and Spain
    (D) Germany, France, Spain, and Italy

14. The Soviet Union under Joseph Stalin witnessed all of the following *except*
    (A) collectivization of farms and increased industrialization.
    (B) the siege of Leningrad during World War II.
    (C) political repression and executions.
    (D) the Hungarian revolt and the invasion of Czechoslovakia.

15. The year 1066 is the date of
    (A) the invasion of England by the Norman king William.
    (B) the beginning of the English Reformation.
    (C) the Children's Crusade.
    (D) Caesar's triumph in the Gallic Wars.

16. The term *chivalry* refers to
    (A) a code of laws developed by Hammurabi.
    (B) a blend of Christian and military ideals.
    (C) a technique of mounted warfare.
    (D) the Eastern influence on Western thought.

17. What major political change occurred in South Africa in 1991?
    (A) Apartheid was outlawed.
    (B) Nelson Mandela was released from prison.
    (C) Whites passed a referendum to share political power with blacks.
    (D) All of the above

18. The French term *détente* was used to describe
    (A) efforts to relax tension between the Soviet Union and the United States.
    (B) the first of several nuclear test-ban treaties.
    (C) the crisis that followed the French student and worker strikes of 1968.
    (D) an informal alliance between France and Britain in the years before World War I.

19. NATO was formed
    - (A) in 1919 to maintain security in Europe against revived German military power.
    - (B) in 1948 to promote cooperation between Latin America and the United States.
    - (C) in 1949 by the United States and Western Europe to counter the Soviet threat.
    - (D) in 1960 to overthrow the South Vietnamese government.

20. What was the Reign of Terror?
    - (A) The imprisonment and execution of opponents of the French Revolution
    - (B) The elimination of the political opposition under Stalin
    - (C) The expulsion of Jews from Spain
    - (D) The rise of the Medicis to power in Florence

21. The Victorian Age, the height of the British Empire, covered the years
    - (A) 1640–1688.
    - (B) 1790–1820.
    - (C) 1837–1901.
    - (D) 1930–1948.

22. The Hundred Years' War between France and England led to all of the following *except*
    - (A) the decimation of the French nobility.
    - (B) the consolidation of the power of the French king.
    - (C) the expulsion of England from all but a tiny area of continental Europe.
    - (D) the end of the monarchy in England.

23. Who was Benito Mussolini?
    (A) An Italian dictator and head of the Fascist
        Party
    (B) The leader of the Italian Communist Party in
        the 1930s
    (C) The leader of the first government of Italy fol-
        lowing World War II
    (D) A leading figure in the art world of Renais-
        sance Venice

24. What happened at the Ukrainian (then Soviet)
    town of Chernobyl in 1986?
    (A) A POW camp containing World War II sol-
        diers was discovered.
    (B) The remains of the so-called missing link were
        found.
    (C) An asteroid collided with Earth.
    (D) A nuclear reactor melted down.

25. What were the Crusades?
    (A) Exploratory expeditions by Europeans
        through Africa and the Far East
    (B) Campaigns by government forces against
        Protestants in Germany and France
    (C) Attempts by Europeans to wrest the Holy
        Land from the Muslims
    (D) Trials and executions of so-called infidels in
        Spain

26. The European powers fought each other in World
    War I during the years
    (A) 1914–1918.
    (B) 1917–1918.
    (C) 1917–1921.
    (D) 1914–1921.

27. Who was Genghis Khan?
    (A) The leader of the Huns who terrified Europe in
        the 300s
    (B) The leader of the Visigoths who sacked Rome
        in 410
    (C) The leader of the Mongols who conquered
        Persia and much of China in the 1200s
    (D) The leader of the Chinese who led the Long
        March in the 1930s

28. The Boer War was a conflict between
    (A) blacks and Dutch settlers in southern Africa.
    (B) Belgians and the indigenous people of the Bel-
        gian Congo.
    (C) the British government in India and the Indi-
        ans.
    (D) Dutch-settler republics in southern Africa and
        the British.

29. The empire of Alexander the Great included
    (A) Russia, Italy, Greece, and Palestine.
    (B) Asia Minor, Syria, Egypt, and Greece.
    (C) Britain, Gaul, Iberia, and Asia Minor.
    (D) Arabia, Egypt, Gaul, and Asia Minor.

30. The area that became Israel in 1948 had formerly
    been known as
    (A) Palestine.
    (B) Jordan.
    (C) Syria.
    (D) Arabia.

31. The opening of the Berlin Wall followed
    (A) a West German rally calling for reunification.
    (B) the sudden death of East German leader Erich
        Honecker.
    (C) mass protests and an exodus of East Germans
        to the West.
    (D) the breakup of the Soviet Union.

32. The French Revolution was *not* a result of
    (A) inequality among the classes of society.
    (B) rising taxes and prices of food and clothing.
    (C) the influx of immigrants from eastern Europe.
    (D) the weak monarchies of Louis XV and Louis
        XVI.

33. The Thirty Years' War broke out because of
    (A) religious differences between Protestants and
        Catholics in seventeenth-century central Europe.
    (B) clashes between Yorkists and Lancastrians in
        fifteenth-century England.
    (C) the death of Czar Peter the Great in the eigh-
        teenth century.
    (D) the feud between Pope Boniface VIII and
        Philip IV of Spain in the thirteenth century.

34. In a historical context, the term *Holocaust* refers to
    (A) the pogroms that took place in Russia under the nineteenth-century czars.
    (B) the Great Fire of 1871 that destroyed much of Chicago.
    (C) the explosions of the atomic bombs of Hiroshima and Nagasaki.
    (D) the systematic murder of 6 million Jews by the Nazis.

35. The Vikings were
    (A) traders from Denmark.
    (B) explorers from Britain.
    (C) troubadours from Gaul.
    (D) warriors from Scandinavia.

36. Napoleon Bonaparte is *not* known for
    (A) codifying French law.
    (B) freeing the serfs.
    (C) becoming emperor of France.
    (D) losing a vital battle at Waterloo.

37. The Spanish Armada was defeated by the
    (A) Americans under Theodore Roosevelt.
    (B) Germans under Adolf Hitler.
    (C) English under Elizabeth I.
    (D) French under Napoleon.

38. Tiananmen Square on June 4, 1989, was reminiscent of
    (A) Prague, Czechoslovakia, on August 20, 1968.
    (B) Paris, France, on July 13, 1789.
    (C) Dien Bien Phu, Vietnam, on May 5, 1954.
    (D) Petrograd, Russia, on October 24, 1917.

39. Which of these did *not* contribute to the Cold War?
    (A) The division of Germany into two separate states
    (B) The German-Soviet Nonagression Pact
    (C) The Soviet Union's development of the atomic bomb
    (D) The suppression of the revolt in Hungary

40. Who was Joan of Arc?
    (A) A French peasant who was burned at the stake for witchcraft
    (B) The mistress of King Louis XIV
    (C) The mother of King Richard Lionheart and King John
    (D) The queen of France responsible for the St. Bartholemew's Day massacre

41. The Berlin Wall was built to
    (A) keep the Mongol invaders out of Germany.
    (B) halt the advance of Russian troops.
    (C) protect Berlin against the peasant uprisings in Germany.
    (D) stop the flow of refugees from East Germany to the West.

42. What was the Weimar Republic?
    (A) The wartime German government under Adolf Hitler
    (B) The post–World War I German government
    (C) The Austrian government after the fall of the Hapsburgs
    (D) The government established in East Germany after World War II

43. The Holy Roman Empire existed from
    (A) 31 B.C.E. to the 400s.
    (B) 800 to the early 1800s.
    (C) 527 C.E. to 1453.
    (D) 1 C.E. to the 1500s.

44. What did Adolf Hitler and British Prime Minister
    Neville Chamberlain agree on at Munich in 1938?
    (A) To permit Germany to occupy parts of
        Czechoslovakia
    (B) To release Germany from its responsibility to
        pay reparations for World War I
    (C) To permit Germany to annex Austria
    (D) To form a German-British alliance against the
        Soviet Union

45. For which of the following is Julius Caesar *not*
    known?
    (A) Invading Britain
    (B) Being assassinated while attending a session of
        the Roman Senate
    (C) Persecuting Christians
    (D) Establishing the 365-day calendar

46. The Industrial Revolution is generally considered
    to have begun
    (A) in the United States at the start of the nine-
        teenth century.
    (B) in Germany in the middle of the nineteenth
        century.
    (C) in France following the French Revolution.
    (D) in Great Britain at the end of the eighteenth
        century.

47. Which of the following was *not* a feature of the Byzantine Empire?
    (A) The widespread use of mosaics in art
    (B) Intense devotion to the Eastern Orthodox church
    (C) The worship of Buddha in Zen monasteries
    (D) Codification of the laws in Justinian's Code

48. The Sino-Japanese War was fought
    (A) between Japan and England over control of the opium trade.
    (B) between Japan and China over control of Korea.
    (C) between Japan and the United States over control of the Philippines.
    (D) between Japan and Siam over control of trade in the South China Sea.

49. Why was the Magna Carta written?
    (A) To bring an end to the Hundred Years' War
    (B) To declare America's independence from Great Britain
    (C) To limit the power of King John of England
    (D) To prevent Julius Caesar from becoming emperor

50. The Easter Rebellion of 1916 took place
    (A) in St. Petersburg, Russia, in an attempt to overthrow the czar.
    (B) in Dublin, in an effort to gain independence from Great Britain for Ireland.
    (C) in Berlin, in protest against the rising toll of World War I.
    (D) in Beijing, in an attempt by Chinese republicans to overthrow the child emperor Pu-Yi.

TEST 2:
Explanatory Answers

1. The correct answer is (C). Simón Bolívar made his name during the Venezuelan revolution of 1810. For the next fifteen years, he helped lead resistance to Spanish rule in Ecuador, Peru, and Upper Peru (later renamed Bolivia). In 1819, he became president of a country that is now divided into Colombia, Ecuador, and Venezuela.

2. The correct answer is (A). Athens fought the Peloponnesian League, a band of city states loyal to Sparta, from 460 to 445 B.C.E. and again from 431 to 404 B.C.E. The Spartans then dominated Greece until the onset of Theban rule in 370 B.C.E.

3. The correct answer is (B). Apartheid aimed at the complete separation of all racial groups in South Africa: whites, blacks, and people of Indian descent. To this end, many black Africans were resettled in "homelands"—often areas of little economic value—and forced to travel long distances to jobs in predominantly white areas. Black Africans were not, however, forbidden to own businesses.

4. The correct answer is (A). The February Revolution in France overthrew King Louis Philippe and marked the beginning of a period of nationalistic uprisings throughout Europe. Hapsburg Austria was faced with revolutions in Hungary, Bohemia, and Italy.

5. The correct answer is (D). In 1936, Germany signed treaties with Italy and with Japan. These led to the Berlin Pact of 1940. Opposition to and defeat of the Axis powers came from the Allies, led by Great Britain, the United States, France, the Soviet Union, and China.

6. The correct answer is (B). Operation Just Cause was the military code name for the 1989 invasion of Panama by U.S. forces. The aim of the operation was to capture General Manuel Noriega, the Panamanian dictator, whom a U.S. court had convicted of drug running and money laundering. However, in the initial attack, the general was not captured, 23 U.S. soldiers were killed, and 200 were wounded. About 50 Panamanian soldiers and over 200 civilians died, according to official U.S. reports, but by some accounts the number of civilian deaths was more than 3,000. The invasion was condemned by the UN General Assembly in December 1989. Noriega took shelter in the Vatican mission, but in January 1990, he surrendered to U.S. forces. He was tried in the United States, and in July 1992, he was sentenced to 40 years in prison.

7. The correct answer is (D). In his desire to divorce Catherine of Aragon and marry Anne Boleyn, Henry VIII defied the authority of the Roman Catholic Church. His resulting excommunication led him to create a separate Church of England, of which, by the Act of Supremacy in 1534, he became the head.

8. The correct answer is (C). The writings of the German political economist Karl Marx (1818–1883) profoundly influenced Lenin's Communist movement in the Soviet Union. Besides writing the *Communist Manifesto* and *Das Kapital,* Marx headed the First International, a Socialist labor federation founded in London in 1864.

9. The correct answer is (D). The term *Third World* was coined to label economically underdeveloped nations in Asia, Africa, and Latin America, usually nations that desired to remain unaligned either to the First World (capitalist) nations or to the Second World (socialist) nations. *Fourth World* is a recent appellation given to countries with an annual per capita income under $300.

10. The correct answer is (A). Gandhi (1869–1948) led the movement against British rule in India, using a systematic program of nonviolent protest and refusal to support British policies. His techniques of passive resistance were later utilized by civil rights protestors in the United States and in other countries. In 1947, India was granted independence and divided into West and East Pakistan and India. Gandhi was assassinated in 1948 by a Hindu fanatic who opposed his desire to reconcile Hindus and Muslims.

11. The correct answer is (B). Charlemagne, king of the Franks, conquered vast portions of western and central Europe in the years 773–798. In 800, at Rome, he was crowned emperor of the western Roman Empire by Pope Leo III.

12. The correct answer is (A). As chairman of the Chinese Communist party and leader of the struggle against the Nationalist Kuomintang, Mao led his Red Army on the Long March in 1934–1935 and established Communist control in the northwestern provinces. Not until after World War II did the Communists gain control of the Chinese government, forcing Chiang Kai-shek and the Nationalists to flee to Taiwan.

13. The correct answer is (B). Spain, France, England, Portugal, and the Netherlands all established vast colonial empires during the Age of Exploration. Motivated by desire for wealth and power, the governments of these countries sponsored colonization in Asia, the Americas, and Africa.

14. The correct answer is (D). Joseph Stalin led the Soviet Union from the death of Lenin in 1924 until his own death in 1953. His five-year plans called for stepped-up industrial production and collectivized agriculture. Stalin's paranoia about opposition led to a series of purge trials and executions. Both the Hungarian revolt (1956) and the invasion of Czechoslovakia (1968) took place after his death.

15. The correct answer is (A). The Norman Conquest of England, led by William the Conqueror, resulted in the end of Anglo-Saxon rule.

16. The correct answer is (B). Chivalry flourished during the time of the Crusades. The key ideals of a chivalrous knight were love of God, loyalty to his lord, courtesy, courage, and chastity.

17. The correct answer is (D). In 1989, F. W. de Klerk was elected president of South Africa on a platform of reform in apartheid laws. In 1991, he announced plans to legalize Black political opposition and lift the ban on the African National Congress, the principal Black opposition party. Shortly afterward, Nelson Mandela, the leader of the ANC, was released after twenty-eight years in prison, and the Population Registration Act, which required registration of all South Africans on the basis of color, was repealed. White-only voters passed a referendum reforming apartheid laws and allowing political power to be shared with Blacks. Nevertheless, actual change was slow to come to South Africa, and bloody conflicts arose between Black factions, particularly the two largest, the Inkatha Freedom Party and the ANC.

18. The correct answer is (A). *Détente* (literally "relaxation") was a term used in the 1960s and 1970s to describe attempts to lessen the tensions of the Cold War. Strategic Arms Limitation Talks (SALT) were part of this effort.

19. The correct answer is (C). The North Atlantic Treaty Organization is an alliance formed to defend against possible aggression by the Soviet Union and its allies. The original members included the United States, Canada, France, Great Britain, Iceland, Italy, Denmark, Norway, Portugal, Belgium, Luxembourg, and the Netherlands. Greece, Turkey, Germany, Poland, the Czech Republic, Spain, and Hungary joined later.

20. The correct answer is (A). In 1793, a dictatorship was established in France under the auspices of the Committee of Public Safety, led by Maximilien Robespierre. The government was centralized, the military was strengthened, and thousands of suspected counterrevolutionaries were executed. The overthrow of Robespierre in 1794 ended the Terror.

21. The correct answer is (C). Victoria reigned through most of the nineteenth century, a period that saw British industrial supremacy and the extension of British rule to one-quarter of the world's land area.

22. The correct answer is (D). The war, which lasted from 1337 to 1453, devastated the population of France as it destroyed British power on the Continent. War, famine, and the plague decimated the nobility in France, creating an opportunity for the consolidation of royal power.

23. The correct answer is (A). Mussolini (1883–1945) founded the National Fascist party in Italy in 1921. In 1922, he was asked to form a government by King Victor Emmanuel III. By 1928, he had established himself as dictator. In the 1930s, he sent Italian troops to invade Ethiopia and Albania; during World War II he was an ally of Hitler.

24. The correct answer is (D). On April 28, 1986, Scandinavian scientists detected high levels of radiation in the air over much of Scandinavia. Gradually, over the next several weeks, the Soviet Union revealed that there had been a major accident at the nuclear reactor at Chernobyl, in Ukraine. The cool-

ing system had malfunctioned, causing the uranium fuel to melt. Hydrogen gas was emitted and ignited, causing an explosion; the reactor cone was exposed, and large amounts of radiation were released. Five years later, radiation levels were still considered highly unsafe within a 60-kilometer radius of the site, and there was a dramatic rise in thyroid disease, anemia, cancer, and immunity problems in the local population.

25. The correct answer is (C). A particularly brutal series of military campaigns, the Crusades were holy wars that pitted European Christians against Muslims between the years 1096 and 1291. Besides draining the treasuries of European countries, the Crusades saw areas of the Middle East change hands numerous times between Crusaders and Muslim Turks and Egyptians.

26. The correct answer is (A). Following the assassination of Austrian archduke Franz Ferdinand at Sarajevo in 1914, Europe was plunged into a four-year war that pitted Germany, Austria, Hungary, Bulgaria, and the Ottoman Empire against Great Britain, France, Russia, and, eventually, twenty-nine other countries. The war in Europe ended officially on Armistice Day, November 11, 1918.

27. The correct answer is (C). Led by Genghis Khan, the Mongol army, known for its fierceness and love of warfare, fought on horseback with bows and arrows. The Mongols captured Beijing, most of Persia, and Russian Turkestan in the 1200s.

28. The correct answer is (D). When gold was discovered in southern Africa in the 1880s, Britain tried to annex the Dutch (Boer) republic of the Transvaal. In 1899, war broke out between Britain and the Transvaal and another Boer republic, the Orange Free State. By 1902, both republics were subjugated; they later became part of the British-ruled Union of South Africa (today's Republic of South Africa).

29. The correct answer is (B). In 336 B.C.E., Alexander, educated by Aristotle, became ruler of Greece and Macedonia. He conquered Asia Minor, then moved on to the Middle East and Africa. When he died in 323 B.C.E., at the age of thirty-three, he had conquered most of the Mediterranean region.

30. The correct answer is (A). In 1947, the United Nations voted to divide Palestine into separate Jewish and Arab states. Displaced Palestinians won Arab support, and Israel was attacked by several Arab nations in 1948. Although outnumbered, the Israelis won the war; the Arab section of Palestine was then absorbed by Jordan. Palestinians, still without a homeland, continue to protest—sometimes violently—the loss of their country.

31. The correct answer is (C). The division of Germany into East and West was a pivotal symbol of the Cold War. The Wall was built across Berlin in 1961 to prevent East Germans from escaping to the West. In August 1989, Hungary removed its barbed wire border with Austria, and suddenly

East Germans, who before could only travel as far as another Communist state, could move to the West through Hungary. A huge exodus began. Then, in October, Soviet leader Mikhail Gorbachev arrived for an anniversary ceremony marking forty years of the East German state. Tens of thousands of Germans took to the streets of East Germany's main cities, embarrassing party chief Erich Honecker, who was forced to resign. On November 4, East Germany agreed to allow its citizens to leave for the West via Czechoslovakia. In effect, this decision rendered the Wall irrelevant. On November 7, the East German cabinet resigned, and on November 9, the new party chief, Egon Krenz, officially opened the borders, and the Wall came down.

32. The correct answer is (C). Economic conditions in France for the artisanal and peasant classes grew steadily worse under Louis XV and Louis XVI. Meanwhile, the noble classes increased their power at the expense of the weak monarchy, frustrating the aspirations of a rising merchant class. Finally in 1789 the monarchy found itself bankrupt and was obliged to call a gathering of notables, the States General, to remedy the situation. When this group met, the representatives of the merchant class, called the Third Estate, reconstituted themselves as a National Assembly and set about drafting a constitution. Meanwhile in Paris, a crowd of shopkeepers and laborers stormed the Bastille Prison, inaugurating a full-scale revolution.

33. The correct answer is (A). The Thirty Years' War began in 1620 as a Protestant revolt against the Holy Roman Emperor. Protestants of Germany, Denmark, and Sweden entered the war, and later France, though mostly Catholic, came in on the side of the Protestants. The war ended in 1648 with the Peace of Westphalia, which changed boundaries throughout central Europe and opened the way for the rise of Prussia.

34. The correct answer is (D). Adolf Hitler's master plan required the elimination of "racially inferior" people, focusing on Jews but including Slavs, gypsies, and others. The Nazis' "Final Solution" was the annihilation of all Jews in Europe. By the end of World War II, at least 6 million Jews had died, most in Nazi concentration camps.

35. The correct answer is (D). The Vikings, or Norsemen, were Scandinavians known for their fearlessness and brutality in warfare. They were seafarers, and in the ninth and tenth centuries they terrorized the coasts of Britain, Russia, and France.

36. The correct answer is (B). In 1799, Napoleon assumed supreme power in the French government. As head of state, his most important work was the revision and codification of French law called the Napoleonic Code. After proclaiming himself emperor in 1804, he began wars with Austria, Great Britain, Russia, and Prussia. In 1814, he was defeated and forced to abdicate, but in 1815, he returned from exile for a last campaign that ended in a final defeat by the British and Prussians at Waterloo.

37. The correct answer is (C). The "sea dogs" of England—captains such as Francis Drake and Walter Raleigh—challenged the Spanish monopoly of trade with the Americas. Angered by this and by the execution of the Catholic Mary Queen of Scots by the English Protestants under Elizabeth I, Philip of Spain sent his Armada in 1588 to conquer England. The English fleet, smaller but swifter than the Spanish, was victorious.

38. The correct answer is (A). Inspired by democratic reforms in Poland, the Philippines, and the Soviet Union, students throughout China began meeting in small groups to discuss reform. The sudden death of Hu Yaobang, former Party chief and one-time heir apparent to Deng Xiaoping, led to large-scale demonstrations by students who respected Hu's tolerance for intellectuals and for change. On April 19, 1989, nearly 10,000 students took over Tiananmen Square in Beijing. The number grew tenfold in two days' time and became embarrassing to the government, which alternated between threats and promises. On May 13, a group of students began a hunger strike. During a visit by Mikhail Gorbachev a few days later, more than one million citizens of Beijing marched in the streets, calling for Deng's resignation and for democratic reforms. Martial law was declared on May 20, and Deng ousted his protégé, Zhao Ziyang, for his attempts at a peaceful solution. From that point, the finale was assured. On June 4, trucks and tanks filled with People's Liberation Army soldiers

stormed the city, randomly shooting citizens and firing into the crowd in Tiananmen Square. As many as 5,000 people were killed, and leaders of the movement were arrested or forced into exile. China's steadily improving relations with the rest of the world were thrown into turmoil by the brutal crackdown. Although it was bloodier, this abrupt ending to a democratic crusade was similar to the sudden end of the Prague Spring, as Warsaw Pact tanks rolled in to quash that budding reform movement. The other dates refer to *successful* revolutions: the formation of the Paris Commune, the battle that marked the end of French rule in Vietnam, and the October Revolution, in which the Bolsheviks seized power.

39. The correct answer is (B). After World War II, Soviet-style governments were set up in the countries occupied by Soviet troops, including the eastern portion of Germany. Increasing antagonism between this Soviet bloc and the West soon led to the formation of opposing military alliances: the Warsaw Pact in the East and NATO in the West. Tensions mounted further when the Soviet Union exploded its own atomic bomb—breaking NATO's monopoly on atomic weapons—and when it forcibly suppressed a revolt in Hungary in 1956. (The German-Soviet Nonaggression Pact, signed in 1939, signaled the start of World War II.)

40. The correct answer is (A). Joan of Arc, a fifteenth-century French peasant girl, claimed she spoke to angels who told her to lead the French armies

against the English in the Hundred Years' War. She won the confidence of the heir to the French throne, and in 1429, she led the French forces that defeated the English at Orléans. Soon afterward, however, Joan was captured by the English, convicted of witchcraft, and burned at the stake.

41. The correct answer is (D). After Germany was divided into separate Communist and non-Communist states, refugees from the East poured into West Berlin. To stop this flow of people, in 1961, the East German government built a wall around the western portion of the city.

42. The correct answer is (B). Following the collapse of the German monarchy at the end of World War I in 1918, a German national assembly met in Weimar to draft a constitution. The resulting so-called Weimar Republic was unpopular; it signed the Versailles Treaty and allowed runaway inflation. Adolf Hitler, the Republic's last chancellor, abolished it in 1934.

43. The correct answer is (B). The coronation in 800 of Charlemagne as Emperor of the West by Pope Leo III established the Holy Roman Empire. After the death of Charlemagne's son, the empire broke up, to be reestablished in 962 by Otto the Great as a confederation of German and northern Italian territories. The empire existed in various forms, ruled by emperors from almost every European country, until Napoleon abolished it in the early 1800s.

44. The correct answer is (A). At Munich, Chamberlain, believing that Hitler's territorial ambitions

could thus be satisfied, agreed to permit German occupation of the Czech border zones. This policy of "appeasement" was a failure; less than a year later World War II began when Germany invaded Poland.

45. The correct answer is (C). Julius Caesar (101–44 B.C.E.) was a Roman general and consul who led the conquest of Gaul (France) and an invasion of Britain. After defeating his rival, Pompey, he gained supreme power in Rome, being appointed dictator for life in 45 B.C.E. His accomplishments included reform of the Senate, expansion of the empire, and establishment of the Julian calendar, which is almost the same calendar that we use today. His power so threatened the conservative families of Rome that in 44 B.C.E., he was assassinated in the precincts of the Senate by a group of his own friends and subordinates, to whom his grandiose ambitions had become intolerable.

46. The correct answer is (D). Beginning in Great Britain at the end of the eighteenth century, the Industrial Revolution changed the world. Mechanization of production, the growth of a class of factory workers, improvements in living standards, the development of new forms of transportation, and the rise of labor unions are among the results of the economic changes that started taking place in the late 1700s.

47. The correct answer is (C). In 330, the Roman emperor Constantine transferred the seat of power

to Constantinople, a new city built on the site of
Byzantium on the Bosporus. In 395, the empire was
divided into western and eastern halves, and after
the extinction of the western empire, the eastern
(Byzantine) empire continued on until it was conquered by the Ottoman Turks in 1453. The empire
is generally thought to have reached its zenith
under Justinian (527–565), who drafted a famous
code of laws. Byzantine culture was characterized
by intense devotion to the Eastern Orthodox
Church and by distinctive styles in architecture and
art, particularly the widespread use of mosaics.

48. The correct answer is (B). In the late 1800s, Japan
and China each wanted to rule Korea and periodi-
cally intervened in the country. In 1894, a rebellion
broke out, and when China and Japan both sent in
troops, the situation grew into a war. The Chinese
were defeated; by the Treaty of Shimonoseki,
Korea achieved nominal independence. Japan was
given compensation in money and territory, including Formosa (Taiwan).

49. The correct answer is (C). As king, John was a failure: during his reign many of England's continental
possessions were lost, and crushing taxes were levied
on the nobles. In 1215, the nobles forced John to sign
the Magna Carta ("Great Charter"), which limited
his power to tax, required jury trials, and forbade the
seizure of property without compensation.

50. The correct answer is (B). In Dublin on April 24
through 29, 1916, the Irish Republican Brother-

hood led the so-called Easter Rebellion against British rule. Hoped-for German aid never materialized, and the revolt was suppressed. Not until 1922 did the southern portion of Ireland gain its independence; Northern Ireland, where a majority of the population is Protestant, remains associated with Britain as part of the United Kingdom.

TEST 3
WE THE PEOPLE: CIVICS

The people's government, made for the people, made by the people, and answerable to the people . . .

—DANIEL WEBSTER

1. The War Powers Act prevents the president from
   (A) declaring war on Third World nations.
   (B) sending armed forces into hostilities for longer than a specified period without the approval of Congress.
   (C) shipping arms to be used in a foreign war.
   (D) acting as head of state in times of war.

2. How is the number of representatives from each state in the House of Representatives determined?
   (A) By the area of the state
   (B) By the wealth of the state
   (C) By the population of the state
   (D) By the amount of exports the state produces

3. What is a junta?
   (A) A group of Communists who meet regularly for political discussion
   (B) A council controlling the government after a revolutionary seizure of power
   (C) An organization that campaigns for a particular presidential candidate
   (D) The Spanish parliament

4. The National Organization for Women (NOW) works to
   (A) pay tuition for disadvantaged women in college.
   (B) strengthen laws against drunk driving.
   (C) establish equal rights for women under the law.
   (D) abolish abortion in the United States.

5. The role of a presidential primary is to do which of the following?
   (A) Select the president of the United States
   (B) Nominate a party candidate
   (C) Elect the vice president of the United States
   (D) Elect delegates to a party's national convention and express candidate preference

6. One function of the FBI is to
   (A) investigate threats to the security of the United States that take place within U.S. borders.
   (B) stop the spread of communism in Central and South America.
   (C) protect the president and vice president.
   (D) coordinate intelligence operations.

7. The Selective Service System is responsible for
   (A) selecting the candidates for president.
   (B) choosing the members of the city council.
   (C) drafting and induction into the armed forces.
   (D) selecting workers in private industry for promotion to government jobs.

8. What was the Stamp Act?
   (A) A law passed by Congress in 1980 raising the price of stamps to 22 cents
   (B) A law passed by the British Parliament in 1765 requiring special stamps on various paper products
   (C) A law passed by Congress in 1941 requiring everyone to carry a stamped identification card
   (D) A law passed by Congress in 1804 requiring that mail bear stamps

9. Which president of the United States has been impeached?
   (A) Richard Nixon
   (B) Ulysses S. Grant
   (C) Andrew Johnson
   (D) Lyndon Baines Johnson

10. What is the function of a jury?
    (A) To decide on the guilt or innocence of a person accused of a crime
    (B) To choose the judge who will preside over a trial
    (C) To protect the life of a person accused of a crime
    (D) To find evidence to prove a person guilty or innocent of a crime

11. In which choice are all those listed members of the president's cabinet?
    (A) Secretary of defense, minority whip, Speaker of the House
    (B) Vice president, secretary of state, chief justice
    (C) Secretary of state, attorney general, secretary of labor
    (D) Secretary of transportation, national security advisor, vice president

12. What happens in a presidential veto?
    (A) The president votes in a national election.
    (B) The senators vote to impeach the president.
    (C) The people vote to choose their president.
    (D) The president refuses to sign a bill into law.

13. The governments of Great Britain, Sweden, and Belgium are examples of
    (A) republics.
    (B) aristocracies.
    (C) constitutional monarchies.
    (D) absolute monarchies.

14. In the case of *Brown* v. *Board of Education of Topeka, Kansas,* the Supreme Court ruled that
    (A) public schools must be desegregated.
    (B) official school prayers were illegal.
    (C) the publication of controversial or "obscene" articles by minors in school newspapers can be suppressed by school authorities.
    (D) children could not work in factories.

15. What is the job of the secretary of state?
    (A) To oversee the defense of the United States
    (B) To oversee the judicial systems of the fifty states
    (C) To take notes in meetings of state
    (D) To handle government affairs involving foreign countries

16. In order, who becomes acting president if the president of the United States dies in office?
    (A) Secretary of state, vice president, national security advisor
    (B) Speaker of the House, vice president, attorney general
    (C) Vice president, Speaker of the House, president pro tempore of the Senate
    (D) Vice president, secretary of state, Speaker of the House

17. Which agency has its offices in the Pentagon?
    (A) CIA
    (B) Department of Defense
    (C) Presidential cabinet
    (D) Department of State

18. The electoral college is
    (A) a school for politicians in Washington, D.C.
    (B) the group representing a presidential candidate at a national convention.
    (C) the group of electors who actually choose the president.
    (D) the name for the votes of citizens in a presidential election before they are tallied.

19. What does the Nineteenth Amendment to the U.S. Constitution state?
    (A) The right to vote shall not be denied because of sex.
    (B) The sale of alcohol is prohibited.
    (C) The government can collect income taxes.
    (D) Slavery shall be abolished.

20. What are the terms in office of these officials: president, senator, representative?
    (A) Eight years, four years, four years
    (B) Four years, six years, two years
    (C) Two years, two years, one year
    (D) Four years, two years, two years

21. When you cast your ballot, you
    (A) nominate a candidate for your party.
    (B) refrain from voting due to religious beliefs.
    (C) choose a political party to which you will belong.
    (D) vote in secret using a machine or a printed form.

22. Alexander Hamilton and other Federalists believed that
    (A) Canada should become part of the Union.
    (B) slavery should be abolished.
    (C) the United States should be ruled by a constitutional monarchy.
    (D) the United States should have a strong central government.

23. The NAACP seeks to
    (A) uphold the rights of African-Americans in the United States.
    (B) protect consumers against fraud.
    (C) make sure medicines are safe and effective.
    (D) ensure world peace.

24. When the Senate ratifies a treaty, it
    (A) votes it down.
    (B) approves it by a two-thirds vote.
    (C) allows the president to veto it.
    (D) changes its wording.

25. What is a naturalized citizen?
    (A) Someone who was born in the United States
    (B) Someone whose parents were born in the United States
    (C) An immigrant who applies for citizenship and passes a test
    (D) An immigrant who has lived in the United States for at least five years

26. The landmark Supreme Court case *Plessy* v. *Ferguson*
    (A) gave African Americans equal rights under the law.
    (B) required "separate but equal" treatment for whites and African-Americans.
    (C) freed slaves in Southern states.
    (D) established quotas for hiring minorities in federal positions.

27. The Voting Rights Act of 1965
    (A) eliminated literacy tests for voters.
    (B) required literacy tests for voters.
    (C) gave eighteen-year-olds the vote.
    (D) gave African-Americans the vote.

28. The right of parties in a case to appeal a decision
    means
    (A) the trial must begin again with brand-new evi-
        dence.
    (B) the jury may reconsider their decision for
        thirty days.
    (C) the decision may be reversed or upheld by a
        higher court.
    (D) the decision was unwarranted and did not
        stand up to scrutiny.

29. What is the Bill of Rights?
    (A) The first ten amendments to the Constitution
    (B) The first paragraph of the Declaration of Inde-
        pendence
    (C) The code of laws of the thirteen colonies
    (D) Any constitution created by a state government

30. The historic separation of church and state in the
    United States
    (A) makes it possible for schools to teach creation-
        ism.
    (B) enables the Senate to begin each day with a
        prayer.
    (C) forbids the support with public funds of reli-
        gious groups.
    (D) means that Christmas is not a federal holiday.

31. The system of checks and balances was designed to
    (A) make it easier for Congress to pay for federal programs.
    (B) keep one branch of government from overpowering another.
    (C) assign the enforcement of laws to the judicial branch.
    (D) allow the chief executive to select a cabinet.

32. To be a democracy, a country *must*
    (A) have a constitution and elected representatives.
    (B) provide economic equality and equal opportunity.
    (C) allow each citizen one vote on each issue.
    (D) None of the above

33. You may sue someone for libel if that person
    (A) publishes something that is incorrect.
    (B) publishes a lie that injures you personally or professionally.
    (C) uses your name without your consent.
    (D) publishes your writing without your consent.

34. Which statement best expresses the primary tenet of socialism and communism?
    (A) Economic equality is preferable to private control of resources.
    (B) The people belong to the state.
    (C) Commerce should be free of governmental interference.
    (D) The acquisition of empire is the lifeblood of the system.

35. What is a prime minister?
    (A) The head of state in Great Britain
    (B) A high-ranking member of the aristocracy
    (C) The leader of the Anglican Church
    (D) The head of a parliamentary government

36. If you oppose capital punishment, you do not want
    (A) convicted criminals to face the death penalty.
    (B) physical punishment of students by teachers.
    (C) heads of state to face impeachment.
    (D) unreasonable search and seizure.

37. A nation with a bicameral legislature
    (A) is run by a premier and cabinet.
    (B) is run by the direct vote of the people.
    (C) has two legislative houses.
    (D) has two political parties.

38. According to the decision in the 1973 Supreme Court case *Roe* v. *Wade,*
    (A) segregation in public schools violates equal protection.
    (B) a wife may charge her husband with rape and assault.
    (C) the Constitution protects the rights of the unborn.
    (D) states may not forbid abortion in the first two trimesters.

39. The Iowa caucuses are held in order to
    (A) select a candidate for president.
    (B) send delegates to party conventions.
    (C) determine which party has more support.
    (D) allow voters to indicate issues of concern.

40. The Alien and Sedition Acts of 1798 did all of the
    following *except*
    (A) prohibit criticism of the government.
    (B) require fourteen years' residency for natural-
        ization.
    (C) allow the president to deport or arrest "dan-
        gerous" immigrants.
    (D) restrict the immigration of non-Europeans.

41. Strictly defined, liberalism versus conservatism
    means
    (A) change versus preservation of the status quo.
    (B) government control versus individual free-
        dom.
    (C) secular humanism versus religious fundamen-
        talism.
    (D) equal opportunity versus individualism.

42. Which of the following is *not* an example of civil
    disobedience?
    (A) Boycotting
    (B) Passive resistance
    (C) Hijacking
    (D) Nonpayment of taxes

43. A writ of habeas corpus is intended
    (A) to allow a prisoner to hire a lawyer at the pub-
        lic's expense.
    (B) to suspend civil liberties in times of war.
    (C) to prevent arbitrary imprisonment and ensure
        judicial review.
    (D) to prevent defendants from having to incrimi-
        nate themselves.

44. Which of these is always true of the U.S. Congress?
    (A) The majority party in the Senate also leads the House.
    (B) The House and Senate may be led by different parties.
    (C) If one party leads the House, another leads the Senate.
    (D) No one party may dominate either house.

45. If defendants in a case invoke the Fifth Amendment, or "plead the Fifth," they
    (A) are asking for extra time to prepare a case.
    (B) are invoking the right not to testify against themselves.
    (C) are refusing to answer all questions posed by the judge.
    (D) can be retried later for the same offense.

46. Which of the following is *not* true of bills in the U.S. Congress?
    (A) Bills become laws if they are approved by Congress and the president.
    (B) Only the House can initiate a bill asking for higher taxes.
    (C) If a bill is not passed in one session of Congress, it dies.
    (D) The Senate may not add to or change a bill from the House.

47. What is a nomination?
    (A) An executive's selection of an appointee
    (B) A party's selection of a candidate for office
    (C) All of the above
    (D) None of the above

48. The case of *Miranda* v. *Arizona* gave suspects in a crime
    (A) the ability to plead guilty to a lesser charge.
    (B) the right to due process and judicial review.
    (C) the right to be informed of their rights.
    (D) money to hire an attorney to represent them.

49. The U.S. attorney general has all of these duties *except*
    (A) running the Department of Justice.
    (B) advising the president in legal matters.
    (C) nominating Supreme Court justices.
    (D) overseeing cases that involve the government.

50. A defense attorney represents the accused, and a prosecuting attorney represents
    (A) the victim.
    (B) the state.
    (C) the convicted.
    (D) the court.

TEST 3:
Explanatory Answers

1. The correct answer is (B). In 1973, during the Vietnam War, Congress passed the War Powers Act over President Richard Nixon's veto. The Act stated that the president must consult with Congress before sending U.S. armed forces into hostilities for longer than a specified period of time.

2. The correct answer is (C). Whereas each state has two senators, the number of representatives per state depends on the population of the state. However, the Reapportionment Act of 1929 set the permanent number of House members at 435.

3. The correct answer is (B). *Junta* is a Spanish word meaning "joined." A junta is a committee or council that controls the government after a revolution. Often, a junta is run by the military. Some historic examples of juntas include those formed in Spain in 1808 and in 1930, in Egypt in 1952, and in Nicaragua and El Salvador in 1979.

4. The correct answer is (C). NOW, founded in 1966, seeks to end discrimination against women in all sectors of society. It favors liberalization of abortion laws, engages in litigation, and works actively in politics.

5. The correct answer is (D). Presidential primaries, both more numerous and more important now

than in the past, are used to select delegates, either pledged or unpledged, to go to a party's national convention, where the presidential candidates are nominated.

6. The correct answer is (A). Both the Federal Bureau of Investigation (FBI) and the Central Intelligence Agency (CIA) are charged with protecting the security of the United States. However, the difference is that the FBI is limited to investigating security threats that take place within U.S. borders. Another function of the FBI is to investigate criminal cases in which suspects have crossed state lines.

7. The correct answer is (C). From 1940 to 1973, the Selective Service System oversaw the drafting and induction of men into the armed forces. In 1973, the armed forces became all volunteer, and the system was placed on standby. However, in 1980, registration for the draft was reinstated.

8. The correct answer is (B). In 1765, the British Parliament passed the Stamp Act, requiring colonists in America to use special stamps, highly taxed, on items such as calendars, newspapers, and contracts. The Act was repealed in 1766 because of strong opposition by the colonists.

9. The correct answer is (C). Impeachment, or charging a public official with a crime in a trial before a competent tribunal, has been a possibility for only three U.S. presidents: Andrew Johnson in 1868, Richard Nixon in 1974, and Bill Clinton in 1998. Johnson was impeached, but was acquitted in a

trial before the Senate. Nixon resigned before he could be impeached. In 1998, Clinton was impeached by the House of Representatives, but he was acquitted by the Senate in 1999.

10. The correct answer is (A). A jury, usually twelve people chosen for their impartiality, has the job of deciding whether a person accused of a crime is guilty or innocent. A *grand jury,* which consists of thirteen to twenty-three people, decides if a person held for a crime should go to trial.

11. The correct answer is (C). There are now fourteen members of the cabinet: secretary of state, secretary of the treasury, secretary of defense, attorney general, secretary of the interior, secretary of agriculture, secretary of commerce, secretary of labor, secretary of health and human services, secretary of housing and urban development, secretary of transportation, secretary of energy, secretary of education, and secretary of veteran's affairs. Cabinet rank members include the vice president, the White House chief of staff, the administrator of the Environmental Protection Agency, the U.S. Trade Representative, and the directors of the Office of Management and Budget and the Office of Homeland Security.

12. The correct answer is (D). When a president vetoes a bill—refuses to sign it into law—he returns it to the House or Senate and explains why he vetoed it. The bill can be passed over the veto if two-thirds of the Congress vote to do so.

13. The correct answer is (C). A constitutional monarchy is a government headed by a king or queen whose power is limited by a constitution.

14. The correct answer is (A). *Brown* v. *Board of Education* was a suit brought by the Brown family of Topeka, Kansas, whose children were forced to go to segregated schools. In 1955, the Supreme Court ruled segregation unconstitutional and charged local schools with the responsibility for integrating.

15. The correct answer is (D). The Department of State is older than the U.S. Constitution. The secretary of state is the highest-ranking executive officer after the president and is responsible for developing foreign policy and handling foreign affairs.

16. The correct answer is (C). If the president dies in office, first the vice president, then the Speaker of the House, then the president pro tempore of the Senate, then the secretary of state become acting president.

17. The correct answer is (B). The Department of Defense is housed in the Pentagon, a five-sided building located in Arlington, Virginia.

18. The correct answer is (C). Electors, the total of whom make up the electoral college, are usually chosen at state party conventions. The number of electors in each state is equal to its total of U.S. senators and representatives. When citizens vote in a presidential election, they are voting for a group of electors representing their candidate. Whichever party wins a majority of votes in a state sends its

electors to Washington, where on the first Monday after the second Wednesday in December, they cast their ballots to choose the president. Because of this process, it is possible to elect a president who has a minority of popular votes, as happened in 1876 with Rutherford B. Hayes, in 1888 with Benjamin Harrison, and in 2000 with George W. Bush.

19. The correct answer is (A). The Nineteenth Amendment gave women the vote by stating that voting rights could not be denied because of gender.

20. The correct answer is (B). A president's term in office is four years; a senator's, six years; and a representative's, two years. Senators and representatives can be reelected indefinitely; a president can serve only two terms.

21. The correct answer is (D). There are two kinds of ballots in the United States: one on which candidates are listed by the office for which they are running and one on which candidates are listed by political party. When you cast your ballot, you vote in secret for one or more people listed on the ballot.

22. The correct answer is (D). Federalists, who believed in a strong federal government, opposed states' rights advocates who wanted power to remain with the states. During the writing of the U.S. Constitution, this conflict came to a boil; a compromise was reached by which the House of Representatives represents the people, and the Senate represents the states.

23. The correct answer is (A). The NAACP, or National Association for the Advancement of Colored People, was formed in 1909 by African-American rights activists led by W. E. B. DuBois. It works to achieve equality for African-Americans.

24. The correct answer is (B). A treaty is ratified if it is approved by a two-thirds majority in the Senate. A constitutional amendment, however, can be ratified in two ways: by a positive vote by legislators in three-quarters of the states or by a positive vote in conventions in three-quarters of the states.

25. The correct answer is (C). To become a naturalized citizen, an immigrant must live in the United States for at least five years and then file an application for citizenship. An applicant is tested on U.S. history, government, and the Constitution before becoming a citizen.

26. The correct answer is (B). *Plessy v. Ferguson* (1896) upheld a Louisiana law that called for "separate but equal" accommodations for whites and African-Americans on passenger trains.

27. The correct answer is (A). In addition to ending the literacy and character test requirement in states where less than half of the voting-age population was registered, the Voting Rights Act allowed the attorney general to determine when federal registration of voters was needed to comply with the Fifteenth Amendment ("The right of citizens . . . to vote shall not be denied or abridged . . . on account of race, color, or previous condition of servitude").

28. The correct answer is (C). The right to an appeal means that the decision of a lower court may be challenged, and the case may be heard again by a higher court, up to and including the Supreme Court.

29. The correct answer is (A). The absence of certain guaranteed rights in the U.S. Constitution as originally written led to ten amendments in 1791. These amendments cover such issues as freedoms of speech and religion, right to bear arms, and right to a speedy trial.

30. The correct answer is (C). Based on the First Amendment's guarantee of freedom of religion, the separation of church and state implies that public support of any religious organization is unconstitutional. This policy means that prayer in schools is unacceptable, and there can be no national religion. Varying interpretations of the First Amendment have kept the issue alive into our own time.

31. The correct answer is (B). The Constitution prescribes a separation of powers among the three branches of government—executive, legislative, and judicial. Few actions may be taken by any branch without the approval of one of the other branches.

32. The correct answer is (D). *Democracy* means "rule by the people." In a direct democracy, such as the one in ancient Athens, each citizen (free males in the case of Athens) votes directly on issues. In a representative democracy, government is run by

representatives elected by the people. In a social democracy, individuals have equal access to public resources without discrimination. In an economic democracy, individuals have equal opportunity and often share the resources. Historically, the concepts of liberty and equality have been keys to the democratic ideal, but differing emphases on one concept or the other have led to different applications of that ideal.

33. The correct answer is (B). To be libelous, a publication must be unjust and must expose the subject to public contempt or cause the subject professional harm.

34. The correct answer is (A). Communism and socialism have in common the belief that economic laws can be made that benefit the people as a whole rather than individuals. Substituting communal ownership for private property is believed to ensure equal opportunity.

35. The correct answer is (D). The chief executive of a parliament or cabinet is called a prime minister. The prime minister is often head of the majority party. (The head of state in Great Britain is the king or queen.)

36. The correct answer is (A). The term *capital punishment* refers to the imposition of the death penalty for particular crimes. Many countries and some states have eliminated the death penalty, and controversy remains over whether or not execution constitutes "cruel and unusual punishment."

37. The correct answer is (C). *Bicameral* means "two chambers," and it refers to those legislatures that are made up of two houses. The British Parliament, for example, is composed of the House of Lords and the House of Commons; the U.S. Congress is divided into the House of Representatives and the Senate.

38. The correct answer is (D). The 1973 ruling legalized abortions during the first six months of pregnancy. However, in 1977, Congress eliminated abortion from those medical operations covered by Medicaid except when needed to save the life of the pregnant woman or to terminate a pregnancy caused by rape or incest.

39. The correct answer is (B). A caucus is a form of primary. In Iowa, delegates to local party conventions are picked in political meetings open to the voting public. Those delegates are expected, but not required, to vote for a particular candidate at the party's national convention.

40. The correct answer is (D). Passed to limit the power of the Jeffersonian Republicans who supported France's position in Franco-American disputes, the Alien and Sedition Acts increased the federal government's power. They enabled the executive to expel any objectionable aliens, lengthened requirements for naturalization, and declared written or spoken criticism of the government to be treasonous. Jefferson's reply, written with James Madison, was "The Kentucky and Virginia Resolutions" of

1798 and was to become the foundation of the states' rights movement.

41. The correct answer is (A). Modern conservatism arose in response to the changes brought about by the French Revolution and industrialism in Europe. It emphasized the preservation of the old order. Liberalism was intended to favor free development of the individual through progressive reform and limited government. Both terms have undergone significant redefinition. Conservatism now implies freedom from government intervention (or maintenance of the economic status quo), whereas liberalism has come to imply government protection (or social and economic change through legislation).

42. The correct answer is (C). The essay "Civil Disobedience" (1849) by Henry David Thoreau calls on citizens to withdraw from cooperation with their governments when those governments undertake acts with which those citizens disagree. Other famous proponents of this idea were Mahatma Gandhi in India and Martin Luther King, Jr. in the United States.

43. The correct answer is (C). Anyone detaining a prisoner is required to bring that prisoner to court and state the reason for his or her arrest. If the judge considers the cause sufficient, the prisoner may or may not be released on bail. If the cause is insufficient, the prisoner must be freed at once.

44. The correct answer is (B). The Senate majority leader is in charge of allocating time and determin-

ing the priorities in business conducted in the Senate. The House majority leader leads party debate in the House and assists the Speaker. The House and the Senate are often controlled by the same party, and that party may be the same as the chief executive's party. However, the legislature may be split, or both houses may be controlled by a party other than the one in control of the White House.

45. The correct answer is (B). The Fifth Amendment holds that no one may be tried for a capital crime unless indicted by a grand jury; that "double jeopardy," or standing trial twice for the same offense, is prohibited; that life, liberty, or property may not be taken without due process of law; and that no one need be "a witness against himself."

46. The correct answer is (D). Although only the House of Representatives may initiate a bill involving raising money, the Senate may amend that bill before approving it. If a bill is approved by the House in one form and by the Senate in another, a joint committee with members from both houses must hammer out the differences before the final bill goes to the president.

47. The correct answer is (C). In the United States, primaries and caucuses enable a party to nominate a single candidate for office. The executive also has the power to nominate people for positions in the judiciary and cabinet.

48. The correct answer is (C). *Escobedo* v. *Illinois* (1964) held that an accused man was denied due

process when police refused his request to call a lawyer and his confession was later used as evidence. This case paved the way for *Miranda* v. *Arizona* (1966), which stated that before questioning may take place, suspects must be informed of their rights to remain silent and contact an attorney.

49. The correct answer is (C). The U.S. attorney general is the head of the Department of Justice and a member of the cabinet. Although an attorney general may advise the president on potential nominees, the president alone may appoint federal and Supreme Court justices.

50. The correct answer is (B). A prosecuting attorney, who may be a district attorney or a state's attorney, represents the state in criminal cases involving state law. In federal cases the prosecutor is a U.S. attorney, who represents the federal government.

TEST 4

SPACESHIP EARTH: GEOGRAPHY

I have always read that the world, both land and water, was spherical.

—CHRISTOPHER COLUMBUS

Questions 1–3 refer to the following map.

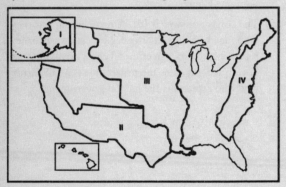

1. The Louisiana Purchase is the section of the above map labeled
   (A) I
   (B) II
   (C) III
   (D) IV

2. The original thirteen colonies are the section of the map labeled
   (A) I
   (B) II
   (C) III
   (D) IV

3. The forty-ninth state is in the section of the map labeled
   (A) I
   (B) II
   (C) III
   (D) IV

4. What is the capital of New York State?
   (A) New York City
   (B) Buffalo
   (C) Albany
   (D) None of the above

5. In which city is the Kremlin located?
   (A) St. Petersburg
   (B) Moscow
   (C) Warsaw
   (D) Berlin

6. Which countries all belong to the Common Market?
   (A) Belgium, Denmark, France, Great Britain, Ireland, Italy, Luxembourg, the Netherlands, Germany, Greece, Portugal, Spain, Sweden, Finland, and Austria
   (B) Great Britain, Ireland, and Australia
   (C) Bulgaria, Ukraine, Germany, Hungary, Poland, Rumania, and Russia
   (D) Denmark, France, Norway, Portugal, Spain, and Sweden

7. The equator is to latitude as which of the following is to longitude?
   (A) Tropic of Cancer
   (B) Tropic of Capricorn
   (C) International date line
   (D) Prime meridian

8. Which of the following is *not* true of the Nile River?
   (A) It is the longest river in the world.
   (B) It empties into the Mediterranean Sea.
   (C) It is the main source of water for Senegal.
   (D) The Aswan Dam is built across it.

9. The Pacific Northwest is made up of which states?
   (A) Washington, Oregon, and part of Idaho
   (B) Oregon and California
   (C) Idaho, Montana, and part of Washington
   (D) California and Arizona

10. Where is Libya?
    (A) In the Middle East, bordering Syria and Lebanon
    (B) In the Middle East, bordering Saudi Arabia
    (C) In northern Africa, bordering Egypt
    (D) In Asia, bordering Brunei

11. What is the capital of Germany?
    (A) Bonn
    (B) Berlin
    (C) Munich
    (D) Vienna

12. What do Guam and Puerto Rico have in common?
    (A) They are both islands in the Caribbean.
    (B) Their residents are U.S. citizens.
    (C) They are both constitutional monarchies.
    (D) They are both south of the equator.

13. The Thirty-eighth Parallel is the line of latitude that marks
    (A) the northern tip of the Oregon Territory.
    (B) the division of Korea after World War II.
    (C) the location of the Panama Canal.
    (D) the line of German defenses in World War I.

14. Which of the following is *not* true of the Mississippi River?
    (A) It divides Kansas from Oklahoma.
    (B) It flows from north to south.
    (C) It ends in Louisiana at the Gulf of Mexico.
    (D) It forms the western border of Illinois.

Questions 15–17 refer to the following map.

15. The line running from north to south represents
    (A) the Great Divide.
    (B) the Mason-Dixon line.
    (C) the San Andreas fault.
    (D) the Oregon Trail.

16. The capital of this state is
    (A) Sacramento
    (B) Los Angeles
    (C) San Francisco
    (D) San Diego

17. The southernmost city on this map is
    (A) Sacramento.
    (B) Los Angeles.
    (C) San Francisco.
    (D) San Diego.

18. Which country is *not* an island chain?
    (A) Fiji
    (B) Philippines
    (C) Indonesia
    (D) Myanmar

19. Which of the following countries does *not* border Israel?
    (A) Iran
    (B) Lebanon
    (C) Jordan
    (D) Egypt

20. What are the Himalayas?
    (A) The mountains that link western and eastern Europe
    (B) A mountain range in Tanzania containing Mount Kilimanjaro
    (C) The highest mountains in the world, located in Asia
    (D) The often impassable mountains of Afghanistan

21. Spanish is the primary language of all of these countries *except*
    (A) Cuba and the Dominican Republic.
    (B) Venezuela and Guatemala.
    (C) Colombia and Argentina.
    (D) Haiti and Brazil.

22. Which of the following states does *not* border Iowa?
    (A) Nebraska
    (B) North Dakota
    (C) Wisconsin
    (D) Missouri

Questions 23–25 refer to the following map.

23. Mexico is the section of the map labeled
    (A) I
    (B) II
    (C) III
    (D) IV

24. Venezuela is the section of the map labeled
    (A) I
    (B) II
    (C) III
    (D) IV

25. Panama is the section of the map labeled
    (A) I
    (B) II
    (C) III
    (D) IV

Questions 26–28 refer to the following map.

26. Scandinavia is the section of the map labeled
    (A) I
    (B) II
    (C) III
    (D) IV

27. The United Kingdom is the section of the map labeled
    (A) I
    (B) II
    (C) III
    (D) IV

28. Iberia is the section of the map labeled
    (A) I
    (B) II
    (C) III
    (D) IV

29. The country once known as ancient Mesopotamia
    is now
    (A) India and Pakistan.
    (B) Egypt and parts of Sudan and Ethiopia.
    (C) Iraq and parts of Iran, Syria, and Turkey.
    (D) Israel.

30. Suez, Erie, and Panama are names of
    (A) socialist republics.
    (B) rivers.
    (C) mountain ranges.
    (D) canals.

31. The Alps run through which of the following
    countries?
    (A) France, Austria, Switzerland, and Italy
    (B) Spain, France, Belgium, and Switzerland
    (C) Germany, Austria, Holland, and Denmark
    (D) Switzerland, Italy, Hungary, and Poland

32. Which countries do *not* border Brazil?
    (A) Guyana and Venezuela
    (B) Ecuador and Chile
    (C) Bolivia and Paraguay
    (D) Peru and Argentina

33. What country was once known as Persia?
    (A) Syria
    (B) Egypt
    (C) Afghanistan
    (D) Iran

34. What is the capital of Ethiopia?
    (A) Addis Ababa
    (B) Harar
    (C) Nairobi
    (D) Pretoria

35. Where is the headquarters of the United Nations?
    (A) Washington, D.C.
    (B) Paris, France
    (C) New York City, NY
    (D) Brussels, Belgium

Questions 36–38 refer to the following map.

36. Japan is the section of the map labeled
    (A) I
    (B) II
    (C) III
    (D) IV

37. China is the section of the map labeled
    (A) I
    (B) II
    (C) III
    (D) IV

38. Vietnam is the section of the map labeled
    (A) I
    (B) II
    (C) III
    (D) IV

39. What is the capital of Texas?
    (A) Houston
    (B) Austin
    (C) Dallas
    (D) Texas City

40. What is the capital of Canada?
    (A) Toronto
    (B) Ontario
    (C) Ottawa
    (D) Quebec

41. Erie, Superior, Huron, Michigan, and Ontario are
    names of
    (A) the Finger Lakes.
    (B) the Great Lakes.
    (C) the bodies of water in the British Lake District.
    (D) the lakes of the Ozarks.

42. What is Vatican City?
    (A) A free state within Rome where the pope lives
    (B) The capital of Italy
    (C) A city now known as Istanbul, where the East-
         ern patriarch lives
    (D) The capital of the Netherlands

43. Which countries belong to the British Common-
    wealth of Nations?
    (A) Greenland, Singapore, India, and Taiwan
    (B) Trinidad and Tobago, Tonga, Canada, and
         New Zealand
    (C) Jamaica, Ireland, Zaire, and Rumania
    (D) Australia, Iceland, Barbados, and Tierra del
         Fuego

44. What is the largest state in the United States?
    (A) Hawaii
    (B) Texas
    (C) Alaska
    (D) California

45. Which city is *not* in the Northern Hemisphere?
    (A) Mexico City
    (B) New York City
    (C) Calcutta, India
    (D) Sydney, Australia

Questions 46–48 refer to the following map of the western portion of the former Soviet Union.

46. What is the name of the area labeled I?
    (A) Siberia
    (B) Russia
    (C) Ukraine
    (D) Soviet Union

47. The area labeled IV is home to a high concentration of
    (A) Kurds.
    (B) Russians.
    (C) Muslims.
    (D) Armenians.

48. The area known as the Baltic States is labeled
    (A) I
    (B) II
    (C) III
    (D) IV

49. What is the capital of Brazil?
    (A) Rio de Janeiro
    (B) Brasilia
    (C) São Paulo
    (D) Caracas

50. Which of the following is *not* true of the Amazon
    River?
    (A) It was named for a tribe of warrior women.
    (B) It runs through Peru and Brazil.
    (C) It is the longest river in the world.
    (D) It carries more water than any other river.

TEST 4:
Explanatory Answers

1. The correct answer is (C). In 1803, the United States purchased land west of the Mississippi from France for around $27 million. The new territory was over 800,000 square miles in area.

2. The correct answer is (D). These British colonies revolted against England and became the United States. They included New Hampshire, Massachusetts, Rhode Island, Connecticut, New York, New Jersey, Pennsylvania, Maryland, Delaware, North Carolina, South Carolina, Virginia, and Georgia.

3. The correct answer is (A). Alaska became the forty-ninth state in 1959, and Hawaii became the fiftieth state later that year.

4. The correct answer is (C). Albany, a city on the Hudson River, has been the capital of New York State since 1797.

5. The correct answer is (B). From 1918 to 1989, the Kremlin housed the administration of the Soviet Union in the capital city, Moscow. A *kremlin* was a medieval walled city. Moscow's Kremlin dates from 1156.

6. The correct answer is (A). The Common Market, or European Economic Community, was established in 1957 to simplify trade among Western European nations. Denmark, Great Britain, and

Ireland joined in 1973. In the 1980s, Greece, Portugal, and Spain joined, and in the 1990s, Sweden, Finland, and Austria became members.

7. The correct answer is (D). The equator is an imaginary circle around the earth designated 0° latitude. The prime meridian is a similar great circle through the poles designated 0° longitude.

8. The correct answer is (C). The Nile runs north from sources in Burundi through Rwanda to Sudan, where its branches, the Blue Nile and the White Nile, converge. The Aswan Dam helps to supply hydroelectric power and irrigation for much of southern Egypt. The river passes through Cairo and forms a huge delta before emptying into the Mediterranean.

9. The correct answer is (A). The Pacific Northwest is an area that encompasses Washington, Oregon, and part of Idaho. The area was home to the Nez Percé, Yakima, Chinook, Bannock, Klamath, and Modoc tribes during the first white explorations by James Cook in the 1770s and Lewis and Clark in 1805–1806.

10. The correct answer is (C). Libya is bordered by the Mediterranean on the north, Egypt and Sudan on the east, Niger and Chad on the south, and Tunisia and Algeria on the west.

11. The correct answer is (B). Before 1990, Bonn was the capital of West Germany. However, when West and East Germany were reunited, Berlin was named the new capital.

12. The correct answer is (B). Guam, an island in the West Pacific, and Puerto Rico, an island in the Caribbean, were both ceded to the United States by the Spanish in 1898. Puerto Rico is a self-governing country, but Guam is administered by the U.S. Department of the Interior. Residents of both islands are U.S. citizens, but they are not empowered to vote in U.S. elections.

13. The correct answer is (B). Following World War II, the United States occupied Korea south of the Thirty-eighth Parallel, and the Soviet Union occupied the region to the north. Both countries withdrew in 1949, but forces from the north invaded the south in 1950, leading to the Korean War.

14. The correct answer is (A). The Mississippi flows between Minnesota and Wisconsin, Iowa and Illinois, Missouri and Kentucky, Arkansas and Tennessee, and Louisiana and Mississippi. It enters the Gulf of Mexico south of New Orleans.

15. The correct answer is (C). The San Andreas fault marks the edges of two geologic plates that slide along each other and cause earthquakes throughout much of California.

16. The correct answer is (A). Sacramento was settled in 1839 and grew rapidly during the California gold rush of 1849. It became the state capital in 1854.

17. The correct answer is (D). San Diego is not far from the southern border of the United States. The compass rose on a map indicates north (N), south (S), east (E), and west (W).

18. The correct answer is (D). Myanmar (formerly Burma) is bordered by India, China, Thailand, Laos, and the Bay of Bengal.

19. The correct answer is (A). Israel's borders are with Syria on the north, Jordan on the east, Egypt on the south, and the Mediterranean on the west.

20. The correct answer is (C). The Himalayas run through Pakistan, India, Tibet, Nepal, Sikkim, and Bhutan. Mount Everest, usually considered the highest mountain in the world at 28,208 feet, is found in the southern range.

21. The correct answer is (D). French is the official language of Haiti, although Creole is widely spoken. This stems from the influx in the 1600s of French planters, who imported slaves from Africa and went on to make Haiti one of the largest producers of coffee and sugar. When Toussaint L'Ouverture, a former slave, overthrew the government and abolished slavery, Haiti became only the second independent country in the Americas, the United States being the first. Portugal ruled Brazil for centuries, and at one time Rio de Janeiro was the capital of the Portuguese empire. Brazil became a republic in 1889, and Portuguese remains the official language.

22. The correct answer is (B). Iowa is bordered by six states: Minnesota on the north, Wisconsin and Illinois on the east, Missouri on the south, and Nebraska and South Dakota on the west.

23. The correct answer is (A). Mexico is the southernmost country in North America. Its northern bor-

der is with the United States; it is bordered on the south by Belize and Guatemala.

24. The correct answer is (D). Venezuela, a republic in northern South America, shares borders with Colombia on the west, Brazil on the south, and Guyana on the east.

25. The correct answer is (C). Because of its location, Panama was chosen as the most likely prospect for a canal linking the Caribbean and the Pacific. Its northern neighbor is Costa Rica, and its southern border is with Colombia.

26. The correct answer is (B). Scandinavia includes the countries Denmark, Sweden, Norway, and Finland.

27. The correct answer is (A). The United Kingdom includes England, Scotland, Wales, and Northern Ireland.

28. The correct answer is (C). Iberia includes the countries Portugal and Spain.

29. The correct answer is (C). Ancient Mesopotamia, the cradle of civilization, where the Tigris and Euphrates rivers flow, extended from the Persian Gulf north to the mountains of Armenia and from the Zagres Mountains west to the Syrian desert. The earliest settlements in Mesopotamia date from about 5000 B.C.E. Today, the region includes portions of Iran, Turkey, Syria, and Iraq.

30. The correct answer is (D). The Suez Canal is a waterway connecting the Gulf of Suez with the

Mediterranean. The Panama Canal connects the Atlantic Ocean with the Pacific Ocean. The Erie Canal connected the Hudson River with Lake Erie but fell into disuse with the rise of the railroads.

31. The correct answer is (A). The Alps are a mountain system that runs through France, Switzerland, northern Italy, Germany, Austria, Slovenia, and Croatia.

32. The correct answer is (B). Brazil is bordered by French Guiana, Suriname, Guyana, Venezuela, Colombia, Peru, Bolivia, Paraguay, Argentina, and Uruguay.

33. The correct answer is (D). The country that had been called Persia since ancient times was officially renamed Iran in 1935. In 1978, a revolution in Iran overthrew the ruler, or Shah, and the Ayatollah Khomeini, a Muslim holy man, led the country until his death in 1989.

34. The correct answer is (A). In 1889, the city of Addis Ababa was made the capital of Ethiopia. Ravaged by war and famine, the country remains economically and industrially underdeveloped.

35. The correct answer is (C). The UN is based in New York. It was founded in October 1945, and has more than 150 members. Its aims are to maintain peace, to promote equal rights, to develop international cooperation, and to encourage respect for human rights.

36. The correct answer is (D). Japan is a string of islands in the Pacific, including the islands of

Hokkaido, Honshu, Shikoku, and Kyushu. Its capital is Tokyo.

37. The correct answer is (B). The People's Republic of China is bordered by North Korea, Mongolia, Kazahkstan, Russia, Tajikistan, Kyrgyzstan, Vietnam, Laos, Myanmar, Bhutan, Nepal, Pakistan, Afghanistan, Sikkim, and India. Its capital is Beijing.

38. The correct answer is (C). Vietnam, an ancient country, was ravaged by war for decades following World War II. Divided for more than twenty years into North Vietnam and South Vietnam, it was reunited in 1976 when troops from the north captured the city of Saigon in the south. Vietnam's capital is Hanoi.

39. The correct answer is (B). In 1870, after Texas was admitted to the Union, Austin was named its capital.

40. The correct answer is (C). Canada is divided into ten provinces and two territories: Alberta, British Columbia, Manitoba, New Brunswick, Newfoundland, Northwest Territories, Nova Scotia, Ontario, Prince Edward Island, Quebec, Saskatchewan, and Yukon Territory. Ottawa, its capital, was founded in 1827 and became the capital in 1867.

41. The correct answer is (B). The Great Lakes of North America comprise the largest body of fresh water in the world. They were formed by glaciers at the end of the Ice Age and were explored by Samuel de Champlain and Robert LaSalle in the seventeenth century.

42. The correct answer is (A). Vatican City, the residence of the pope and the headquarters of the Roman Catholic Church, is located within the boundaries of the city of Rome. It has been an independent state with its own currency and citizenship since 1929.

43. The correct answer is (B). The Commonwealth of Nations was established in 1931 and consists of more than forty sovereign and associated states, including Great Britain. Most of the member states have their own governments, but a few, such as Nevis-St. Kitts and St. Lucia, are governed by Great Britain. There is no formal constitution for the Commonwealth, but all members acknowledge the British monarch as its head and can consult with one another on common problems.

44. The correct answer is (C). The largest state in the United States is Alaska, with an area of 570,833 square miles. The next largest is Texas with an area of 262,015 square miles.

45. The correct answer is (D). The Northern Hemisphere is the half of the earth that lies north of the equator. The Southern Hemisphere lies south of the equator. Australia is in the Southern Hemisphere.

46. The correct answer is (B). Siberia is only one part of the vast republic of Russia, which contains three-fourths of the territory of the former Soviet Union, one-half of its population, and two of its major cities—Moscow and St. Petersburg. President Boris Yeltsin is faced with a crumbling infrastructure and

economic stagnation, despite Russia's potential as a cornucopia of natural resources. Ukraine is the area labeled III. It is bounded on the west by Moldava, now contemplating reunification with Rumania, and on the north by Belarus, still a Communist stronghold.

47. The correct answer is (C). Clockwise from the north, these republics are Kazakhstan, Kyrgyzstan, Tajikistan, Uzbekistan, and Turkmenistan. Together with Azerbaijan, directly to the west of the Caspian Sea, these nations house over 50 million Muslims. These republics now must decide whether to choose a Western, democratic form of government or to follow an Islamic model such as that in Iran. The republics that abut Azerbaijan are predominantly Christian: Armenia to the west and Georgia to the northwest.

48. The correct answer is (B). From west to east, these republics are Lithuania, Latvia, and Estonia. The Baltics were independent between the World Wars but were overrun once more by the Soviet Union in 1940. Lithuania declared its independence again in 1990, but it took more than a year for the three states to be recognized by the rest of the world. Although their pattern of domination and independence is similar, the republics have very different populations and histories. Lithuania was a powerful state in the Middle Ages and united with Poland in 1569 to try to avoid Russian takeover. Latvia was controlled at various times by Poland and Sweden before being taken over by Russia.

Estonia was run by the Danes, the Teutonic Knights, and the Swedes before passing to Russia.

49. The correct answer is (B). The capital of Brazil, Brasilia, is one of the newest cities in the world. It was founded in 1960 when officials decided to move the capital inland to encourage development of the interior of the country.

50. The correct answer is (C). The Amazon, which originates in northern Peru, flows across Brazil before emptying into the Atlantic. It is the second-longest river in the world but carries more water than any other river. It was named by explorer Francisco de Orellana, who claimed to have seen female warriors on its banks.

TEST 5
WORTH
A THOUSAND WORDS:
ART AND ARCHITECTURE

... Art, admired in general, is always actually personal.

—MARIANNE MOORE

1. What is the monument in the above photo?
   (A) Hadrian's Wall
   (B) The Great Wall of China
   (C) The Iron Curtain
   (D) The Berlin Wall

2. Who was Christopher Wren?
   (A) An English painter in the nineteenth century
   (B) A sixteenth-century Dutch landscape artist
   (C) An English architect of the seventeenth century
   (D) An eighteenth-century Belgian sculptor

3. This is a sculpture of
   (A) *David* by Michelangelo.
   (B) *King Solomon* by Bernini.
   (C) *Moses* by Michelangelo.
   (D) *John the Baptist* by Rodin.

4. Ionic, Doric, and Corinthian are styles of
   (A) still lifes.
   (B) church naves.
   (C) stained glass.
   (D) columns.

5. This picture shows a
   (A) Grecian column.
   (B) Mayan temple tower.
   (C) American Indian totem pole.
   (D) Persian ornamental staff.

6. For what is Edgar Degas best known?
   (A) His landscapes of the French countryside
   (B) His paintings of dancers
   (C) His abstract sculptures
   (D) His graceful Gothic cathedrals

7. What is this edifice?
   (A) The Roman forum
   (B) The Greek Parthenon
   (C) The temple at Delphi
   (D) The Colosseum in Rome

8. For what are these artists known: Alfred Eisen-
   staedt, Margaret Bourke-White, and Ansel Adams?
   (A) Their photography
   (B) Their portraits
   (C) Their sculptures
   (D) Their landscapes

9. What is this statue called?
   (A) *Winged Victory*
   (B) *Aphrodite*
   (C) *Venus de Milo*
   (D) *The Rape of the Sabine Women*

10. A pietà is a depiction of
   (A) Christ on the cross.
   (B) the dead Christ held by Mary.
   (C) an angel announcing the birth of Christ to Mary.
   (D) the baptism of Christ by John the Baptist.

11. This is the church called
    (A) St. Peter's.
    (B) St. Paul's.
    (C) Westminster Abbey.
    (D) Ste. Chapelle.

12. How is a fresco made?
    (A) By carving from marble or stone
    (B) By fusing colored glass to a metal ground
    (C) By firing colored glass rods together and cut-
        ting them in sections
    (D) By painting on wet plaster and allowing it
        to dry

13. This is a typical example of art from
    (A) ancient Egypt.
    (B) sixteenth-century Holland.
    (C) Renaissance Italy.
    (D) ancient Greece.

14. For what stylistic trait is Rembrandt best known?
    (A) The use of pointillism in painting
    (B) The subtle use of light and shadow in painting
    (C) The development of the baroque in architec-
         ture
    (D) The development of photorealism in painting

15. This picture shows
    (A) a piece of cloisonné enamel.
    (B) an illuminated manuscript.
    (C) a mosaic.
    (D) a triptych.

16. The great museum of Paris is called
    (A) the Metropolitan Museum of Art.
    (B) the National Gallery.
    (C) the Uffizi.
    (D) the Louvre.

17. What is this picture called?
    (A) *Portrait of Diane de Poitiers*
    (B) *The Jewish Bride*
    (C) *Arrangement in Grey and Black No.1: The Artist's Mother*
    (D) *The Seated Woman*

18. Pieter Breughel the Elder is best known for his
    (A) portraits of kings and queens.
    (B) sculptures of children at play.
    (C) paintings showing seasonal scenes of peasant life.
    (D) frescoes of the life of St. Francis of Assisi.

19. This picture depicts
    (A) an Oriental pagoda.
    (B) a Hindu temple.
    (C) a Romanesque church.
    (D) a Moslem mosque.

20. What are some of the identifying features of a Gothic cathedral?
    (A) Rounded arches, small windows, flying buttresses
    (B) Domed roof, colonnades, elaborate tympanum
    (C) Thin walls, pointed arches, large windows
    (D) Simple lines, heavy vaults, mosaic roof

21. This painting is found in
    (A) St. Paul's in London.
    (B) the Louvre in Paris.
    (C) Notre Dame in Paris.
    (D) the Sistine Chapel in the Vatican.

22. Jacob van Ruisdael, John Constable, and William Turner are best known for their
    (A) book illustrations.
    (B) portraits.
    (C) still lifes.
    (D) landscapes.

23. Andy Warhol is best known for the style known as
    (A) cubism.
    (B) pop art.
    (C) fauvism.
    (D) dadaism.

24. The Great Sphinx is
    (A) a Greek god to whom a huge temple was built.
    (B) a Roman emperor of whom a giant statue was
        built.
    (C) an Egyptian statue that stands near the Pyra-
        mids.
    (D) the name of the largest Egyptian pyramid.

25. The painting above depicts
    (A) a pietà.
    (B) an adoration.
    (C) an annunciation.
    (D) a crucifixion.

26. For what are these men known: Federico Fellini, Ingmar Bergman, and John Huston?
   (A) Developing the movement called pop art
   (B) Directing classic films
   (C) Experimenting with still photography
   (D) Perfecting the art of portraiture

27. The painting above is a typical
   (A) landscape.
   (B) trompe l'oeil.
   (C) altarpiece.
   (D) still life.

28. The art of inlaying colored tile and gold in mosaics typifies
    (A) Byzantine art of the sixth century.
    (B) Egyptian art around 4000 B.C.E.
    (C) Flemish art of the 1400s.
    (D) Nigerian art of the ninth century.

29. What is this building?
    (A) The Pitti Palace, built in the fifteenth century in Florence
    (B) Notre Dame, built in the twelfth to fourteenth centuries in Paris
    (C) The Pantheon, built in the first century B.C.E. in Rome
    (D) Hampton Court Palace, built in the sixteenth century near London

30. Which artist helped initiate the era of abstract expressionism?
    (A) Paul Gauguin
    (B) Jackson Pollock
    (C) Georgia O'Keeffe
    (D) Henri de Toulouse-Lautrec

31. This photograph shows
    (A) the Brooklyn Bridge.
    (B) London Bridge.
    (C) the Golden Gate Bridge.
    (D) the Bridge of Sighs.

32. Frank Lloyd Wright is famous for
   (A) stressing horizontal lines and "organic" architecture.
   (B) designing tall columns of steel and glass.
   (C) introducing energy efficiency to housing.
   (D) merging Gothic and Romanesque features with modern materials.

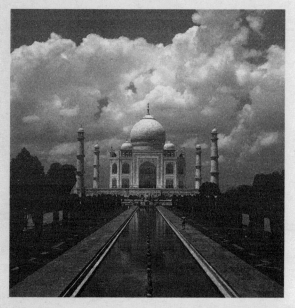

33. This example of Islamic architecture is known as
   (A) the Alhambra.
   (B) Santa Sophia.
   (C) the Qutab Minar.
   (D) the Taj Mahal.

34. Like the Egyptian pyramids, the Mayan pyramids
    (A) house crypts.
    (B) are made of stone or mud blocks.
    (C) contain carvings and paintings.
    (D) All of the above

35. Pablo Picasso's painting *Guernica* was created as a response to
    (A) the beauty of the Spanish countryside.
    (B) the horrors of fascism and war.
    (C) the world of the poor.
    (D) his rejection by Spanish society.

36. The style called rococo was known for its
    (A) grand scale and dramatic flair.
    (B) intricate and delicate decoration.
    (C) emphasis on line and symmetry.
    (D) use of themes from Norse and Roman mythology.

37. What is this statue?
    (A) *The Sleeping Muse* by Brancusi
    (B) *Adam* by Lombardo
    (C) *Recumbent Figure* by Moore
    (D) *The Thinker* by Rodin

38. The Parthenon is
    (A) a Doric temple dedicated to Athena in Athens.
    (B) a temple for worship of all gods in Rome.
    (C) a bridge connecting the Left Bank to Île de la
        Cité in Paris.
    (D) a museum housing European masterpieces in
        St. Petersburg.

39. Who painted this work?
    (A) Rembrandt
    (B) Holbein
    (C) Leonardo da Vinci
    (D) Michelangelo

40. The term *bas-relief* refers to a
    (A) style of painting.
    (B) weaving technique.
    (C) kind of sculpture.
    (D) ceramic glaze.

41. What is the significance of this group of stones?
    (A) They were brought to England from Africa by
        Caesar's army.
    (B) The structure was built by hand by Egyptian
        slaves.
    (C) They may be the ruins of an arena designed by
        Alexander.
    (D) Their arrangement indicates a possible astro-
        nomical function.

42. Artists painting in the traditional Japanese style are
    likely to use
    (A) tempera on rice paper.
    (B) ink on paper or silk.
    (C) watercolor on canvas.
    (D) acrylics on oiled paper.

43. This mask is typical of the traditional art of
    (A) Pakistan.
    (B) West Africa.
    (C) the Seminole Indians.
    (D) Persia.

44. Which of these groups of painters are known for
    their portraits?
    (A) Reynolds, Stuart, Gainsborough
    (B) Turner, Constable, Delacroix
    (C) Monet, Renoir, Pissarro
    (D) Dürer, Bosch, Correggio

45. Name the painter and the subject of this portrait.
    (A) James Whistler; John Ruskin
    (B) Vincent van Gogh; Vincent van Gogh
    (C) Dante Gabriel Rossetti; Raphael
    (D) Mary Cassatt; Paul Cézanne

46. Which of these artists are known for their sculp-
    ture?
    (A) Smith, Giacometti, Duchamp
    (B) Dubuffet, Johns, Klee
    (C) Magritte, Dali, Chagall
    (D) Rivera, Klimt, Hopper

47. Which of these artists painted the work *American Gothic?*
    (A) Grandma Moses
    (B) José Orozco
    (C) Dorothea Lange
    (D) Grant Wood

48. What is an aqueduct?
    (A) A technique of etching that produces a wash effect
    (B) A conduit built to carry water
    (C) A deep well drilled into water-bearing rock
    (D) An ornate shrub often pictured in Greek and Roman art

49. This painting is representative of
    (A) the Ashcan School.
    (B) primitivism.
    (C) the Hudson River School.
    (D) German expressionism.

50. What is this building?
    (A) Mount Vernon
    (B) The White House
    (C) The Capitol
    (D) Monticello

TEST 5:
Explanatory Answers

1. The correct answer is (B). The Great Wall of China, 1,500 miles long, was built in the third century B.C.E. by the Ch'in dynasty to protect the country from Central Asian nomads. It averages twenty-five feet in height, and space shuttle astronauts claim it is the only landmark they can see from space.

2. The correct answer is (C). Sir Christopher Wren's (1632–1723) prominence was the result of a disaster—the Great Fire of London of 1666, which burned down St. Paul's Cathedral. Commissioned to rebuild the church, Wren designed it in the Roman baroque style, with a dome like that of St. Peter's.

3. The correct answer is (A). Michelangelo was a Renaissance sculptor, painter, and designer who believed that an artist's job, "like God's," was to "make men." His *David*, completed in 1504, is considered one of the greatest statues of the Renaissance.

4. The correct answer is (D). While Doric, Ionic, and Corinthian are actually names of three Greek orders of architecture, their differences are reflected in the columns used in temple building. The Doric column is grooved or fluted and has a simple flaring capital. The Ionic column is also fluted but has a capital with a large scroll. The Corinthian column is smooth, and the capital is decorated with shoots and leaves.

5. The correct answer is (C). The picture shows a Haida Indian chieftain's house with a totem pole in front. The pole is carved to show plants, animals, and inanimate objects and depict legends that act both as a history of the tribe and a method of identifying the family.

6. The correct answer is (B). Degas, one of the best-known Impressionist painters (though he always denied being an Impressionist), usually painted people. He executed many paintings of dancers, performing or in class, as well as statues of dancers in motion.

7. The correct answer is (D). The Colosseum, completed in 80 C.E., is one of the largest single buildings in the world. It held fifty thousand spectators and was used for gladiatorial games.

8. The correct answer is (A). Alfred Eisenstaedt (1898–1995) was a photographer who completed more than 1,500 assignments for *Life* magazine in the 1930s and 1940s. Margaret Bourke-White (1906–1971) also photographed for *Life*. She was the only American to record the Nazi bombing of Moscow and is known for her photographs of concentration camps. Ansel Adams (1902–1984) was a landscape photographer whose photographs of the Far West show nature on a grand scale.

9. The correct answer is (C). The statue is called *Venus de Milo* and was sculpted in the first century B.C.E. It was found on Melos Island in Greece and is thought to belong to a group of statues that also included a Cupid.

10. The correct answer is (B). A pietà depicts Christ
    taken from the cross and held by Mary. One of the
    most famous pietàs is the statue by Michelangelo,
    now housed in St. Peter's in Rome.

11. The correct answer is (A). Originally built in 326,
    St. Peter's, erected on the burial site of the apostle
    Peter in Rome, was rebuilt in the sixteenth and sev-
    enteenth centuries. Much of the present-day build-
    ing was designed by Michelangelo and Bernini. St.
    Peter's is a basilica, with a domed roof; it is where
    the pope offers Mass when he is in Rome.

12. The correct answer is (D). A fresco is a painting
    made on wet plaster so that the plaster absorbs the
    pigment. One of the most famous frescoes is
    Leonardo da Vinci's *Last Supper*, in Milan. Unfor-
    tunately, this fresco has faded and been damaged
    by pollution, and is no longer on public display.

13. The correct answer is (A). The picture shows the
    third gold coffin of Tutankhamen, or King Tut.
    This coffin was made of solid gold and set inside
    two other coffins, both made of wood covered in
    gold leaf.

14. The correct answer is (B). Rembrandt van Rijn, a
    Dutch painter of the seventeenth century, is known
    for the way he used light and shadow in his paint-
    ings. Such masterpieces as *The Man with the
    Golden Helmet* and *The Night Watch* clearly show
    that he is one of the great geniuses of Dutch art.

15. The correct answer is (B). In the Middle Ages,
    before the invention of the printing press, manu-

scripts were copied by hand, usually by monks, who were among the few literate groups of the time. Because most manuscripts were religious in nature, the monks painted, or illuminated, them with illustrations, believing that the beauty of their work added to the glory of God.

16. The correct answer is (D). Originally a palace, the Louvre was made a museum after the French Revolution. It houses Leonardo da Vinci's *Mona Lisa*, the *Venus de Milo,* Whistler's painting of his mother, and thousands of other great works of art.

17. The correct answer is (C). James McNeill Whistler (1834–1903) was an American who lived in Paris and London. He promoted the idea of art for art's sake, insisting that painting had no mission to fulfill and did not have to tell a story. His best-known painting, often called "Whistler's Mother," is actually titled *Arrangement in Grey and Black No. 1: The Artist's Mother.*

18. The correct answer is (C). Pieter Breughel the Elder (1525–1569) painted some of the earliest depictions of peasant life in European art, often concentrating on the ways in which the seasons affected his subjects. His sons Jan and Pieter the Younger were also painters and frequently used a style similar to their father's.

19. The correct answer is (A). Pagodas, found in China, Korea, and Japan, are used as Buddhist shrines, tombs, or memorials. They are usually built of wood or brick. This pagoda in Kyoto, Japan, dates from 951 C.E.

20. The correct answer is (C). Gothic architecture, a style typical of the European Middle Ages, produced a lighter, higher building than did the Romanesque style that preceded it. Pointed arches and vaults helped take the strain from the walls and allowed for larger windows and higher ceilings. High Gothic cathedrals such as the one at Chartres in France have flying buttresses to reduce the strain further, complex rib vaulting, and elaborate decorative carvings.

21. The correct answer is (D). The ceiling of the Sistine Chapel, painted by Michelangelo between 1508 and 1512, depicts scenes from the Creation in the Old Testament. The section pictured shows God giving Adam the spark of life.

22. The correct answer is (D). Jacob van Ruisdael (c. 1629–1682) was a Dutch landscape painter of the seventeenth century. Constable (1776—1837) and Turner (1775–1851) were both British; Constable believed landscape painting should be the result of observation, whereas Turner often linked his landscapes with literary themes or historical events in the Romantic style.

23. The correct answer is (B). Pop art was a movement of the 1950s and 1960s whose imagery was based on American mass media, and Andy Warhol was one of the most prominent artists of this movement. Fauvism was a movement of the turn of the century that included heavy outlines, primitive forms, and flat planes of color. Cubism, which developed at the same

time, is identified by the angles and facets that make up its forms. Dadaism was an often nihilistic movement whose advocates felt that all values were made meaningless by World War I.

24. The correct answer is (C). The Great Sphinx is a statue guarding the Pyramids at Giza. It is in the shape of a lion with a human head, probably that of the pharaoh Chephren, and stands sixty-five feet high.

25. The correct answer is (C). *Annunciation*, or "announcement," refers to the moment when the Archangel Gabriel tells the Virgin Mary that she is carrying the Son of God. It is a common motif of European painting, especially painting of the Middle Ages and Renaissance. This example was painted between 1430 and 1445 by Fra Angelico.

26. The correct answer is (B). Federico Fellini (1920–1993) was an Italian director best known for his strange, often surrealistic films, such as *La Dolce Vita, Satyricon,* and, recently, *And the Ship Sailed On.* Bergman (b. 1918), a Swedish director, has among his works *Smiles of a Summer Night, The Seventh Seal, Cries and Whispers,* and *The Magic Flute,* a film version of Mozart's opera. John Huston (1906–1987), an American, directed the films *The Maltese Falcon, The African Queen,* and, just before his death, the film version of James Joyce's "The Dead."

27. The correct answer is (D). Since ancient times, people have painted inanimate objects, but during the

Renaissance, such paintings became a genre of their own. Masters of the art over the centuries include the van Eycks, Rubens, Rembrandt, the Peales, and Cézanne, whose *Pears and Peaches* is shown here.

28. The correct answer is (A). Mosaics, composed of inlaid colored glass, marble, tile, or gemstone, are used in many cultures. The Romans used them to decorate floors, and pre-Columbian art contains examples of this craft. The construction of Santa Sophia in Constantinople (now Istanbul) marked the pinnacle of the art form. Magnificent gold mosaics may still be seen there today.

29. The correct answer is (B). *Notre Dame de Paris* is an example of early Gothic architecture. It was begun in 1163 but was not completed until the fourteenth century. Its famous gargoyles were added much later.

30. The correct answer is (B). Jackson Pollock (1912–1956), influenced by the Surrealists, created a style of abstract art sometimes called "action painting." In rapid, rhythmic motions, he dripped or threw paint onto canvases, creating swirling patterns of color.

31. The correct answer is (C). The Golden Gate Bridge was built across San Francisco Bay in the 1930s. At 9,266 feet in length, it is one of the longest suspension bridges in the world.

32. The correct answer is (A). The American architect Frank Lloyd Wright (1869–1959) developed a the-

ory of architecture stressing the needs of the people who used it. His unadorned, clean-looking buildings contained functional rooms that allowed interaction both with the rest of the building and with the landscape outside.

33. The correct answer is (D). The Taj Mahal in Agra, India, was designed by a Turk and built to house the tomb of Mumtaz Mahal by her husband, Shah Jahan. Construction took from 1630 to 1648. The dome, minarets, and intricate decoration mark it as Islamic in style.

34. The correct answer is (D). Egyptian pyramids were built around 2700 B.C.E.–2200 B.C.E. to preserve the mummified bodies of rulers. Mayan pyramids of the Yucatán and Central America were constructed some 3,000 years later. Like the Egyptian pyramids, they were decorated, and they often contained tombs. Whereas the Egyptian pyramids had steep triangular sides. Mayan pyramids were built of steeply stepped blocks and often rose to ritual chambers at the summit.

35. The correct answer is (B). Pablo Picasso (1881–1973) was a Spanish painter, sculptor, and graphic artist whom many believe is the foremost influence in twentieth-century art. His enormous painting, *Guernica* (1937), was a response to the bombing of the ancient capital of the Basques during the Spanish Civil War.

36. The correct answer is (B). Fanciful ornamentation, shellwork, and airy asymmetry distinguished rococo

art and architecture of the eighteenth century from the heavy baroque style of the seventeenth century.

37. The correct answer is (D). Auguste Rodin (1840–1917) was a French sculptor known for his work in bronze and marble. *The Thinker* was intended to be part of a great pair of doors called *The Gates of Hell,* but the doors were never finished.

38. The correct answer is (A). Built around 440 B.C.E., the Parthenon on the Acropolis in Athens housed vast quantities of sculpture depicting scenes from Greek mythology. In 1806, the Earl of Elgin removed many of the ancient friezes and sculptures from the Parthenon to England, where they remain in the British Museum, to the dismay of many Greeks.

39. The correct answer is (C). Arguably the most famous painting in the world, *Mona Lisa* (1503) now hangs in the Louvre. Because of his excellence in the areas of painting, sculpture, architecture, engineering, and music, Leonardo da Vinci is often considered the model of the Renaissance man.

40. The correct answer is (C). Bas-relief is a type of sculpture in which the form projects only slightly from the surrounding surface and is not wholly separated from it.

41. The correct answer is (D). The group of stones is called Stonehenge, and it is an ancient monument in the south of England, that dates back perhaps 4,000 years. The stones are thought to have served

a religious purpose, possibly involving the movements of the sun and stars. Although there are many theories, no one is really sure how the ancients moved the stones to this location.

42. The correct answer is (B). Traditional Japanese painting, beginning in the eighth century, was done with Chinese ink or watercolor on silk or paper. The paintings were either horizontal or vertical scrolls.

43. The correct answer is (B). Masks are used in the religious and social rituals of many cultures. This mask is a Chokwe Mwana Pwo mask, worn by men in ceremonies that represents female ancestors and emphasizes beauty.

44. The correct answer is (A). Many painters in the eighteenth and nineteenth centuries made a living painting portraits in order to support their other, less lucrative work. Joshua Reynolds (1723–1792) painted more than 2,000 portraits of English notables. Gilbert Stuart (1755–1828), an American, is best known for his paintings of George Washington, including the one reproduced on the $1 bill. Thomas Gainsborough (1727–1788) was known for his portraits but preferred landscape painting. *The Blue Boy* is one of his most famous works.

45. The correct answer is (B). Vincent van Gogh's (1853–1890) *Self-portrait with Palette* shows his characteristic linear brush strokes and heavy application of paint. Most of van Gogh's work was done in the two years before his death in 1890, years during which he went progressively mad.

46. The correct answer is (A). David Smith (1906–1965), an American, worked in steel and wrought iron. Alberto Giacometti (1901–1966) was a Swiss Surrealist who sculpted elongated forms in bronze. Marcel Duchamp (1887–1968), the French painter, was among the first to exhibit "found objects" or "ready-mades" as art.

47. The correct answer is (D). Grant Wood's stylized paintings of midwestern landscapes and people came to national attention through the Federal Arts Project of Franklin D. Roosevelt's administration. *American Gothic* was painted in 1930.

48. The correct answer is (B). An aqueduct is a pipeline or conduit that carries water from a source to where it is needed. The long, arched structures built during the Roman Empire to house conduits may still be seen in many parts of Europe.

49. The correct answer is (C). Romantic paintings of the American landscape were the product of the Hudson River School of the nineteenth century. *Fields and Streams* by Thomas Doughty is an example of the Hudson River School. It contains typical elements of the Hudson River style: grand scale, vast sky, and detailed foreground. The Ashcan School was a group of eight American painters of different styles who banded together in the early 1900s to introduce modern European painters to the American public. Their penchant for painting everyday city scenes led to their title. At around the same time, German Expressionists were using art

to express emotion and inner feeling rather than surface or objective reality. Primitivism refers to a simple, naïve style such as that of Grandma Moses (1860–1961).

50. The correct answer is (C). The Capitol is built on a hill in Washington, D.C., on a site selected by George Washington and the architect Pierre L'Enfant. Many architects worked on the building over time, but much of their work was destroyed by fire in the War of 1812. In 1830, the building was finished, although the dome and wings were not added until the 1860s. The Capitol is home to the seat of the U.S. legislature.

TEST 6
THE FOOD OF LOVE: MUSIC

Music is the universal language of mankind.

—HENRY WADSWORTH LONGFELLOW

1. Which of these instruments is *not* in the woodwind family?
   (A) Flute
   (B) Bassoon
   (C) Trombone
   (D) Oboe

2. Ludwig van Beethoven's work includes
   (A) nine symphonies and several piano concertos.
   (B) nine books of madrigals and three operas.
   (C) three nocturnes and two choral pieces.
   (D) four scherzos and dozens of polkas and mazurkas.

3. What is a hymn?
   (A) A composition for male voices
   (B) A special kind of religious song
   (C) A tune composed for closed-mouth vocalization
   (D) A primitive kind of folk song

4. The development of the chord is part of the history of
   (A) cadence.
   (B) harmony.
   (C) pitch.
   (D) ligature.

5. Which of these are considered origins of jazz?
   (A) Spirituals, Caribbean music, work songs
   (B) Soul, rock and roll, rap
   (C) Folk songs, atonality, program music
   (D) Country dances, baroque music, monody

6. Which list arranges vocal ranges from highest to lowest?
   (A) Contralto, soprano, countertenor, baritone, bass
   (B) Soprano, mezzo-soprano, contralto, tenor, baritone, bass
   (C) Treble, tenor, contralto, baritone, countertenor
   (D) Soprano, contralto, tenor, bass, baritone

7. Handel's *Messiah* is an oratorio, which means that
   (A) it is performed outdoors.
   (B) it does not use a full orchestra.
   (C) it calls for no staging or costumes.
   (D) it uses soloists in lieu of a chorus.

8. Louis Armstrong is known for
   (A) his clarinet playing and orchestration.
   (B) astonishing fingering feats on piano.
   (C) an improvisatory trumpet and vocal style.
   (D) inventing the form called "be-bop."

9. From the sixteenth century, the word *ballad* has referred to
   (A) a dance for two partners.
   (B) any simple melody for piano or guitar.
   (C) a very short piece of music.
   (D) a story told in song.

10. An octave is
    (A) a group of eight players.
    (B) the complete work of a composer.
    (C) an interval of eight notes.
    (D) the distance between thumb and little finger on the piano.

11. Who was Enrico Caruso?
    (A) An Italian operatic tenor
    (B) A Spanish cellist
    (C) A composer of twelve-tone music
    (D) A conductor of the New York Philharmonic

12. W. S. Gilbert and Sir Arthur Sullivan are known for their
    (A) operas based on the lives of British heroes.
    (B) Broadway musical comedies.
    (C) orchestral arrangements for films.
    (D) comic operettas.

13. What is a waltz?
    (A) A dance involving changes of partner
    (B) A very slow form of polka
    (C) Dance music with three beats to the bar
    (D) A stately dance in 2/4 time

14. The kind of sonata written by Beethoven or Mozart
    (A) has one movement and is performed by an orchestra.
    (B) has three or four movements and is performed by one or two instruments.
    (C) is in the same form as a sonata written by Bach or Handel.
    (D) is a vocal work containing arias and recitatives.

15. George Balanchine is primarily known as which of the following?
    (A) A dancer
    (B) A composer
    (C) A choreographer
    (D) A pianist

16. If one line of music is in counterpoint with another,
    (A) it harmonizes with the line but has a tune of its own.
    (B) it parallels the line one octave higher or lower.
    (C) it repeats each phrase in a minor key.
    (D) it exactly reverses the melody of the other.

17. An overture originally was
    (A) the first movement in a symphony.
    (B) lesser vibrations when a string is plucked.
    (C) a solo piece for piano or voice.
    (D) the opening to an oratorio or opera.

18. What is the difference between rhythm and tempo?
    (A) Rhythm involves speed, and tempo involves loudness.
    (B) Rhythm involves pitch, and tempo involves accent.
    (C) Rhythm involves beat, and tempo involves speed.
    (D) There is no difference; they both involve rate and pitch.

19. Which of these instruments is *not* in the percussion family?
    (A) Xylophone
    (B) Castanet
    (C) Snare drum
    (D) Banjo

20. Duke Ellington's style of composing was novel in its
    (A) emphasis on tightly structured collective improvisation.
    (B) lack of notation and reliance on impromptu creation.
    (C) elegant and unemotional arrangements of classic tunes.
    (D) integration of Eastern harmonics and Western rhythms.

21. *Swan Lake* is likely to be part of the repertoire of which of the following?
    (A) A marching band
    (B) A ballet company
    (C) An opera company
    (D) A chamber group

22. Among the compositions of John Philip Sousa is
    (A) "The Stars and Stripes Forever."
    (B) "Maple Leaf Rag."
    (C) "Rule Britannia."
    (D) "Honeysuckle Rose."

23. What is a choir?
    (A) A symphony for mixed voices
    (B) A vocal group that performs only church music
    (C) A group of singers or the place in which they sing
    (D) A song to celebrate a religious holiday or feast day

24. The word *flamenco* refers to
    (A) a particular kind of music from Spain.
    (B) a folk dance of southern France.
    (C) a style of Portuguese folk song.
    (D) a popular Cuban ballroom dance.

25. Among the compositions of Giuseppe Verdi are
    (A) *The Barber of Seville, Cenerentola,* and *William Tell.*
    (B) *Aïda, Otello,* and *Il Trovatore.*
    (C) *Lohengrin, Parsifal,* and *Tristan und Isolde.*
    (D) *La Bohème, Madame Butterfly,* and *Tosca.*

26. Bach, Telemann, and Handel were composers of the
    (A) classical period.
    (B) baroque period.
    (C) romantic period.
    (D) rococo period.

27. What is a melody?
    (A) A logical succession of single musical notes
    (B) A structure of chords
    (C) A body of singers with several performers for
        each part
    (D) A written symbol used to represent duration
        and pitch

28. The composer of the *Brandenburg Concertos*, the
    Mass in B Minor, and *The Well-Tempered Clavier* is
    (A) Philip Glass.
    (B) Peter Ilyich Tchaikovsky.
    (C) Johann Sebastian Bach.
    (D) Ludwig van Beethoven.

29. For what was Billie Holiday best known?
    (A) Her interpretation of the roles of Aïda and
        Mimi in *La Bohème*
    (B) Collaborating with Oscar Hammerstein to
        write *South Pacific*
    (C) Interpreting and singing the blues and popular
        music
    (D) Winning the Brussels Music Competition at
        the age of twelve

30. *Afternoon of a Faun*, *Les Sylphides*, and *Parade* are
    all
    (A) ballets.
    (B) operas.
    (C) cantatas.
    (D) None of the above

31. Igor Stravinsky composed which of the following?
    (A) *Der Rosenkavalier, Salomé,* and *Don Quixote*
    (B) *The Moldau, Czech Dances,* and *The Bartered Bride*
    (C) *The Firebird, The Rites of Spring,* and *Petroushka*
    (D) *The Heir Apparent* and *Maharajah*

32. What is a symphony?
    (A) A vocal work with instrumental accompaniment
    (B) An orchestral work, usually in three or four movements
    (C) A dance in slow 3/4 time with syncopated rhythms
    (D) A sacred text set to music for chorus, soloists, and orchestra

33. *Das Rheingold, Die Walküre, Siegfried,* and *Die Götterdämmerung* are
    (A) a series of ballets by Peter Ilyich Tchaikovsky.
    (B) a group of cantatas by Johann Sebastian Bach.
    (C) a cycle of operas by Richard Wagner.
    (D) a collection of symphonies by Ludwig van Beethoven.

34. What is chamber music?
    (A) Instrumental music limited to a few performers
    (B) Opera performed in a small room, or chamber
    (C) Organ music performed in the chamber adjoining a church nave
    (D) A work in several movements intended for evening entertainment

35. Which instruments belong to the brass family?
    (A) Violin, viola, cello, bass
    (B) Harpsichord, piano, accordion, organ
    (C) Flute, oboe, bassoon, clarinet
    (D) Cornet, trombone, tuba, flügelhorn

36. Johannes Brahms was a master of
    (A) the symphony.
    (B) chamber music.
    (C) the sonata.
    (D) All of the above

37. What is a concerto?
    (A) A work in which a soloist contrasts with other
         instruments
    (B) A small group of performers playing different
         instruments
    (C) A dance in 3/4 time that came into popularity
         during the eighteenth century
    (D) A song for two or three voices to a text about
         the birth of Christ

38. When a musical piece builds to a crescendo,
    (A) a chorus joins in.
    (B) it gets louder.
    (C) the wind section joins in.
    (D) it gets quieter.

39. Among Aaron Copland's compositions are
    (A) *The Three-Cornered Hat* and *Nights in the Gardens of Spain.*
    (B) *Krazy Kat, Skyscrapers,* and *Adventures in a Perambulator.*
    (C) *Billy the Kid, Rodeo,* and *Appalachian Spring.*
    (D) *Shaneurs* and *At Dawning.*

40. When and where might you have danced the minuet?
    (A) England in the sixteenth century
    (B) France in the seventeenth century
    (C) Germany in the nineteenth century
    (D) Italy in the fourteenth century

41. What is harmony?
    (A) The bass line in a choral piece
    (B) A recurring theme in a musical composition symbolizing an idea or object
    (C) The structure and relationships of chords
    (D) A change of key

42. *Eugene Onegin, Romeo and Juliet,* and *Sleeping Beauty* are compositions by
    (A) Frédéric Chopin.
    (B) Giacomo Puccini.
    (C) Richard Strauss.
    (D) Peter Ilyich Tchaikovsky.

43. The string section of an orchestra includes
    (A) xylophone, triangle, and cymbals.
    (B) bassoon, piccolo, oboe, and flute.
    (C) cello, viola, double bass, and violin.
    (D) lute, guitar, theorbo, and chitarrone.

44. *La Traviata, Carmen,* and *Madame Butterfly* are
    examples of
    (A) operas.
    (B) ballets.
    (C) études.
    (D) symphonies.

45. *Don Giovanni, Eine kleine Nachtmusik,* and *The
    Magic Flute* are works by
    (A) Ludwig van Beethoven.
    (B) Gian-Carlo Menotti.
    (C) Wolfgang Amadeus Mozart.
    (D) Henry Purcell.

46. What is a synthesizer?
    (A) A wind instrument similar to the oboe
    (B) An electronic apparatus that can produce
        musical sounds
    (C) A device used by composers to vary the stress
        on notes
    (D) The section of an organ that increases or
        diminishes the volume of sound

47. Which of these composers wrote during the roman-
    tic period?
    (A) Haydn, Mozart, and Gluck
    (B) Monteverdi, Vivaldi, and Scarlatti
    (C) Schubert, Brahms, and Mendelssohn
    (D) Bartok, Debussy, and Schoenberg

48. George Gershwin is the composer of
    (A) *Orpheus in Hades* and *Tales of Hoffman.*
    (B) *Porgy and Bess, Rhapsody in Blue,* and *An American in Paris.*
    (C) *Schelomo, Baal Shem,* and *Sacred Service.*
    (D) *The Three-Penny Opera, Down in the Valley,* and *Mahagonny.*

49. Chopin is best known for
    (A) operas and symphonies.
    (B) ballets and chorales.
    (C) mazurkas and études.
    (D) All of the above

50. The sitar, the tabla, and the sarangi are all
    (A) dances from Indonesia.
    (B) musical instruments from India.
    (C) musical instruments from Japan.
    (D) Middle Eastern religious chants.

TEST 6:
Explanatory Answers

1. The correct answer is (C). At one time, all wood-wind instruments were made of wood. Even when made of metal, woodwinds share certain qualities: They are essentially tubular, with holes along the length of the tube. The holes are covered or uncovered to produce notes of different pitches. Oboes, clarinets, flutes, piccolos, saxophones, bagpipes, and recorders are all woodwinds. The trombone, which has a very different mouthpiece from a woodwind, is a member of the brass family.

2. The correct answer is (A). Beethoven (1770–1827) was a pianist in Bonn and Vienna. At the end of the eighteenth century, he began to lose his hearing, and from that time on he concentrated on composing. His music brought drama and expressiveness to the old classical forms. His nine symphonies, five piano concertos, one violin concerto, and countless chamber pieces still form a major part of the classical repertoire.

3. The correct answer is (B). For centuries, hymns were written in Latin and sung by priests. Not until the Reformation of the sixteenth century did the idea that ordinary people could sing in praise of God catch on. Chorales and psalms became popular in the reformed churches, and composers began to write specifically for the church.

4. The correct answer is (B). A chord is a group of notes played at the same time. At one time, melody was played as a single line or harmonized by octaves so that high C and middle C notes might be played at the same time, for example. In the eleventh century, lines of melody sometimes moved in parallel fifths so that middle C and G would be sounded together, for example. Chords were a later invention, based on the concept that every note could form the root of a series of harmonic notes. A common chord is a chord including the root (C, for example), the third above it (E), and the fifth above it (G).

5. The correct answer is (A). Basic jazz forms use syncopated rhythms, improvisation, and certain select harmonic sequences. The origins of jazz are many, but key among them are work songs, blues, gospel, spirituals, ragtime, and various Latin styles.

6. The correct answer is (B). Female voices are divided by pitch into three classes: soprano (the highest), mezzo-soprano, and contralto. The highest adult male voice is the countertenor, followed by tenor, baritone, and bass. The highest boy's voice is treble, followed by alto.

7. The correct answer is (C). An oratorio is something like an opera, except that it is usually performed without action or scenery. The chorus plays a large part in any oratorio, linking arias sung by soloists with stretches of choral music. In a true oratorio, the theme is religious.

8. The correct answer is (C). Louis Armstrong (1900–1971) came from the New Orleans jazz tradition. He played trumpet on riverboats before moving to Chicago and then New York, where he played in Fletcher Henderson's big band. He triumphed as a solo player with his own bands in the 1920s and 1930s and then went on to a career that included scat singing and movie roles.

9. The correct answer is (D). A ballad is a song based on a narrative poem. Traditional folk songs such as "Barbara Allen" and "The Ballad of Casey Jones" are ballads.

10. The correct answer is (C). *Octo* is a root meaning "eight," and an octave is the eight notes that make up a scale. Acoustically, a note one octave above another has twice its frequency. These intervals of eight notes are a key element of Western music.

11. The correct answer is (A). Caruso (1873–1921) had an astonishing range and great power, but his real fame derives from the fact that he was the first great opera star to be recorded and thus was the first to live on after his career ended.

12. The correct answer is (D). Sir Arthur Sullivan, an English composer, teamed with lyricist W. S. Gilbert in the 1870s and 1880s to create such popular operettas as *The Mikado, The Pirates of Penzance,* and *H.M.S. Pinafore.* Gilbert and Sullivan were so successful that impresario Richard D'Oyly Carte constructed a theater called the Savoy expressly for their work.

13. The correct answer is (C). A waltz is a piece of music in 3/4 time, usually meant for dancing. Derived from peasant dances of Austria and Bavaria, it reached the height of its popularity in the mid-1800s.

14. The correct answer is (B). The baroque sonata, such as those composed by Handel and Bach, is a work for solo instrument made up of several movements. The classical sonata, such as those composed by Beethoven and Mozart, is written for keyboard or for keyboard and one other instrument. It may have three or four movements. The first movement is in "sonata form," which means that it consists of a musical statement containing several themes, a section that elaborates on the themes, and a section that returns to the original statement.

15. The correct answer is (C). Balanchine (1904–1983) was a dancer with Diaghilev and his Ballets Russes before moving to the United States in 1933. He helped to found the School of American Ballet and worked as artistic director and principal choreographer of the New York City Ballet for more than thirty years. His choreography emphasized form over story and featured movement applied over the musical structure of a piece.

16. The correct answer is (A). Counterpoint is a form of harmony in which melodies are played in conjunction with one another or interwoven. In the simplest form, a fixed melodic line is written, and a note is written to harmonize with each note of the

fixed line. More elaborate forms use inversions, in which an upper part becomes a lower part and vice versa, and imitations, where the second part repeats the first part while the first part continues.

17. The correct answer is (D). *Overture* is from the French word *ouverture,* or "opening." It once referred exclusively to orchestral music that opened an opera or oratorio, but in the nineteenth century the term was applied to short, independent orchestral compositions in sonata form, now called concert overtures.

18. The correct answer is (C). Rhythm is the beat of a piece of music and the pattern of notes that make up that beat. *Tempo* means "time" in Italian, and the word is used to describe the pace at which a piece is to be played.

19. The correct answer is (D). Percussion instruments are those instruments whose sound derives from a tap or blow from the player. Percussion was not in use in orchestras except in special effects until the late nineteenth century. Percussion instruments include drums, bells, triangles, cymbals, pianos, xylophones, and rattles. The banjo is a member of the string family.

20. The correct answer is (A). Considered one of the foremost composers of the twentieth century, Ellington (1899–1975) perfected a form of jazz that combined intricately structured written work with improvisation. Working with many of the best artists in the jazz world, Ellington created compo-

sitions around the talents of his band members, allowing their creativity to merge with his structure in a process of collaborative composition that many artists today try to emulate. Pieces such as "Mood Indigo" and "Take the A Train" were immensely popular, and Ellington's musicianship and composing ability helped make jazz a recognized art form.

21. The correct answer is (B). Tchaikovsky's three ballets, *Swan Lake*, *Sleeping Beauty*, and *The Nutcracker*, choreographed by Lev Ivanov and Marius Petipa, are among the most famous and popular of all ballets in the classical repertoire.

22. The correct answer is (A). Sousa led the U.S. Marine Corps band for twelve years in the late 1800s and then went on to lead his own band. He is famous for composing dozens of marches, of which "The Stars and Stripes Forever" is perhaps the best known.

23. The correct answer is (C). A choir is simply a group of singers, and the word may also refer to the part of a cathedral between the sanctuary and the nave used by singers in a church choir.

24. The correct answer is (A). A mournful song from Andalusia, Spain, is the basis for flamenco. The rhythm and melody derive from Arabic music of Spain's Moorish conquerors. The dance that accompanies this music is highly dramatic and energetic.

25. The correct answer is (B). All of the works listed are operas, but only these three are by Giuseppe

Verdi (1813–1901), one of the greatest opera com-
posers of all time. Other operas by Verdi include
Rigoletto, La Traviata, Don Carlo, Macbeth, and
Falstaff. The other operas listed are by Rossini,
Wagner, and Puccini.

26. The correct answer is (B). Baroque music was, like
the architecture of the time, both lavish and precise. Johann Sebastian Bach (1685–1760), George
Frederick Handel (1685–1759), and Georg Telemann (1748–1831) were three of the best-known
composers of the period. Opera, oratorio, cantata,
suite, sonata, and fugue originated during this
time.

27. The correct answer is (A). A melody is usually a
simple strand of music that is developed in a musical composition against a harmonic background.

28. The correct answer is (C). Johann Sebastian Bach
(1685–1750), a German composer of the eighteenth century, incorporated the forms of German
music, the Italian concerto, and French dance
music into his compositions. He brought the forms
of fugue, suite, and canon to their greatest expres-
sion. More than one thousand of his compositions
survive.

29. The correct answer is (C). Billie Holiday
(1915–1959), also known as Lady Day, had a
unique singing style and method of interpreting the
blues. One of her best-known songs, "Strange
Fruit," is the story of a lynching; she invests the
song with a vibrant power that brings out the truth

in the words. Critics often compare her singing voice to a horn, but in phrasing and in feeling, she moves far beyond the range of any instrument. She died at 44, a victim of drug addiction.

30. The correct answer is (A). Prélude à l'après-midi d'un faune (1890) by Debussy, *Les Sylphides* (1909) from music by Chopin, and *Parade* (1917) by Eric Satie are ballets, or dances, in which performers dance to music to tell a story or set a mood. All three ballets were commissioned by Sergei Diaghilev of the Ballets Russes; *Afternoon of a Faun* was choreographed as a vehicle for the great dancer Nijinsky.

31. The correct answer is (C). Igor Stravinsky (1882–1971) was a composer whose ballets, such as *The Firebird, The Rites of Spring,* and *Petroushka,* commissioned by Diaghilev, earned him his fame. He used dissonance, polytonality, and asymmetrical rhythm to produce a distinctive sound.

32. The correct answer is (B). Symphonies evolved from the Italian operatic overture of the seventeenth century, which had three movements. After the mid-eighteenth century, a fourth movement was often added. Mozart, Beethoven, and Brahms were masters of the symphonic form.

33. The correct answer is (C). *Der Ring des Nibelungen* is a series of four operas by Richard Wagner that took twenty-eight years to produce. The operas tell of a ring made by dwarves that gives its owner mas-

tery of the world, of the love of Siegfried and
Brünnhilde, and of the way in which the curse of
the ring kills Siegfried and drives Brünnhilde to her
own death.

34. The correct answer is (A). Chamber music was
originally intended to be played in a room in a
house, rather than a church or hall. Now it usually
refers to music written for a few performers, each
playing a different part; it emphasizes clarity and
balance.

35. The correct answer is (D). Brass instruments are
wind instruments that transmit a tone by the vibration of the player's lips. They include trumpet,
French horn, trombone, tuba, cornet, flügelhorn,
saxhorn, and sousaphone. They are usually made
of brass today, though in the past they were made
of wood, horn, and glass.

36. The correct answer is (D). Johannes Brahms
(1833–1897) was a German composer, a contemporary of Liszt and Schumann. He was a conductor
and music director for the Prince of Lippe-Detmold.
His compositions include four symphonies, con-
certi, sonatas, character pieces, and chorales.

37. The correct answer is (A). *Concerto* is a term that
has gone through several meanings. Until the early
eighteenth century, it was a vocal work with instrumental accompaniment. Bach's *Third Brandenburg*
was a concerto for several instruments. A *concerto
grosso* provides instrumental solos, and the solo
concerto, now the best-known type, has a solo

instrument against an orchestra. The one point that all concertos have in common is that they provide a musical contrast: between voice and orchestra, instrument and orchestra, or instrument and instrument.

38. The correct answer is (B). *Crescendo* is an Italian term that means "increasing." Music that builds to a crescendo gets louder. The term does not specify a degree of loudness.

39. The correct answer is (C). Born in 1900, Aaron Copland is one of America's greatest composers. He has written three symphonies, chamber music, ballets, an opera, piano music, and music for films. The other pieces mentioned are by Manuel de Falla, John Carpenter, and Percy Atherton.

40. The correct answer is (B). The minuet is a French dance in 3/4 time, introduced around 1650. It was used often in ballets and instrumental pieces until Beethoven quickened its tempo and it became the scherzo.

41. The correct answer is (C). Harmony, once a term that meant music, now means the relationship of chords and their structure and function. Traditional harmonic theory began in the baroque era and lasted until the late nineteenth century when composers began to find alternatives to traditional harmony.

42. The correct answer is (D). Tchaikovsky (1840–1893) was a Russian composer known for his romantic compositions. He wrote eleven operas,

seven symphonies, four suites, more than one hundred songs, and some of today's best-loved ballets.

43. The correct answer is (C). The string section of the orchestra is made up of instruments on which gut or metal wire is bowed, plucked, struck, or rubbed, producing a sound. These instruments include, in order of size, violin, viola, cello, and double bass.

44. The correct answer is (A). *La Traviata* (1853) by Guiseppe Verdi, *Carmen* (1875) by Georges Bizet, and *Madame Butterfly* (1904) by Giacomo Puccini are all operas—stage works that are completely or mostly sung. Opera began in Italy, where a group of composers, using the idea of Greek drama with its cadences and chorus, began setting words to music. *Euridice* (1600) by Jacopo Peri is considered the first opera. Some of the best-known composers of opera are Verdi, Wagner, Mozart, and Puccini.

45. The correct answer is (C). Mozart (1756–1791) was an Austrian whom many consider to be the greatest composer of all time. He began composing at the age of 5 and wrote his first symphony at 9. He was influenced by Bach, Handel, and Haydn. In all, he wrote more than 600 works, and his mastery of all classical forms makes his work the epitome of classical music.

46. The correct answer is (B). The synthesizer, invented by Robert Moog in 1965, produced a revolution in electronic composition. The system, usually with a keyboard, can memorize, change, and play musical sounds.

47. The correct answer is (C). The romantic period is said to have lasted from about 1820 to 1910. National styles of composition grew popular, and the role of the orchestra became more important. Romantic composers were concerned with the musical past and used influences from the past to write lyrical compositions. As Romantics in philosophy and literature changed their emphases from the universal to the individual, so too in music romanticism focused on the composer as creator and the performer as interpreter, a trend that continues today.

48. The correct answer is (B). George Gershwin (1898–1937) was an American composer whose concert works join the sounds of jazz with those of traditional orchestration. His opera *Porgy and Bess* is a love story set among a group of African-American workers in South Carolina; it was considered the first successful American opera. The other works listed are by Jacques Offenbach, Ernest Bloch, and Kurt Weill.

49. The correct answer is (C). Frédéric Chopin (1810–1849), a composer of the Romantic school, wrote mostly for the piano. He composed fifty-one mazurkas, twelve polonaises, seventeen waltzes, and twenty-seven études, as well as nocturnes, sonatas, and ballads.

50. The correct answer is (B). Indian music is based on a system of melodic modes called ragas and rhythms called talas. Each raga is performed at a

certain time of day or of the year. Indian instruments include the sitar (a large lute), the sarod (a short-necked lute), the sarangi (a stringed instrument), the tabla (a set of drums), and the tamboura (a droning lute).

TEST 7
ALL'S RIGHT
WITH THE WORLD:
MYTH AND RELIGION

Religion in its humility restores man to his only
dignity, the courage to live by grace.

—GEORGE SANTAYANA

1. What is Original Sin?
   (A) The first sin that a person commits in his or
       her life
   (B) Any sin resulting from disobedience of the Ten
       Commandments
   (C) Sin resulting from Adam's and Eve's eating of
       the forbidden fruit
   (D) Any one of the Seven Deadly Sins

2. What is Mecca?
   (A) The holy city of Islam
   (B) A directional point on the compass to which
       religious believers bow when praying
   (C) The Egyptian goddess of the River Nile
   (D) The Buddhist heaven

3. Isis, Re, and Osiris are all
   (A) Hindu prophets.
   (B) Mayan gods.
   (C) Scandinavian warrior-gods.
   (D) Egyptian gods.

4. Who was John the Baptist?
   (A) The author of the Gospel according to St. John
   (B) The man who baptized Christ
   (C) One of the twelve apostles of Christ
   (D) All of the above

5. Mount Olympus and Asgard are
   (A) locations of temples to Apollo.
   (B) sites of religious pilgrimages.
   (C) legendary homes of the gods.
   (D) two of the great pyramids.

6. Why was Job considered to be so patient?
   (A) He withstood Satan's testing and kept his faith
       in God.
   (B) He followed Christ despite the mockery of his
       family.
   (C) He waited for Moses when Moses went to
       speak with God.
   (D) He did not protest when God refused to accept
       his sacrifice.

7. What is the Quran?
   (A) The ark in which the Jewish holy book is kept
   (B) The church built over Christ's tomb in Jerusalem
   (C) The name for Moses' Ten Commandments
   (D) The holy book of Islam

8. Aphrodite (Venus) was the goddess of
   (A) erotic love and marriage.
   (B) war.
   (C) the hunt and wild animals.
   (D) the hearth.

9. Methodist, Presbyterian, and Unitarian are names of
   (A) the Gospels.
   (B) Protestant sects.
   (C) levels in the Catholic hierarchy.
   (D) Anglican sects.

10. What was Charon's job?
    (A) He held the world on his shoulders.
    (B) He had to find and bring back the Golden Fleece.
    (C) He was responsible for answering the Sphinx's riddle.
    (D) He ferried the dead across the River Styx to Elysium.

11. The story of Noah involves
    (A) the journey out of slavery in Egypt to Israel.
    (B) the denial of Christ before his crucifixion.
    (C) an ark built to escape a flood inflicted by God.
    (D) a wrestling match with an angel.

12. Who was Thor?
    (A) The Roman god of healing
    (B) The Greek god of eloquence and good fortune
    (C) The Norse god of thunder
    (D) The war god of the Assyrians

13. What is the Torah?
    (A) A valley near Jerusalem where the dead are buried
    (B) The first five books of the Old Testament
    (C) A feast that celebrates the harvest season
    (D) The candle that burns between Easter and Ascension Day

14. Athena (Minerva) was the goddess of
    (A) war, wisdom, and crafts.
    (B) the waters and the rainbow.
    (C) the harvest.
    (D) fertility and wine.

15. Matthew, Mark, Luke, and John were
    (A) saints of the Middle Ages who were killed by Muslims.
    (B) the first kings in the Middle East to convert to Christianity.
    (C) evangelists who wrote gospels on Jesus' life.
    (D) apostles who followed Jesus.

16. For what is Lazarus known?
    (A) Writing the book of the Apocalypse
    (B) Being raised from the dead by Jesus
    (C) Returning home as the prodigal son
    (D) Aiding a man who was robbed by thieves

17. What is a phoenix?
    (A) A bird that rises from its own ashes
    (B) A bird that feeds on elephant calves and pos-
        sesses a huge egg
    (C) A sea monster that makes dangerous whirlpools
        when surfacing
    (D) A monster that is part lion, part goat, and part
        serpent

18. What was the result of the building of the Tower of
    Babel?
    (A) God flooded the earth for forty days and
        nights.
    (B) God demanded that Abraham sacrifice his
        son.
    (C) God appeared as a burning bush to express his
        anger.
    (D) God confounded the speech of men so that
        they could not understand each other.

19. A Dionysian celebration, or Bacchanalia, is
    (A) a solemn feast during which a goat is slaugh-
        tered to worship the gods.
    (B) a dance at which young virgins are picked as
        wives by warriors.
    (C) a revel in which wine and sex are the foremost
        entertainment.
    (D) a religious rite honoring Dionysus in which
        candles, signifying eternal life, are burned.

20. The Good Samaritan was
   (A) the man who gave Jesus wine as he hung on the cross.
   (B) a man who helped the victim of a brutal robbery.
   (C) another name for John, who comforted Mary after the Crucifixion.
   (D) a man who gave away all of his riches to follow Jesus.

21. In Greek and Roman mythology, the supreme god was known as
   (A) Apollo.
   (B) Hades or Pluto.
   (C) Mars or Ares.
   (D) Zeus or Jupiter.

22. On Yom Kippur, worshippers
   (A) celebrate the freeing of Jews from slavery in Egypt.
   (B) commemorate the victory of the Maccabees over the Assyrians.
   (C) celebrate the new year.
   (D) fast to atone for their sins.

23. In the Book of Revelation, Armageddon is
   (A) the place where the last battle between good and evil will take place.
   (B) the horseman of the Apocalypse representing Death.
   (C) another name for the Antichrist.
   (D) the mountain on which Jesus stood when Satan tempted him.

24. The nine goddesses of the arts were called
    (A) the Graces.
    (B) the Harpies.
    (C) the Muses.
    (D) the Sirens.

25. What did the thirty pieces of silver buy?
    (A) Jesus' robe as he hung on the cross
    (B) Judas's betrayal of Christ
    (C) The food for the Last Supper
    (D) Joseph's freedom from Potiphar

26. In the Bible, what is the significance of the god Baal?
    (A) He is denounced as a false god.
    (B) He takes over the kingdom of heaven.
    (C) He represents greed and love of money.
    (D) He causes a great flood.

27. Our word *narcissism* derives from a myth about
    (A) a young woman who cared more for objects than for love.
    (B) a man who fell in love with his own reflection.
    (C) a couple torn apart by Zeus and Aphrodite.
    (D) the goddess of spring.

28. What was the Holy Grail?
    (A) The shroud covering the dead Christ
    (B) A sliver of the true cross
    (C) The staff carried by Jesus as he traveled to Jerusalem
    (D) A mythic talisman sought by the knights of the Round Table

29. The Garden of Eden represents
    (A) a state of innocence.
    (B) the path to righteousness.
    (C) life after death.
    (D) the uninterrupted dream.

30. In the story of Cain and Abel, Cain
    (A) was slain by Abel, who denied the deed.
    (B) killed his brother out of jealousy.
    (C) was the only son of Adam and Eve.
    (D) sacrificed Abel to the Lord out of piety.

31. What was the title given to Siddhartha Gautama?
    (A) Huitzilopochti
    (B) Apostle
    (C) Buddha
    (D) Krishna

32. Martin Luther is known for
    (A) working with the civil rights movement.
    (B) founding the Church of England.
    (C) leading the Protestant Reformation.
    (D) ruling the Holy Roman Empire.

33. What do these names have in common: Elohim, Allah, and Brahma?
    (A) They are all names of prophets.
    (B) They are all names for God.
    (C) They are all found in the Bible.
    (D) They are all found in the Quran.

34. The Ten Commandments given to Moses by God include
    (A) laws forbidding murder and theft.
    (B) freedom of speech.
    (C) prophecies about the coming of Christ.
    (D) descriptions of the apocalypse.

35. In Greek and Roman mythology, Phoebus Apollo was
    (A) the god of music and of light.
    (B) the ruler of the underworld.
    (C) the brother of Zeus (Jupiter).
    (D) the motherless god of wisdom.

36. The phrase *Immaculate Conception* refers to
    (A) the belief that Jesus was the son of God.
    (B) the concept that true believers can be saved.
    (C) the idea that Mary was free from Original Sin.
    (D) a movement of mystics and alchemists in the 1700s.

37. According to Islam, Muhammad was
    (A) the last of the prophets, following Abraham, Moses, and Jesus.
    (B) the one true god, whom all Muslims must obey without question.
    (C) the eighth incarnation of the great god Vishnu.
    (D) the author of the *Tao-te-ching*.

38. What was the kingdom of the god Poseidon?
    (A) The heavens
    (B) The land of the dead
    (C) The ocean
    (D) None of the above

39. Sodom and Gomorrah were
    (A) wicked people.
    (B) cities.
    (C) prophets.
    (D) Hindu gods.

40. Eros was the god of
    (A) athletic ability.
    (B) art.
    (C) peace.
    (D) love.

41. What do these names have in common: Leviticus, Deuteronomy, and Ruth?
    (A) They are all names of prophets.
    (B) They are all apostles of Christ.
    (C) They are books of the Old Testament.
    (D) They are characters in the New Testament.

42. The phrase *Achilles' heel* refers to
    (A) the fulfillment of a prophecy despite a person's will.
    (B) a traitorous act against a former friend or leader.
    (C) the tendency to follow a leader blindly into battle.
    (D) a point of vulnerability on an otherwise strong person.

43. When Pandora's box was opened,
    (A) the first woman was created.
    (B) the Muses were set free.
    (C) evil was released into the world.
    (D) the winds and clouds flew out.

44. What is the goal of Hinduism?
    (A) Divine assistance
    (B) Freedom from rebirth and suffering
    (C) Spiritual ecstasy
    (D) Worldwide recognition of the power of prayer

45. What is Ramadan?
    (A) The festival of lights in Jewish tradition
    (B) A manifestation of the Great Spirit of the Sioux
    (C) The largest Mayan temple, dedicated to
        Kulkulcán
    (D) The ninth month of the Muslim year

46. Daedalus designed
    (A) the Minotaur and the Gorgons.
    (B) the Parthenon.
    (C) a labyrinth and a method of flight.
    (D) the palace of the gods.

47. The story of David and Goliath represents
    (A) the triumph of the slave over his oppressor.
    (B) the power of the righteous against all odds.
    (C) the discovery of an honorable man.
    (D) the loss of innocence and the building of an
        empire.

48. Because of her beauty, Helen of Troy
    (A) was stolen from her husband and precipitated
        a war.
    (B) displeased the goddess Athena and was con-
        demned to die.
    (C) became the symbol of unrequited love.
    (D) was adored by Lancelot and caused the fall of
        a kingdom.

49. The story of the prodigal son is a parable about
    (A) a child who shows remarkable talent in music.
    (B) the unforgiving nature of man and God.
    (C) predictions made by a soothsayer about a young prince.
    (D) a repentant sinner's return to his father's house.

50. The adventures of Theseus included
    (A) a war against the Amazons.
    (B) the killing of the Minotaur.
    (C) removing a sword from under a stone.
    (D) All of the above

TEST 7:
Explanatory Answers

1. The correct answer is (C). According to Christian theology, Original Sin is held by all people at birth and results from Adam and Eve's disobedience to God in eating the fruit of the Tree of Knowledge. Original Sin can be removed by baptism.

2. The correct answer is (A). Mecca, a city in what is now Saudi Arabia, was the birthplace of Muhammad and is the holiest city of the Islamic religion. Pious Muslims are urged to journey to Mecca at least once in their lifetimes. Muslims, when praying, face in the direction of Mecca.

3. The correct answer is (D). In Egypt, the sun was venerated as the greatest god and was called Re. Osiris was the god of the funerary cult, a hero who had died and been resurrected. Isis was the wife and sister of Osiris; she was the patron goddess of mariners.

4. The correct answer is (B). John the Baptist, born to St. Elizabeth late in her life, heralded the coming of Christ in his sermons in the wilderness. He baptized Christ, beginning his ministry. He was imprisoned by Herod Antipas for denouncing Herod's marriage to his brother's wife and was beheaded at the request of Salome, Herod's stepdaughter.

5. The correct answer is (C). On the border of Thessaly and Macedonia stands Mt. Olympus, 9,800 feet high, purported to be the home of the Greek gods. Asgard, on the other hand, is not a real place but is supposed to be the center of the universe, according to Norse mythology. The gods lived in its many halls and mansions, the most famous of which was Valhalla.

6. The correct answer is (A). Job was tested by Satan, who took his wealth and his children and afflicted him with boils; however, Job kept his patience and his faith, as God knew he would, and eventually God rewarded him.

7. The correct answer is (D). The Quran is considered by Muslims to be the word of God, revealed to Muhammad by the angel Gabriel. It has its basis in the Judeo-Christian tradition and was transmitted orally for hundreds of years before it was written down.

8. The correct answer is (A). Aphrodite (Venus in Roman mythology) was the Greek goddess of love and marriage. She was born from the foam that bubbled about the severed parts of the castrated Uranus. She was the wife of Hephaestus and the lover of Ares; her child was Eros. The gods of the other areas mentioned are Ares (Mars), Artemis (Diana), and Hestia (Vesta).

9. The correct answer is (B). John Wesley was the founder of Methodism, which began at Oxford University in the 1720s. The name was originally

used derisively because the group of believers was so regular in their meetings and prayers. Presbyterianism is another Protestant sect, based on the Calvinist creed, which states that salvation is predetermined. The presbyters, or elders of the church, govern the church for the members. Unitarianism, also a Protestant sect, rejects the idea of the Trinity and holds that God is one being. It affirms reason, conscience, tolerance, and a belief in the universal brotherhood of man.

10. The correct answer is (D). Charon, the ferryman of the River Styx, ferried the dead to the fields of Elysium, a land of perfect happiness. Greek dead were customarily buried with a coin in their mouth, payment for Charon. The idea of crossing a river to reach the land of the dead is older than Greek mythology; it appears in Egyptian and Mesopotamian mythology as well.

11. The correct answer is (C). Noah, one of the few faithful left on Earth, was told by God that civilization would be destroyed by a flood that would last forty days and nights. Noah built an ark and populated it with two of each kind of animal. His family rode out the flood with the creatures. Most religions and mythologies, including Hinduism and Babylonian, Greek, and Hittite mythology, have a flood story.

12. The correct answer is (C). The Norse god Thor was the son of Odin, leader of the gods. He was the most widely worshipped of Norse gods and was

known as man's protector. The word *Thursday* comes from his name.

13. The correct answer is (B). The Torah is the first five books of the Old Testament. It is also the word used for the scroll, kept in every Jewish synagogue, on which these five books, or Pentateuch, are written. In Christianity, these five books are referred to as Genesis, Exodus, Leviticus, Numbers, and Deuteronomy.

14. The correct answer is (A). Born fully armed from the head of Zeus, Athena (Minerva in Roman mythology) was the goddess of war and helped to defeat the giants when they stormed Olympus. She was also the goddess of wisdom and of handicrafts. The city of Athens was named after her, and the Parthenon was dedicated to her.

15. The correct answer is (C). The evangelists who wrote the Gospels are generally supposed to have been different people from the original apostles and to have written their works up to seventy years after the crucifixion. The Gospel of Matthew is the most complete account of Jesus' sayings and is called the Gospel of the Son of David; the Gospel of Mark is an account of Jesus' actions and is called the Gospel of the Son of God. St. Luke wrote the Acts of the Apostles as well as a Gospel, which is called the Gospel of the Saviour; St. John's Gospel is the most spiritual of the four and is called the Gospel of the Word.

16. The correct answer is (B). Lazarus, a New Testament figure who was the brother of Mary and

Martha of Bethany, died and was raised from the dead by Jesus four days later.

17. The correct answer is (A). The phoenix, a mythical Arabian bird, builds a pyre every five hundred years and immolates itself. A new phoenix then rises from the ashes and, some say, flies with the remains of its parent to Heliopolis in Egypt. The idea of a bird that burns itself and is reborn also appears in myths of the Aztecs and Mayans, the Chinese, and the Japanese.

18. The correct answer is (D). The story of the Tower of Babel is a Biblical explanation for the differences among languages. Determined to reach heaven and see God, Noah's descendants built a huge tower; but God, displeased with their presumption, struck all of mankind with the inability to understand one another's speech.

19. The correct answer is (C). Dionysus, or Bacchus in Roman mythology, was the son of Zeus and a mortal woman. He introduced wine to the world, but when driven mad by Hera, he wandered the Earth inciting his followers to wild, drunken revelry.

20. The correct answer is (B). The story of the Good Samaritan is a parable from the Gospel of St. Luke. It tells of a man stripped and wounded by thieves and of the Samaritan who found and took care of him. Jesus' message after the parable was "Go and do thou likewise." Nowadays, "Good Samaritan" is a phrase that describes anyone who helps someone in need.

21. The correct answer is (D). Zeus (Jupiter or Jove in Roman mythology) was the king of the gods. He was the son of Chronos and Rhea, husband to Hera, and father, by various goddesses and humans, of the Graces, Persephone, Apollo, Artemis, Athena, Ares, Hermes, Dionysus, Heracles, Perseus, Helen, and Clytemnestra.

22. The correct answer is (D). Yom Kippur, the Day of Atonement, falls on the tenth day of the seventh month in the Jewish calendar. It is the last of ten days of atonement, which begin on Rosh Hashanah, the Jewish new year.

23. The correct answer is (A). St. John the Divine, a prisoner on the Greek island of Patmos, had a vision in which he saw the Day of Judgment. This prompted him to write the Book of Revelation, a description of the end of the world and the triumph of Christ. Before Judgment Day, the forces of good and evil will fight on the plain of Armageddon.

24. The correct answer is (C). The Muses, the nine daughters of Zeus and Mnemosyne, were Calliope, muse of the epic; Clio, muse of history; Erato, muse of erotic poetry; Euterpe, muse of lyric poetry; Melpomene, muse of tragedy: Polyhymnia, muse of hymns; Terpsichore, muse of dance; Thalia, muse of comedy; and Urania, muse of astronomy.

25. The correct answer is (B). Judas Iscariot, one of Christ's disciples, betrayed Jesus for thirty pieces of silver by identifying him with a kiss in the Garden of Gethsemane. As a result, Jesus was arrested,

tried, and crucified; in remorse, Judas returned the money and hanged himself. The story of the betrayal at Gethsemane is told in the gospels of Mark and Matthew.

26. The correct answer is (A). Baal was the name of various gods of the Canaanites—gods who required human sacrifice. Denounced by the prophets as false gods, Baal became equated with evil. *Beelzebub,* from *Baal,* is a name for the devil.

27. The correct answer is (B). Narcissus was a beautiful and vain young man. When he rejected the love of the nymph Echo, she pined away until only her voice remained. In punishment, he was forced by a goddess to fall in love with his own reflection. He too pined away for love, leaving only a small flower in his place.

28. The correct answer is (D). There are many theories about the Grail. Once it was assumed to be the chalice from which Christ drank at the Last Supper. Joseph of Arimathea caught some drops of the crucified Christ's blood in the chalice, and it sustained him through imprisonment and hardship. The chalice then passed through various hands until at last it reached Sir Galahad of King Arthur's Round Table. More recent theories claim that the Grail was an ancient fertility symbol. Whatever its origin, the quest for the Grail is one of the great Western literary themes, appearing in works from Chrétien de Troyes' *Perceval* (c. 1185) to T. S. Eliot's *The Waste Land* (1922).

29. The correct answer is (A). Adam and Eve were
    placed by God in the Garden of Eden and told to
    eat freely of all of the trees but the Tree of Knowl-
    edge of Good and Evil. The serpent convinced Eve
    that to eat of that tree would not harm her but
    would make her "like God, knowing good and
    evil." Eve ate the fruit and gave some to Adam.
    God recognized their sin, cursed them, and
    expelled them from the garden.

30. The correct answer is (B). Cain was the first son of
    Adam and Eve, and Abel was their second son.
    Abel was a shepherd, while Cain farmed and grew
    crops. Abel sacrificed a lamb to God, thereby satis-
    fying the requirement of a blood sacrifice that
    proved true faith. Cain offered the fruits of his har-
    vest, but his offering was rejected. In fury, Cain
    killed Abel, was cursed, and was driven east of
    Eden and marked for life. Cain thus was the first
    murderer and Abel the first martyr, according to
    Judeo-Christian tradition.

31. The correct answer is (C). *Buddha,* meaning "the
    enlightened one," was the title given to Siddhartha
    Gautama, founder of the Buddhist religion. Sid-
    dhartha, who lived about the sixth century B.C.E.,
    gave up his princely position and wandered for six
    years seeking enlightenment. While meditating, he
    achieved his goal, and he went on to instruct others
    in the path he had taken. The basic tenets of his
    philosophy are four: the idea that existence is suf-
    fering; that suffering is caused by desire; that nir-

vana, or an end to suffering, is possible; and that there is a path leading to nirvana that involves right action, right resolve, and right concentration.

32. The correct answer is (C). Trained as a lawyer, Luther (1483–1546) became a priest after a religious awakening. Disgusted by the church's sale of pardons for sin (called *indulgences*), Luther protested and was excommunicated. After the Diet of Worms called for his imprisonment, Luther found sanctuary with the Elector Frederick III of Saxony. He continued to write and preach, and his followers, the Protestants, grew in number. His teachings were challenged by John Calvin and Huldreich Zwingli, and the Protestant movement split into factions. However, the Lutherans remained a vital force in northern Europe.

33. The correct answer is (B). Elohim is one of several forms of the name for God in the Old Testament. Allah is the name of God in the Quran. Brahma is the creator in the Hindu trinity.

34. The correct answer is (A). When Moses met God on Mount Sinai, he was given the Law, which listed the principles that were to govern the life of the faithful. Among the commandments were laws that forbade killing, adultery, and theft.

35. The correct answer is (A). Phoebus Apollo, a son of Zeus, was the god of archery and prophecy as well as music. Although Helios was the sun god, Apollo is often associated with the sun, and various myths depict him driving his sun-chariot across the heavens.

36. The correct answer is (C). In Christian thought, all
    people are born with the taint of Original Sin, which
    can be removed only through baptism. The idea that
    Mary was free from such taint has been argued
    through the ages (with noted resistance coming from
    Thomas Aquinas), but Pope Pius IX made the idea
    formal Roman Catholic dogma in 1854.

37. The correct answer is (A). The founder of Islam
    named himself Muhammad in order to fulfill cer-
    tain prophecies in the Old Testament. His teachings
    and those revelations made to him by Allah are set
    down in the Quran, the holy book of Islam. Islam
    is considered a theocracy: thus, the ruler of an
    Islamic nation should be a spiritual leader as well
    as head of government, and division between civil
    and religious law is negligible. In the first few cen-
    turies after Muhammad's death in 632, battles over
    his succession led to a division of Islam into Sunni
    and Shiite sects. The Wahabi sect of Sunni Islam is
    the religion of Saudi Arabia. Shiite Islam is the pre-
    dominant religion of Iran.

38. The correct answer is (C). Poseidon (Neptune in
    Roman mythology) was the god of the sea and the
    brother of Zeus and Hades. He was also in charge
    of horses. The Greeks feared his nasty temper,
    which manifested itself in earthquakes and storms
    at sea. It was Poseidon's wrath that kept Odysseus
    so long at sea in the *Odyssey*.

39. The correct answer is (B). God determined to
    destroy the cities of Sodom and Gomorrah because

of their wicked inhabitants. Abraham asked that the cities be spared if ten good men could be found. When that proved impossible, Lot and his family were the only people allowed to escape. At the last moment, Lot's wife looked back at the burning cities and was turned into a pillar of salt.

40. The correct answer is (D). Early myths claim that Eros (Cupid) was born at the same time as Earth, but the more common tale is that he was the son of Aphrodite, goddess of love. He is often pictured as a child with a bow and a quiver of arrows.

41. The correct answer is (C). The books of the Old Testament are Genesis, Exodus, Leviticus, Numbers, Deuteronomy (the Books of Moses); Joshua, Judges, Ruth, 1 Samuel, 2 Samuel, 1 Kings, 2 Kings, 1 Chronicles, 2 Chronicles, Ezra, Nehemiah, Esther, Job, Psalms, Proverbs, Ecclesiastes, Song of Solomon, Isaiah, Jeremiah, Lamentations, Ezekiel, Daniel, Hosea, Joel, Amos, Obadiah, Jonah, Micah, Nahum, Habakkuk, Zephaniah, Haggai, Zechariah, and Malachi. Some books are named after their authors (e.g., Ezekiel), some are named after the main characters (e.g., Jonah), and others are named for the main plot points (e.g., Exodus). *Leviticus* means "about the Levites"; *Deuteronomy* means "repetition of the law." *Ruth* tells the story of Ruth and her mother-in-law, Naomi.

42. The correct answer is (D). In the *Iliad*, Achilles was a hero who fought against Troy in the Trojan War. At birth, his mother had dipped him in the River

Styx, which made him invincible everywhere except on the heel by which she held him. After Achilles killed Hector in battle, Hector's brother Paris shot Achilles in the heel, killing him.

43. The correct answer is (C). Prometheus's brother, Epimetheus, was supposed to bestow attributes on man and other animals. He ran out of gifts by the time he reached man, and he called on Prometheus to suggest something. Prometheus went to heaven and brought back the gift of fire to give to man. This gift made man stronger than the other animals, and Prometheus's recklessness enraged Zeus so much that he created the first woman, Pandora. Zeus gave Pandora a box that she was to present to the man she married. Epimetheus married Pandora and opened the box, releasing all of the evils that plague man. Other versions of the story claim that Pandora's curiosity led her to open the box. This story may be compared with that of the Garden of Eden.

44. The correct answer is (B). Many religions are covered by our term *Hinduism,* but the primary tenets of these religions are similar. The results of people's actions are their *karma,* and these control their lives in the next stage of rebirth. Pure acts lead to the possibility of *moksha,* or freedom from the cycle. The goal is attained through pilgrimage, worship, mental exercises, and clean living.

45. The correct answer is (D). This is the Muslim Holy Month, commemorating the revelations of the Quran to Muhammad. Muslims are expected to

fast from sunrise to sundown every day during this period.

46. The correct answer is (C). After Daedalus completed the labyrinth in which the Minotaur was to be kept, he and his son were imprisoned by King Minos so that they would not give away the secrets of the maze. Daedalus made wings from feathers and wax for himself and Icarus, and they flew from Crete and headed for Sicily. In his pride at being able to fly, Icarus flew too close to the sun, which melted the wax in his wings. He fell into the sea and was killed.

47. The correct answer is (B). The Philistine giant Goliath challenged the Israelites, but only David agreed to fight. Saul gave him a sword and armor, but David was not used to them and chose to fight with only his sling and five stones. Armed with these and his faith, he struck Goliath in the forehead and killed him. This began an intense rivalry between Saul and David that ended only with Saul's death.

48. The correct answer is (A). Helen was half-divine, being the daughter of Zeus and Leda. In legend, she was stolen from her husband, Menelaus, by Paris. The kidnapping sparked the Trojan War. Helen's legendary beauty led Christopher Marlowe to refer to her as "the face that launched a thousand ships" (1604).

49. The correct answer is (D). One of Christ's parables tells of the sinning son who returns to his father's house to find forgiveness and love awaiting him.

The meaning of the parable is clear: forgiveness of
the repentant sinner is possible in the house of the
Father.

50. The correct answer is (D). Theseus was probably a
real king of Athens, but the myth that surrounds
him far outweighs any real contributions he made.
According to the story, he was brought up by his
mother, who led him to a rock under which the
sword and sandals of his father lay. When he could
move the rock and take the sword and sandals, he
would be worthy of presentation to his father, the
king. Theseus was finally able to move the rock,
and he set out for Athens, having many adventures
along the way. Once he had been recognized by his
father, Theseus resolved to save Athens from the
Cretan Minotaur, to whom fourteen young Atheni-
ans were sacrificed each year. With the help of Ariadne, daughter of King Minos of Crete, he was able
to find his way through the labyrinth and kill the
half-man, half-bull monster. Theseus unheroically
abandoned Ariadne and sailed for home, but his
father, thinking him dead, leaped from a cliff to his
death. King Theseus then did battle with the Ama-
zons, women warriors from the Black Sea region.
He defeated them and made their queen, Hip-
polyta, his bride.

TEST 8
A WELL-TURNED PHRASE: QUOTES, PHRASES, AND APHORISMS

A word is dead
When it is said,
Some say.
I say it just
Begins to live
That day.
—EMILY DICKINSON

1. If a speaker talks *ad infinitum*, he or she
   (A) goes on without limit.
   (B) speaks off-the-cuff.
   (C) appeals to a listener's heart rather than head.
   (D) talks between main presentations.

2. In his "I Have a Dream" speech, Martin Luther King, Jr. refers to
   (A) violence as the correct response to oppression.
   (B) the struggle between the rights of commoners and of kings.
   (C) a world in which children are judged by character, not color.
   (D) a light "which shines over all the land and sea."

3. What is the Golden Rule?
   (A) "As ye would that men should do to you, do ye also to them likewise."
   (B) "To everything there is a season, and a time to every purpose under heaven."
   (C) "It is better to light one candle than curse the darkness."
   (D) "God loves to help him who strives to help himself."

4. "A bird in hand is worth two in the bush" is equivalent in meaning to
   (A) "They will turn and bite the hand that fed them."
   (B) "Good words are worth much, and cost little."
   (C) "Hope is the thing with feathers."
   (D) "He is a fool who leaves things close at hand to follow what is out of reach."

5. The phrase "fiddle while Rome burns" may be applied to people who
   (A) respect higher learning and reward intellectualism.
   (B) ignore human misery while indulging themselves.
   (C) prefer the arts to affairs of state.
   (D) lose hope in the face of disaster.

6. To express optimism in times of disaster, you might say,
   (A) "Every cloud has a silver lining."
   (B) "He who hesitates is lost."
   (C) "Still waters run deep."
   (D) "A rolling stone gathers no moss."

7. "Actions speak louder than words" means
   (A) words outlast deeds.
   (B) deeds are meaningful; talk is cheap.
   (C) a bad action will not go unpunished.
   (D) never act without weighing the consequences.

8. Who said, "The only thing we have to fear is fear itself"?
   (A) Abraham Lincoln
   (B) Winston Churchill
   (C) John F. Kennedy
   (D) Franklin D. Roosevelt

9. "Let sleeping dogs lie" means
   (A) you can't teach an old dog new tricks.
   (B) never listen to the advice of strangers.
   (C) don't ask for needless trouble.
   (D) old ways are better.

10. If a transaction is *bona fide,*
    (A) it favors one party.
    (B) it is made in good faith.
    (C) no one can break the agreement.
    (D) the payment is in cash.

11. A person who has the Midas touch
    (A) cannot make friends.
    (B) has a firm handshake.
    (C) is cold and distant.
    (D) makes money easily.

12. In his soliloquy that begins "To be, or not to be,"
    Hamlet weighs the pros and cons of
    (A) fidelity.
    (B) poetry.
    (C) suicide.
    (D) power.

13. What is a *non sequitur?*
    (A) A statement that does not follow logically
        from prior remarks
    (B) A person who is not affiliated with a particu-
        lar religion
    (C) The failure to honor a contract or personal
        obligation
    (D) An idea that is absurd or unintelligible

14. To "steal (people's) thunder" is to
    (A) poke fun mercilessly and make them look bad.
    (B) cajole them out of a very bad mood.
    (C) avoid them at all costs.
    (D) use their ideas without giving credit.

15. If you wished to remark on familial closeness, you
    might say,
    (A) "Happy families are all alike."
    (B) "Have no friends not equal to yourself."
    (C) "Blood is thicker than water."
    (D) "Familiarity breeds contempt."

16. To perform a deed "by hook or by crook" is to do it
    (A) by any means possible.
    (B) carelessly and without forethought.
    (C) in an unlawful manner.
    (D) with malicious intent.

17. Something that is run-of-the-mill is
    (A) coarse.
    (B) ordinary.
    (C) peculiar.
    (D) refined.

18. "Hobson's choice" refers to
    (A) a choice between two equally terrible events.
    (B) no choice at all.
    (C) an obvious decision.
    (D) an overabundance of options.

19. If people meet briefly and never encounter each other again, they are like
    (A) "little, nameless, unremembered acts."
    (B) "two hearts that beat as one."
    (C) "partners in crime."
    (D) "ships that pass in the night."

20. The phrase *e pluribus unum,* found on the seal of the United States, means
    (A) "in God we trust."
    (B) "from many, one."
    (C) "united we stand."
    (D) "liberty and equality."

21. If you promise to turn over a new leaf, you aim to
    (A) read more in the coming year.
    (B) set aside youthful passions.
    (C) alter your behavior.
    (D) "cultivate (your) garden."

22. When you tell someone, "You can't have your cake and eat it, too," you mean to say,
    (A) "Sweet things never last."
    (B) "Don't put off your work until tomorrow."
    (C) "Finish one thing before starting another."
    (D) "You must make a decision."

23. To warn someone of the foolishness of relying on future gains, you might say,
    (A) "Don't count your chickens before they are hatched."
    (B) "Slow and steady wins the race."
    (C) "Prepare today for the wants of tomorrow."
    (D) "Beware lest you lose the substance by grasping at the shadow."

24. If you "walk the straight and narrow," you
    (A) follow a course laid out by fate.
    (B) lead the "life of Riley."
    (C) do not stray from righteousness.
    (D) give up everything for love.

25. You might use the phrase "The grass is always greener on the other side of the fence" to describe
    (A) discontented people who seek their fortunes far from home.
    (B) politicians who promise followers "a chicken in every pot."
    (C) farmers who prefer planting crops to harvesting them.
    (D) happy children who enjoy the out-of-doors.

26. If you "bury the hatchet," you
    (A) ignore an insult.
    (B) spend too much money.
    (C) hide the evidence of a crime.
    (D) make peace.

27. When you claim that "the road to hell is paved with good intentions," what do you mean?
    (A) Good intentions do not guarantee a good deed.
    (B) Good men as well as bad go to hell.
    (C) Sin can mask itself as good.
    (D) The devil tempts us to forget our good intentions.

28. When someone works or plays too hard, you say he or she
    (A) "makes hay while the sun shines."
    (B) "takes the bitter with the sweet."
    (C) "burns the candle at both ends."
    (D) "can't make a silk purse out of sow's ear."

29. What does "an eye for an eye" mean?
    (A) An act of violence should be punished with equal violence.
    (B) Sight is the most precious of man's senses.
    (C) People must strive to look at life in the same way.
    (D) Any part of you that is not pleasing in God's eyes should be struck off.

30. Those who separate the wheat from the chaff
    (A) use advanced methods in farming.
    (B) separate people by race or religion.
    (C) pick the winners in horse races.
    (D) decide what is important or valuable.

31. The incident or thing that finally causes you to lose control is
    (A) "the lunatic fringe."
    (B) "the last straw."
    (C) "the most unkindest cut of all."
    (D) "Pandora's box."

32. Who are the *hoi polloi?*
    (A) The news media
    (B) The common masses
    (C) The aristocracy
    (D) Royalty

33. Who originally advised men to "turn the other cheek"?
    (A) Moses
    (B) Jesus
    (C) Mahatma Gandhi
    (D) Martin Luther King, Jr.

34. Who said, "Give me liberty or give me death," and under what circumstances?
    (A) Patrick Henry, addressing the Virginia Convention
    (B) Nathan Hale, before his execution for spying
    (C) George Washington, addressing troops at Valley Forge
    (D) Thomas Jefferson, after the reading of the Declaration of Independence

35. What is "the American Dream"?
    (A) Returning to the land of one's ancestors
    (B) The possibility of bettering oneself through individual enterprise
    (C) Spreading democracy throughout the world
    (D) Being the first country to put a station in space

36. People who injure themselves trying to wreak revenge on another are said to
    (A) grin like a Cheshire cat.
    (B) be guilty by association.
    (C) speak softly and carry a big stick.
    (D) cut off their noses to spite their faces.

37. Who is "the Grim Reaper"?
    (A) Jesus
    (B) Death
    (C) Satan
    (D) God

38. The phrase "Fourscore and seven years ago" is the opening to what speech?
    (A) Franklin D. Roosevelt's address to Congress asking for a declaration of war
    (B) Winston Churchill's "Blood, Sweat, and Tears" speech
    (C) Abraham Lincoln's Gettysburg Address
    (D) King Edward VIII's abdication speech

39. What is a *vicious circle*?
    (A) The symbol of something precious and valuable
    (B) A chain of events in which the solution to a problem creates a worse problem
    (C) The solution to a problem found in one brilliant move
    (D) A spectacular display made without effort

40. A person who is warned, "*Caveat emptor!*" should be aware that
    (A) there is a vicious dog on the premises.
    (B) he or she should seize the opportunity to enjoy life.
    (C) the goods or services purchased are not guaranteed by the seller.
    (D) he or she should be careful of what is said and to whom.

41. Who claimed that "no man is an island"?
    (A) John Donne, in "Devotions upon Emergent Occasions"
    (B) William Shakespeare, in Sonnet 97
    (C) Andrew Marvell, in "A Dialogue between the Soul and Body"
    (D) John Milton, in "How Soon Hath Time"

42. What is the difference between the abbreviations *e.g.* and *i.e.?*
    (A) After using e.g. you quote; after using i.e. you paraphrase.
    (B) E.g. refers to years before the birth of Christ; i.e. refers to years after the birth of Christ.
    (C) E.g. is used in footnotes; i.e. is used in bibliographies.
    (D) After using e.g. you list examples; after using i.e. you explain or expand.

43. When you see the handwriting on the wall, you
    (A) are the means of your own defeat.
    (B) are warned of your approaching ruin or defeat.
    (C) leave potential problems undisturbed.
    (D) ignore an act of vandalism or violence.

44. If you are convicted of a crime *in absentia,* you
    (A) were sick at the time of the conviction.
    (B) were innocent of the crime.
    (C) were not present at the conviction.
    (D) fought against the conviction.

45. When you are advised "not to look a gift horse in the mouth," you
    (A) take what is offered with gratitude and without question.
    (B) try to brighten a gloomy situation.
    (C) acknowledge the positive features of someone you dislike.
    (D) leave troublesome issues undisturbed.

46. Who advised Americans to "ask not what your country can do for you; ask what you can do for your country"?
    (A) Franklin D. Roosevelt
    (B) John F. Kennedy
    (C) Martin Luther King, Jr.
    (D) Ronald Reagan

47. If you play the devil's advocate, what are you doing?
    (A) Finding fault with an idea or person supported by someone else
    (B) Going along with the crowd
    (C) Arguing against organized religion
    (D) Blaming someone for the wrongdoing of others

48. A man with a chip on his shoulder is
    (A) confused about a situation.
    (B) suffering from a crippling disease.
    (C) entirely with hope.
    (D) angry for no apparent reason and ready to fight.

49. What is a wolf in sheep's clothing doing?
    (A) Pretending to love animals
    (B) Masking ill will with an outward show of good nature
    (C) Showing a liking for parties and fun
    (D) Running away from danger

50. If a family has a nasty secret that they keep hidden, you say they
    (A) "are on the horns of a dilemma."
    (B) "are riding for a fall."
    (C) "have a skeleton in their closet."
    (D) "have a fly in the ointment."

TEST 8:
Explanatory Answers

1. The correct answer is (A). From the same root as the word *infinity*, the Latin phrase *ad infinitum* means "without end or limit."

2. The correct answer is (C). This speech was the culmination of the March on Washington in 1963. Drawing on texts from the Old Testament and lyrics of spirituals, King called for a world where black and white were equal partners and racism was nonexistent.

3. The correct answer is (A). Christ says this in his Sermon on the Mount, which sets forth his definitions of righteousness, his interpretations of the commandments, and his rules for religious observances.

4. The correct answer is (D). The first quotation is from Cervantes (1547–1616); citation (D) is from Plutarch (c. 46–120 C.E.), who said it some 1,500 years before Cervantes.

5. The correct answer is (B). The emperor Nero blamed Christians for the fire that destroyed most of Rome in 64 C.E. It is believed that he himself set the fire in order to have a reason to persecute the Christians. Nero thought of himself as a great artist and musician. The image of his playing a fiddle while Rome burns is used to illustrate callous disregard for human suffering.

6. The correct answer is (A). Its use in two popular songs of the early 1900s kept the "silver lining" metaphor in the public vocabulary. Lena Ford's "Keep the Home Fires Burning" (1915) and P. G. Wodehouse's "Look for the Silver Lining" (1920) both refer to the silver lining that hints at the sun behind every cloud.

7. The correct answer is (B). In *Henry VIII* Shakespeare wrote, "'tis a kind of good deed to say well: And yet words are no deeds." The implication is that talking is easy, but actions are all that matter. The phrase "easier said than done" is ascribed to Plautus (254–184 B.C.E.).

8. The correct answer is (D). Roosevelt said this in his first inaugural address in 1933. The quote reflects Proverbs 3:25: "Be not afraid of sudden fear." The biblical reference had been paraphrased by many writers, including Montaigne and Thoreau, before being used by Roosevelt in perhaps its most famous wording.

9. The correct answer is (C). Dickens uses this phrase in *David Copperfield,* but in *Troilus and Criseyde,* Chaucer writes, "It is nought good a slepyng hound to wake." The maxim had probably been around for years before Chaucer so recorded it in the late fourteenth century.

10. The correct answer is (B). *Bona fide* is Latin for "good faith," meaning "without deceit." The phrase is often used to mean "genuine" or "authentic."

11. The correct answer is (D). This phrase, ironically, has come to mean something positive, but its original connotation was extremely grave. In Greek mythology Midas was a Phrygian king who asked for and received the power to turn all he touched to gold. He delighted in his gift until he found that he could neither eat nor drink, and he turned his beloved daughter into a cold, lifeless statue. In despair he asked for the power to be removed, and he lived out the rest of his life quietly in the country.

12. The correct answer is (C). In Shakespeare's play, Hamlet, a man of thought rather than action, is driven to despair by the murder of his father by his uncle and his uncle's subsequent marriage to his mother. In this famous speech, Hamlet wonders whether it is better to "suffer the slings and arrows of outrageous fortune" or to die. He decides that the fear of what lies after death keeps most people from taking their own lives.

13. The correct answer is (A). *Non sequitur* is Latin for "it does not follow." In logic, it refers to a kind of fallacy, or inference that does not follow from a given premise. In ordinary speech, it refers to any statement that is not a logical part of the conversation.

14. The correct answer is (D). According to Bartlett's *Familiar Quotations,* in 1709, the playwright John Dennis invented a special effect for a play that was badly received. At a performance of Macbeth some time later, Dennis heard his special effect in use, whereupon he cried, "See how the rascals use me! They will not let my play run, and yet they steal my thunder!"

15. The correct answer is (C). John Ray lists this maxim in *English Proverbs* in 1670. It is used to describe the connection between even the most spiritually distant relatives.

16. The correct answer is (A). In the late fourteenth century, this phrase appeared in *Controversial Tracts* by John Wycliffe, but it had probably been in use for a while. It is thought to stem from methods of gathering firewood—using a hooked pole or a scythe.

17. The correct answer is (B). Henry James speaks of a person "ground in the very mill of the conventional" in *The Portrait of a Lady* (1881). Something that is run-of-the-mill is just like everything else ground in the mill—average.

18. The correct answer is (B). According to Bartlett's *Familiar Quotations*, Hobson was a liveryman who forced his customers to take whichever horse stood nearest the door. The phrase thus refers to lack of choice.

19. The correct answer is (D). Henry Wadsworth Longfellow (1807–1882) penned this image in a poem in *Tales of a Wayside Inn* (1863–1874):

> Ships that pass in the night, and speak
>   each other in passing,
> Only a signal shown and a distant voice in
>   the darkness;
> So on the ocean of life we pass and speak
>   one another.
> Only a look and a voice; then darkness
>   again and silence.

20. The correct answer is (B). This Latin phrase, also found on many U.S. coins, refers to the idea that from people of great diversity was forged a single nation.

21. The correct answer is (C). "Turning over a new leaf" (as in "book," not "tree") was mentioned by Cervantes in *Don Quixote* (1605–1615). It appears earlier in works by Roger Ascham (1570) and Gabriel Harvey (1593). The metaphor relates to starting over on a blank page.

22. The correct answer is (D). "Wouldst thou both eat thy cake and have it?" asked George Herbert in 1633. The proverb was already probably in common usage as a way to point up the impossibility of having things both ways and the need to make a choice.

23. The correct answer is (A). All of these quotations are morals from Aesop's fables, set down about the sixth century B.C.E. Aesop warns his readers that expecting all of their eggs to hatch may prove foolish.

24. The correct answer is (C). In the Sermon on the Mount, Christ tells his listeners about the path to everlasting life: "Wide is the gate, and broad is the way, that leadeth to destruction, and many there be which go in thereat. Because strait is the gate, and narrow is the way, which leadeth unto life, and few there be that find it." André Gide used this ironically in *Strait Is the Gate* (1909), a story of a girl who sacrifices her worldly happiness to that of her sister, only to die without achieving spiritual or earthly joy.

25. The correct answer is (A). This maxim tells of the futility involved in assuming that things are better somewhere else—no matter where you are, the grass is always greener elsewhere.

26. The correct answer is (D). Burying the hatchet was an American Indian tradition signifying peace. Washington Irving used the phrase in *Captain Bonneville* (1837) to describe a peaceful meeting among Indian chiefs.

27. The correct answer is (A). In 1150, Bernard of Clairvaux claimed that "Hell is full of good intentions or desires," meaning that a person's deeds do not necessarily reflect his or her intentions. The idea of the road to hell being "paved" with good intentions wasn't used until Samuel Johnson spoke of it in 1775.

28. The correct answer is (C). To burn (or light) a candle at both ends was a phrase used by Thomas Bacon in 1592; he meant it to express wasted time. The idea of burning a candle at both ends to mean living too hard wasn't used until 1857 when, in a novel called *Two Years Ago* by Charles Kingsley, a character is described as burning "the candle of life at both ends."

29. The correct answer is (A). In Exodus, God tells Moses that "thou shalt give life for life, eye for eye, tooth for tooth, hand for hand," informing him that an act of violence should be punished in equal measure.

30. The correct answer is (D). Those who separate the wheat from the chaff do what farmers have done for centuries: dispose of what is not useful or true and set

aside that which is. In the Gospel of St. Matthew, John the Baptist predicts that Jesus will "burn up the chaff," that is, send the wicked to hell.

31. The correct answer is (B). "The last straw" is a shortened form of "the last straw that breaks the camel's back," first used by Charles Dickens in *Dombey and Son*. The phrase refers to the last incident or piece of information that a person can bear before breaking down in sorrow, anger, or exhaustion.

32. The correct answer is (B). *Hoi polloi* is a Greek phrase meaning "the many." *Hoi polloi* are the masses.

33. The correct answer is (B). In the Gospel of St. Matthew, Jesus says. "Whosoever shall smite thee on thy right cheek, turn to him the other also." This means that violence should not be met with violence, an idea that translated itself into the passive resistance movements led by Gandhi and Martin Luther King, Jr.

34. The correct answer is (A). On March 23, 1775, Patrick Henry addressed the Virginia Convention in Richmond, urging them to fight for their freedom from Great Britain.

35. The correct answer is (B). The American Dream is based on the concept of America as a new Eden, a land where people can redefine themselves, free of the restrictions of society. Such an idea is easily corrupted; F. Scott Fitzgerald's *The Great Gatsby* is one of the best illustrations of how the American Dream can be debased.

36. The correct answer is (D). In *A Classical Dictionary of the Vulgar Tongue,* Francis Grose defines "he who cut off his nose to be revenged of his face" as one who, "to be revenged of his neighbour, has materially injured himself."

37. The correct answer is (B). The Grim Reaper is Death, who mows down men with his scythe. He is described by Henry Wadsworth Longfellow in his poem "The Reaper and the Flowers" (1839): "There is a reaper whose name is Death."

38. The correct answer is (C). In 1863, after the battle at Gettysburg, Pennsylvania, President Abraham Lincoln gave a speech honoring the dead who fell defending the Union. The speech ended, "government of the people, by the people, for the people, shall not perish from the earth."

39. The correct answer is (B). A *vicious circle* is a chain of events in which the solution to a problem causes another problem, and the solution to that problem causes still another problem, and so on.

40. The correct answer is (C). *Caveat emptor* is Latin for "Let the buyer beware." It is a rule of law that stipulates that a purchaser rather than a vendor is responsible for goods or services purchased, except for what is specified in a sales contract.

41. The correct answer is (A). "No man is an island, entire of itself; every man is a piece of the continent, a part of the main" was written by John Donne in 1624. In the same "Meditation," Donne wrote, "Never send to know for whom the bell

tolls; it tolls for thee." Both statements stress the idea that people are linked together and that each person's actions affect others.

42. The correct answer is (D). E.g. is the abbreviation for *exempli gratia,* Latin for "for example"; after using it you would list examples. I.e. is the abbreviation for *id est,* or "that is," after which you would explain or expand on what you were saying.

43. The correct answer is (B). The original handwriting on the wall, "Mene, mene, tekel upharsin," was drawn by God on the wall of Belshazzar's palace in Babylon. In the Old Testament tale, Daniel interpreted the writing, which foretold the ruin of Belshazzar, who had dined from the sacred vessels from the temple of the Israelites.

44. The correct answer is (C). *In absentia* is Latin for "in one's absence." Whatever happens to you *in absentia* occurs while you are absent.

45. The correct answer is (A). A horse's age can be determined by looking at its teeth. Literally, "Don't look a gift horse in the mouth" means "Refrain from insulting the giver by checking the horse's age." In general, the saying means that any gift or offering should be accepted without question.

46. The correct answer is (B). In his inaugural address of 1961, John F. Kennedy urged Americans to act for their country rather than waiting for their country to act for them. The thought comes from a speech made by Oliver Wendell Holmes in 1884, in which he stated that the citizenry should recall

"what our country has done for each of us, and to ask ourselves what we can do for our country in return."

47. The correct answer is (A). The devil's advocate was originally a churchman who had the job of arguing against the sainthood of someone nominated for canonization.

48. The correct answer is (D). If you have a chip on your shoulder, you are ready for a fight. In an 1857 *Harper's Magazine* an anonymous contributor wrote, "A provocation to a fight . . . is placing a chip upon a man's shoulder and daring another to knock it off."

49. The correct answer is (B). The original wolf in sheep's clothing was an invention of Aesop, who used the fable, written around 550 B.C.E., to show that appearances can be deceiving. The idea also appears in the Gospel of St. Matthew, who wrote, "Beware of false prophets, which come to you in sheep's clothing, but inwardly they are ravening wolves."

50. The correct answer is (C). William Makepeace Thackeray (1811–1863) was the first to use the idea of a skeleton to symbolize a shameful secret. He claimed that "there is a skeleton in every house."

TEST 9
OF THEE I SING:
AMERICAN LITERATURE

By American literature . . . we
ought to mean literature written in
an American way, with an
American turn of language and an
American cast of thought.

—STEPHEN BUTLER LEACOCK

1. Who wrote *Cat on a Hot Tin Roof, A Streetcar
   Named Desire,* and *The Glass Menagerie?*
   (A) Eugene O'Neill
   (B) Sam Shepard
   (C) Tennessee Williams
   (D) Edward Albee

2. Langston Hughes was a writer of
   (A) poetry.
   (B) novels.
   (C) plays.
   (D) All of the above

3. An African-American writer known for his antiracist
   essays and novels of African-American life is
   (A) Imamu Amiri Baraka.
   (B) Thomas Pynchon.
   (C) Norman Mailer.
   (D) James Baldwin.

4. The novel for which Nathaniel Hawthorne is best known is
   (A) *The Scarlet Letter.*
   (B) *The Deerslayer.*
   (C) *Maggie: A Girl of the Streets.*
   (D) *Sister Carrie.*

5. The novelist who satirized small-town life, the scientist's search for truth, and evangelism is
   (A) Saul Bellow.
   (B) Sinclair Lewis.
   (C) Nathanael West.
   (D) John Dos Passos.

6. Which of the following is one of the major themes of *The Great Gatsby?*
   (A) The corruption of American innocence through the pursuit of wealth
   (B) The prejudices and injustices of Americans toward American Indians
   (C) The acceptance of death as a part of nature
   (D) The loss of faith and the triumph of science

7. The book that made Ralph Ellison famous is the story of
   (A) life in the Chicago stockyards.
   (B) a boy who is sent to reform school.
   (C) an African-American man's search for identity in the 1930s.
   (D) a drummer and drug addict in the slums of Chicago.

8. Ezra Pound was known for
    (A) his novels of social conscience.
    (B) his pro-Communist essays.
    (C) his deeply religious poems and short stories.
    (D) his poetry, criticism, and political views.

9. Of what kind of poetry are these lines characteristic?
   "I arise from rest with movements swift / As the
   beat of the raven's wings."
    (A) Southern poetry
    (B) Native American poetry
    (C) Haiku
    (D) Romantic poetry

10. A Nobel Prize winner known for his mystical tales
    of Jewish life and folklore is
    (A) Isaac Bashevis Singer.
    (B) Frederik Pohl.
    (C) Saul Bellow.
    (D) Henry Miller.

11. Which of these novels is by writer Toni Morrison?
    (A) *Beloved*
    (B) *Jazz*
    (C) *The Bluest Eye*
    (D) All of the above

12. When you think of E. E. Cummings, what stylistic
    eccentricity comes to mind?
    (A) His use of obscenity in poetry
    (B) His use of onomatopoeia in poetry
    (C) His use of dissonance in poetry
    (D) His use of only lowercase letters in poetry

13. Who is the author of the novels *Ethan Frome* and *The House of Mirth*?
    - (A) Edith Wharton
    - (B) Alice James
    - (C) Alice Walker
    - (D) Carson McCullers

14. Eugene O'Neill is the author of which of the following?
    - (A) *Waiting for Lefty, Awake and Sing!,* and *Golden Boy*
    - (B) *The Emperor Jones, A Long Day's Journey Into Night,* and *The Iceman Cometh*
    - (C) *American Buffalo, The Woods,* and *Glengarry Glen Ross*
    - (D) *True West, Fool for Love,* and *Buried Child*

15. A nineteenth-century writer known for his Romantic poetry and macabre stories is
    - (A) Washington Irving.
    - (B) James Fenimore Cooper.
    - (C) Edgar Allan Poe.
    - (D) Bret Harte.

16. Who was Emily Dickinson?
    - (A) A nineteenth-century novelist who explored women's sexual and emotional dependence
    - (B) A nineteenth-century poet who used the imagery of nature to explore human consciousness
    - (C) A twentieth-century poet who experimented with unusual stanza forms
    - (D) A twentieth-century writer who explored the African-American Midwestern experience

17. Eudora Welty, Flannery O'Connor, and Carson McCullers are all
    (A) poets who focused on the struggle for female independence.
    (B) novelists who wrote satires of midwestern life.
    (C) playwrights who explored the isolation of modern women.
    (D) novelists who wrote about the American South.

18. Winner of both the Pulitzer Prize and the Nobel Prize, John Steinbeck wrote
    (A) *V* and *Gravity's Rainbow.*
    (B) *The Grapes of Wrath* and *Of Mice and Men.*
    (C) *A Death in the Family* and *Let Us Now Praise Famous Men.*
    (D) *Ragtime* and *Loon Lake.*

19. What is the major theme of Thornton Wilder's play *Our Town?*
    (A) Even the smallest moments in life have great value and meaning.
    (B) Life in big cities is spiritually degrading.
    (C) Children are the means of humankind's immortality.
    (D) The American Dream has become meaningless.

20. Why is Walden Pond an important location in American literary history?
    (A) It is the body of water in which Virginia Woolf drowned herself.
    (B) It is the body of water around which the Lake poets lived.
    (C) It is where Henry Thoreau lived and recorded his impressions.
    (D) It is the setting for Charles Kingsley's *The Water Babies*.

21. Who wrote the lines: "The woods are lovely, dark, and deep, / But I have promises to keep, / And miles to go before I sleep"?
    (A) Anne Sexton
    (B) Robert Frost
    (C) A. R. Ammons
    (D) Robert Lowell

22. What is transcendentalism?
    (A) A movement led by Alfred Jarry that stressed the lack of reason in human existence
    (B) A movement led by Jean-Paul Sartre that stated that existence precedes essence
    (C) A movement led by Tristan Tzara that tried to negate all traditional values in the arts
    (D) A movement led by Ralph Waldo Emerson that stressed the divinity of man

23. What do Dashiell Hammett, Raymond Chandler, and Mickey Spillane have in common?
    (A) They are poets in the modernist tradition.
    (B) They are all writers of detective fiction.
    (C) They wrote novels of rural life in the Southeast.
    (D) They are biographers of famous literary figures.

24. Who was the creator of the characters Huckleberry Finn, Tom Sawyer, and Pudd'nhead Wilson?
    (A) Herman Melville
    (B) Hart Crane
    (C) Thomas Wolfe
    (D) Samuel Clemens

25. What belief did the Naturalist movement in America stress?
    (A) The importance of conservation of land and animal life
    (B) The innocence and virtue of man in the state of nature
    (C) The limitations of social conditions and heredity on man's capacity to change
    (D) The free and spontaneous act of literary composition

26. Washington Irving created which of the following characters?
    (A) Diedrich Knickerbocker and Rip van Winkle
    (B) Meg, Beth, Amy, and Jo
    (C) Little Eva and Topsy
    (D) Billy Budd and Queequeg

27. Willa Cather is perhaps best known for her
   (A) stories of life on the New England coast.
   (B) novels that celebrate the American past.
   (C) poems about spiritual growth and doubt.
   (D) essays on the rights of women.

28. *The Sound and the Fury* and *Absalom, Absalom!*
   are two novels by
   (A) Robert Penn Warren.
   (B) William Faulkner.
   (C) Booth Tarkington.
   (D) Katherine Anne Porter.

29. What is a "tall tale"?
   (A) A short novel set on the prairie
   (B) Any tale whose main characters are animals
       with human traits
   (C) An exaggerated anecdote about frontier life
   (D) A stream-of-consciousness story by Edgar
       Allan Poe

30. Herman Melville is famous for his
   (A) tales of life along the Mississippi River.
   (B) poems about the simple pleasures of sport and
       competition.
   (C) novels about sea voyages.
   (D) adventure stories about explorers and pirates.

31. *The Waste Land* and *Four Quartets* are poems by
   (A) Edna St. Vincent Millay.
   (B) Wallace Stevens.
   (C) Carl Sandburg.
   (D) T. S. Eliot.

32. *Uncle Tom's Cabin* was an important influence on
    (A) the Abolitionist movement.
    (B) American isolationists.
    (C) the carpetbaggers.
    (D) the colonial militia.

33. Which of these people wrote in prerevolutionary times?
    (A) Mary Mapes Dodge and William Dean Howells
    (B) Waldo Frank and Josephine Herbst
    (C) Sarah Orne Jewett and George Washington Cable
    (D) Anne Bradstreet and Jonathan Edwards

34. Which of these plays are by Arthur Miller?
    (A) *Death of a Salesman* and *The Crucible*
    (B) *Sweet Bird of Youth* and *The Night of the Iguana*
    (C) *Who's Afraid of Virginia Woolf?* and *The Zoo Story*
    (D) *Our Town* and *The Skin of Our Teeth*

35. Ernest Hemingway's writing style is characterized by
    (A) flowing imagery and poetic diction.
    (B) biting wit and sarcastic humor.
    (C) terseness and understatement.
    (D) sentimentality and use of symbolic structure.

36. Louisa May Alcott is known for her
    (A) somewhat moralistic novels for children.
    (B) unique educational philosophy and ideas for school reform.
    (C) illustrated children's stories about animals.
    (D) strong antislavery sentiment and political speech-writing.

37. Which of these works are by Richard Wright?
    (A) *Notes of a Native Son* and *The Fire Next Time*
    (B) *The 42nd Parallel* and *Manhattan Transfer*
    (C) *Native Son* and *Black Boy*
    (D) *Bronzeville Boys and Girls* and *The Bean Eaters*

38. Which of these lines is attributable to Henry Wadsworth Longfellow?
    (A) "This is the forest primeval. The murmuring pines and the hemlocks."
    (B) "Life is real! Life is earnest! / And the grave is not its goal."
    (C) "Listen, my children, and you shall hear, / Of the midnight ride of Paul Revere."
    (D) All of the above

39. *Slaughterhouse-Five* and *Cat's Cradle* are novels by
    (A) Thomas Pynchon.
    (B) Kurt Vonnegut.
    (C) William Styron.
    (D) Joseph Heller.

40. Henry James's influence on later writers stems from his
    (A) attention to point of view and psychological realism.
    (B) use of regional dialect and historical settings.
    (C) emphasis on heroic traits in handicapped or impoverished characters.
    (D) All of the above

41. What do Sherwood Anderson and Edgar Lee Masters have in common?
    (A) Both wrote about small towns in the Midwest.
    (B) Both started literary magazines in Boston.
    (C) Both published tales based on Cajun legends.
    (D) Both satirized New York and European society.

42. Which of these groups of authors are known for their science fiction?
    (A) Arthur Schlesinger, Daniel Boorstein, Frances Fitzgerald
    (B) Ray Bradbury, Ursula LeGuin, Isaac Asimov
    (C) A. R. Gurney, Lanford Wilson, Beth Henley
    (D) Marjorie K. Rawlings, John Hersey, Pearl Buck

43. Upton Sinclair, Ida Tarbell, and Lincoln Steffens were part of
    (A) the Puritan tradition.
    (B) the school of regionalism.
    (C) the transcendentalist movement.
    (D) the muckraking movement.

44. Walt Whitman's poetry was among the first in America to
    (A) concentrate on rural themes.
    (B) eliminate regular metrical structure.
    (C) apply medievalism to American art.
    (D) emphasize form over emotion.

45. *Rabbit, Run* and *The Centaur* are novels by
    (A) Mary McCarthy.
    (B) Robert Coover.
    (C) John Updike.
    (D) Bernard Malamud.

46. Which of these groups of writers are associated with the Beat movement?
    (A) John Crowe Ransom, Allen Tate, John Gould Fletcher
    (B) Gregory Corso, Jack Kerouac, Allen Ginsberg
    (C) Eugene Debs, Norman Thomas, Robert La Follette
    (D) Abbie Hoffman, Jerry Rubin, Eldridge Cleaver

47. Marianne Moore is known for her
    (A) plays satirizing "the rat race."
    (B) biographies of famous American women.
    (C) ironic poems on everyday subjects.
    (D) financial support of "Lost Generation" writers.

48. Dorothy Parker, E. B. White, and James Thurber were all
    (A) poets.
    (B) playwrights.
    (C) expatriates.
    (D) humorists.

49. Who wrote *Common Sense* and *The Rights of Man?*
    (A) Thomas Paine
    (B) John Adams
    (C) Thomas Jefferson
    (D) Henry Adams

50. *Lolita, Pnin,* and *Pale Fire* are novels by
    (A) Donald Barthelme.
    (B) Edna Ferber.
    (C) Vladimir Nabokov.
    (D) John Barth.

TEST 9:
Explanatory Answers

1. The correct answer is (C). Tennessee Williams (1911–1983) is thought by many to be the best modern American dramatist. He was awarded the Pulitzer Prize for both *A Streetcar Named Desire* (1947) and *Cat on a Hot Tin Roof* (1955); his characters often suffer from loneliness and sexual anxiety that erupts into violence.

2. The correct answer is (D). Langston Hughes (1902–1967) was one of the foremost members of the Harlem Renaissance, a movement of African-American writers that included Zora Neale Hurston, Countee Cullen, and Richard Wright. He was mainly known for his poetry, but he also wrote plays, novels, humorous sketches, short stories, and a two-volume autobiography. His use of African-American dialect led to a revolution in African-American writing, influencing later generations of writers up to the present.

3. The correct answer is (D). James Baldwin (1924–1987) was the author of *Notes of a Native Son* (1955) and *The Fire Next Time* (1963), collections of essays condemning American race discrimination. His novels *Giovanni's Room* (1956), *Another Country* (1962), and *Just Above My Head* (1979) are moving stories of African-American life in America and abroad.

4. The correct answer is (A). Nathaniel Hawthorne
   (1804–1864) was a New Englander, a writer of
   short stories and novels, among which are *The
   House of the Seven Gables* (1851) and *The
   Blithedale Romance* (1852). His story of Puritan
   America, *The Scarlet Letter* (1850), is his masterpiece; it tells of the illicit romance between a married woman and a minister and explores the themes
   of sin, guilt, and hypocrisy. The other novels mentioned are by James Fenimore Cooper, Stephen
   Crane, and Theodore Dreiser.

5. The correct answer is (B). Winner of the Nobel
   Prize in 1930, Sinclair Lewis was a satirist who tar-
   geted small-town America in *Main Street* (1920),
   scientists in *Arrowsmith* (1925), and evangelists in
   Elmer Gantry (1927). *Arrowsmith* was awarded
   the Pulitzer Prize, but Lewis turned it down
   because the award was given to the work that best
   presented "the wholesome atmosphere of American life."

6. The correct answer is (A). *The Great Gatsby* (1925)
   is the story of the rise and fall of Jay Gatsby, a man
   without a real past or emotional ties, and his effect on
   Tom and Daisy Buchanan and on the story's narrator,
   Nick Carraway. The novel is set during the 1920s
   and shows the emptiness of the lives of those who
   lived and prospered in the Jazz Age.

7. The correct answer is (C). *The Invisible Man*
   (1952), winner of the National Book Award, charts
   the journey of an African-American man from the

South to Harlem and his search for personal and racial identity. A poll of two hundred authors and critics taken in 1964 named the book "the most distinguished single work published in the last twenty years."

8. The correct answer is (D). Ezra Pound (1885–1972) was a controversial poet, critic, and essayist. Early in his career he promoted the school of imagism, which stressed metaphor and image. Later he became involved in the Fascist movements of Hitler and Mussolini, broadcasting propaganda from Italy. After World War II he was arrested and committed to an asylum, but he continued to write poetry and essays until his death.

9. The correct answer is (B). This line is from an Eskimo poem in *Beyond the High Hills: A Book of Eskimo Poetry*. Like other Native American poetry, it uses simple, clear images of nature to express emotions and thoughts about life.

10. The correct answer is (A). Isaac Bashevis Singer (1904–1992), born in Poland, emigrated to the United States in 1935. He wrote novels such as *The Family Moskat* (1950), memoirs, and collections of stories for children, the best known of which is *The Fools of Chelm* (1973). His tales, most of which were originally written in Yiddish, reflect Jewish culture and folklore. In 1978, he won the Nobel Prize for literature.

11. The correct answer is (D). Toni Morrison was born Chloe Anthony Wofford in 1931. Her first novel,

The Bluest Eye, was published in 1969 to wide acclaim, and later novels, especially *Beloved* (1988), for which she won the Pulitzer Prize, have won her a large following. Morrison's novels, including her 1992 book *Jazz,* often treat the topic of racism and deal with the myths and realities of African-American life.

12. The correct answer is (D). Although E. E. Cummings (1894–1962) is most often remembered for using only lowercase letters in his poetry, this was only part of his experimentation with the visual form of the poem. He worked with line fragments, unusual punctuation, and verse shapes as well. He also wrote a novel, *The Enormous Room* (1922) and a play, *Him* (1927), and was the author of numerous essays.

13. The correct answer is (A). Edith Wharton (1862–1937) was called "the great and glorious pendulum" by Henry James, perhaps because of the way she moved between society life and the intellectual life that produced her novels, including *The House of Mirth* (1905) and *Ethan Frome* (1911). The former revealed the hypocrisies of high society, while the latter is an almost legendary tale of a couple who live outside society.

14. The correct answer is (B). Eugene O'Neill (1888–1953) was America's first major playwright. He was a four-time Pulitzer Prize winner (in 1920 for *Beyond the Horizon,* in 1921 for *Anna Christie,* in 1928 for *Strange Interlude,* and in

1956 for *A Long Day's Journey Into Night*) and the only American dramatist to win a Nobel Prize. His theater group, the Provincetown Players, staged his early plays in Greenwich Village, but soon O'Neill's work moved to Broadway. He wrote more than thirty plays, most of which explore the raw, primitive self beneath man's civilized veneer. The other plays mentioned are by Clifford Odets, David Mamet, and Sam Shepard.

15. The correct answer is (C). Edgar Allan Poe (1809–1849) became famous with the publication of his poem "The Raven" (1845), which many critics consider an imitation of the British romantic style. His tales of the grotesque, however, established him as an important writer, one who has influenced such later greats as William Faulkner and Vladimir Nabokov.

16. The correct answer is (B). Emily Dickinson (1830–1886) was a New England poet who in her later years became a recluse. She wrote almost 2,000 poems, only seven of which were published in her lifetime. Her short verses, characterized by her use of dashes as punctuation, explored themes of love, death, and immortality.

17. The correct answer is (D). Eudora Welty, born in 1909, is a native of Jackson, Mississippi. Her stories and novels, including *Delta Wedding* (1946) and the Pulitzer Prize–winning *Optimist's Daughter* (1972), tell of small-town life in the South. Flannery O'Connor (1924–1964) set most of her short

stories and novels in the South. She blended religious faith with the grotesque in her novel *Wise Blood* (1952) and the story collection *A Good Man Is Hard to Find* (1955). Carson McCullers (1917–1967) was a Georgian whose novel *The Heart Is a Lonely Hunter* (1940) and collection of stories *The Ballad of the Sad Cafe* (1951) were set in the South and explored human loneliness.

18. The correct answer is (B). John Steinbeck (1902–1968) wrote primarily about the disadvantaged in America. His best-known novel, *The Grapes of Wrath* (1939), is the story of the Joads, an Oklahoma family driven from their dustbowl farm and forced to become migrant workers in California. The other novels mentioned are by Thomas Pynchon, James Agee, and E. L. Doctorow.

19. The correct answer is (A). *Our Town* (1938), which won the Pulitzer Prize, takes place in a small New England town and traces the daily lives of several inhabitants. The play treats themes of love, marriage, birth, and death, and stresses the value of seemingly insignificant moments in life.

20. The correct answer is (C). *Walden* (1854) was written by Henry David Thoreau (1817–1862) during the two years he lived alone in a cabin on the banks of Walden Pond. In the book, Thoreau urges readers to simplify their lives and look to nature for meaning and clarity in life.

21. The correct answer is (B). Robert Frost (1874–1963) was not well known as a poet until he

reached his forties. He wrote in traditional verse forms and developed themes of rural life and nature.

22. The correct answer is (D). Transcendentalism was a movement that began in New England in the nineteenth century. It had its roots in the philosophy of Plato and stressed intuition as the means to understanding reality. Emerson, the leader of the movement, called for transcendentalists to trust only direct experiences; their belief in man's divinity was the key to reliance on self rather than on an external God. The other movements mentioned are absurdism, existentialism, and dadaism.

23. The correct answer is (B). Raymond Chandler (1888–1959) created the detective Philip Marlowe, who solved crimes in *The Big Sleep* (1939), *Farewell My Lovely* (1940), and *The Long Goodbye* (1954). Mickey Spillane, born in 1918, wrote novels of violence and sex starring detective Mike Hammer, such as *I, the Jury* (1947) and *Kiss Me Deadly* (1952). Dashiell Hammett (1894–1961) created detectives Sam Spade in *The Maltese Falcon* (1930) and Nick Charles in *The Thin Man* (1932).

24. The correct answer is (D). Samuel Clemens (1835–1910), who wrote under the pen name Mark Twain, created characters that reflected purely American traits and habits. His greatest character, Huck Finn, is a boy whose adventures on the Mississippi with Jim, a runaway slave, are a

social commentary that condemns slavery and reveals the corruption of the American South.

25. The correct answer is (C). Naturalism, a literary movement that came to America from France at the turn of the century, emphasized the subordination of characters to their environments. Stephen Crane's novel *Maggie: A Girl of the Streets* (1896), Frank Norris's McTeague (1899), and Theodore Dreiser's *Sister Carrie* (1900) are examples of naturalist fiction.

26. The correct answer is (A). Washington Irving (1783–1859) grew up as a wealthy member of New York society, which he satirized in *History of New York*, a burlesque that he claimed was by the historian Diedrich Knickerbocker. The word *knickerbocker* is now used to name any resident of New York State, particularly one descended from the early Dutch settlers. Rip van Winkle is the hero of one tale in *Sketch Book of Geoffrey Crayon, Gent.*, usually considered to be the first collection of short stories in America. Rip falls asleep for twenty years. When he wakes, an old man, he finds his wife dead and the British colonies replaced by the United States. The other characters listed are from works by Louisa May Alcott, Harriet Beecher Stowe, and Herman Melville.

27. The correct answer is (B). The novelist Willa Cather (1876–1947) grew up in Nebraska, and the prairie country is the setting for many of her works. Her best-known novels deal with pioneers and

immigrants in the Midwest—*O Pioneers* (1913), *The Song of the Lark* (1915), and *My Antonia* (1918) among them. Although *Death Comes for the Archbishop* (1927) is set in the Southwest, it also focuses on the American past.

28. The correct answer is (B). The decadence and slow destruction of the Old South are major themes of the novels of William Faulkner (1897–1962). His important works take place in a mythical county in Mississippi and involve several fictional families whose lives interweave. *The Sound and the Fury* (1929) tells the story of the disintegration of the Compson family. The narrative is in four distinct parts, the first three being the stream of consciousness of the three sons, one of whom is retarded. *Absalom, Absalom!* (1936) has multiple narrators, who tell of Thomas Sutpen and his doomed attempts to become a Southern aristocrat in the years preceding the Civil War.

29. The correct answer is (C). Distinguished by rampant exaggeration and humor, tall tales are folk tales of the American frontier. Some, such as the tales of Davy Crockett, have characters based on real heroes. Most, including stories of Pecos Bill and Paul Bunyan, simply celebrate pioneer traits of courage, strength, and inventiveness.

30. The correct answer is (C). Herman Melville (1819–1891) went to sea at the age of eighteen. For the next eight years, he alternated life aboard ships with life as a schoolteacher. Most of his writing is

based on his experiences on whalers in the South Pacific. Novels include *Typee* (1846), *Omoo* (1847), *White-Jacket* (1850), and the powerful *Moby-Dick* (1851), which integrates a symbolic tale of man and fate with realistic scenes of whaling and discussion of its history.

31. The correct answer is (D). Thomas Stearns Eliot (1888–1965) wrote criticism and plays, but he is best known for his poetry. *The Waste Land,* written after World War I, evokes the related legends of the primitive Fisher King and the Holy Grail in its depiction of a sterile and amoral modern world. *Four Quartets* (1943) includes "Burnt Norton," "East Coker," "The Dry Salvages," and "Little Gidding." Through memories of these places, the poet explores time, mortality, and the creative process.

32. The correct answer is (A). *Uncle Tom's Cabin* is a morality tale about life on a plantation. The evil Simon Legree, a Northerner, oversees the slaves and treats them cruelly. Harriet Beecher Stowe (1811–1896) wrote the book in support of the Abolitionist cause, and Abraham Lincoln referred to her as "the little woman who started (the Civil) war." Her book was wildly popular and controversial, and a year after its publication in 1852, she was forced by doubting readers to write *A Key to Uncle Tom's Cabin,* a list of facts about slavery and plantation life.

33. The correct answer is (D). Anne Bradstreet (c. 1612–1672) traveled from England to Massachusetts at

the age of eighteen. The first collection of her poems was published in 1650 in England under the title *The Tenth Muse Lately Sprung Up in America*. She is remembered chiefly for short poems on life in New England, including "On the Burning of Her House" and "To My Dear and Loving Husband." She also wrote an autobiography, *Religious Experiences*. Jonathan Edwards (1703–1758), a pastor and missionary in Massachusetts, is known for his "fire-and-brimstone" sermons, notably "Sinners in the Hands of an Angry God." His evangelicism led to the religious movement known as "The Great Awakening" in 1740–1750, which culminated in a split between Edwards's followers and more liberal churchgoers.

34. The correct answer is (A). *Death of a Salesman* won Miller a Pulitzer Prize in 1949. Its hero is Willy Loman, the quintessential common man, whose seemingly petty failures are raised to the level of tragedy. *The Crucible* was written at the height of the McCarthy era (1953) and told of the Salem witch-craft trials. The other plays listed are by Tennessee Williams, Edward Albee, and Thornton Wilder.

35. The correct answer is (C). In short stories such as "The Snows of Kilimanjaro" (1938) and novels such as *The Sun Also Rises* (1926) and *For Whom the Bell Tolls* (1940), Ernest Hemingway (1899–1961) used a spare, unemotional style punctuated by terse dialogue. His themes include courage, cynicism, and the loss of liberty.

36. The correct answer is (A). The daughter of Bronson
    Alcott, a noted educator and friend to Thoreau and
    Emerson, Louisa May Alcott (1832–1888) grew up in
    a poor household surrounded by books and learned
    people. She wrote melodramas to make ends meet,
    and became editor of a children's magazine in 1867.
    Her most popular novels are based on her own family
    life and include *Little Women* (1869), *Little Men*
    (1871), *Rose in Bloom* (1876), and *Jo's Boys* (1886).

37. The correct answer is (C). Richard Wright
    (1909–1960) achieved recognition with a collection
    of short stories called *Uncle Tom's Children*, which
    won a prize in 1938 as the best work submitted by a
    member of the Federal Writers' Project. The stories
    dealt with racial discrimination in the South. *Native
    Son* (1940) brought Wright lasting fame with its
    depiction of Bigger Thomas, a Chicago slum-dweller
    whose environment is directly linked to his fate.
    Black Boy (1945) is an autobiographical account of
    Wright's Southern boyhood. The other works listed
    are by James Baldwin, John Dos Passos, and Gwen-
    dolyn Brooks.

38. The correct answer is (D). Henry Wadsworth
    Longfellow (1807–1882) was a prolific poet who
    helped to create and maintain many American leg-
    ends in poems such as *The Song of Hiawatha*
    (1855) and *The Courtship of Miles Standish*
    (1858). The lines quoted are from *Evangeline*
    (1847), "A Psalm of Life" (1839), and "Paul
    Revere's Ride" from *Tales of a Wayside Inn* (1874).

39. The correct answer is (B). Kurt Vonnegut was born in 1922 and worked as a freelance writer in the early 1960s before gaining attention as a science fiction novelist. Works such as *Cat's Cradle* (1963) and *Slaughterhouse-Five* (1969), although still concerned with science fiction themes, were atypical of the genre in their use of absurdism and satire.

40. The correct answer is (A). The quintessential novelist, Henry James (1843–1916) is considered one of the greatest technicians of the form. Many of his works treat the "international theme"—the contrast of American and European characters and values. He strove to hone the point of view in his novels and stories so that revelations and insights belong to his characters rather than to an omniscient narrator. Characterization is therefore subtly and deliberately revealed over the course of the narrative. Among his most important works are *The Portrait of a Lady* (1881), *The Wings of the Dove* (1902), *The Ambassadors* (1903), *The Golden Bowl* (1904), and the novella *The Turn of the Screw* (1898).

41. The correct answer is (A). Sherwood Anderson (1876–1941) is best known for his collection of stories of small-town life titled *Winesburg, Ohio* (1919). The book focuses on the psychological dramas behind the scenes of a fictional town. The extraordinary dreams of ordinary people is also the theme of *Spoon River Anthology,* a collection of blank verse by Edgar Lee Masters (1868–1950).

42. The correct answer is (B). Among the popular works of Ray Bradbury (b. 1920) are *The Martian Chronicles* and many short stories. Ursula LeGuin (b. 1929) wrote *Left Hand of Darkness, City of Illusion,* and many other science fiction and fantasy works for children and adults. Isaac Asimov (1920–1992) wrote *I, Robot* and the *Foundation* trilogy, among hundreds of works of fiction and nonfiction.

43. The correct answer is (D). *Muckrakers* was a term used by Theodore Roosevelt to label people concerned with uncovering corruption in business and government. The movement began in 1902 and lasted until World War I. Among the major works of protest to emerge from the movement were Upton Sinclair's *The Jungle* (1906), an exposé of the meat-packing industry; Ida Tarbell's *History of the Standard Oil Company* (1904); and Lincoln Steffens's *Shame of the Cities* (1904).

44. The correct answer is (B). Walt Whitman (1819–1892) wrote poetry that fit natural speech patterns rather than regular metrical structure. His most important work, a collection of poems called *Leaves of Grass* (1855), underwent many revisions and additions during the poet's lifetime. At first ignored by the critics, the book became controversial in time, and Whitman lost a job with the Department of the Interior because of his "immoral" writing. In his celebration of the human body, egalitarianism, and the sexual self, he was certainly ahead of his time.

45. The correct answer is (C). John Updike (b. 1932) is a poet and essayist as well as a fiction writer. His subjects tend to be suburbanites, and although his short stories are quite popular, it is novels such as *Rabbit, Run* (1960) and *The Centaur* (1963) that made his reputation.

46. The correct answer is (B). The Beat movement of the 1950s involved a complicated combination of Eastern mysticism, social nonconformity, sexual freedom, and drug use. Many of the writers associated with the movement were poets, with Allen Ginsberg (1926–1997) and Gregory Corso (1930–2001) among the best known. Jack Kerouac 1922–1969) was a novelist, whose *On the Road* (1957) typifies the rambling style of all of the Beats, poets and fiction writers alike.

47. The correct answer is (C). The poems of Marianne Moore (1887–1972) are unusual in their focus on the whole stanza rather than the line, which makes them read at times like prose rather than poetry. For her subjects she chose animals, machines, buildings, and people, examining each with a scientific eye for detail.

48. The correct answer is (D). Dorothy Parker (1893–1967) wrote acerbic drama reviews for *Vanity Fair* and *The New Yorker* and poems and short stories full of irony and bitter humor, but she is remembered more for her bon mots, one-liners culled from her writing or conversation. These include "Men seldom make passes / At girls who

wear glasses" from "News Item" (1927) and "runs the gamut of emotions from A to B" from a drama review. Elwyn Brooks White (1899–1985) was a columnist for *The New Yorker,* a writer of children's books, a poet, and an essayist. He collaborated with James Thurber (1894–1961) on the book *Is Sex Necessary?* (1929). Thurber worked at *The New Yorker* as well. He wrote "The Secret Life of Walter Mitty," a number of other stories, essays, and a play.

49. The correct answer is (A). A radical pamphleteer, Thomas Paine (1737–1809) believed in the need for reform through revolution. *Common Sense* (1776) called for the secession of the colonies from England and led to the drafting of the Declaration of Independence. *The Rights of Man* (1792) was written in defense of the French Revolution and led to Paine's trial in England as a traitor. He lived in France until he was imprisoned during the Reign of Terror, and he later died in poverty in the United States.

50. The correct answer is (C). Vladimir Nabokov (1899–1977) was born in Russia and moved to the United States in 1940. *Lolita* (1958) is a darkly comic novel about a man's obsessive desire for a very young girl. The title character in *Pnin* (1957) is a semiautobiographical portrait of a professor of Russian literature at an American university. *Pale Fire* (1962) is an experiment in narrative structure, a novel disguised as a poem and commentary.

TEST 10
MIGHTIER THAN
THE SWORD:
WORLD LITERATURE

World literature is . . . a kind of collective body
and a common spirit, a living unity of the heart
which reflects the growing spiritual unity of
mankind.

—ALEXANDER SOLZHENITSYN

1. *Crime and Punishment* and *The Brothers Karamazov* are novels by
   (A) Leo Tolstoy.
   (B) Aleksandr Pushkin.
   (C) Fyodor Dostoevsky.
   (D) Nikolai Gogol.

2. Which of the following plays is *not* by George Bernard Shaw?
   (A) *Man and Superman*
   (B) *Major Barbara*
   (C) *Pygmalion*
   (D) *Antony and Cleopatra*

3. The poems of William Wordsworth can best be described as
   (A) comic and rhetorical.
   (B) lyrical and romantic.
   (C) epic and didactic.
   (D) sentimental and dramatic.

4. James Joyce created which of the following characters?
   (A) Molly Bloom and Stephen Dedalus
   (B) Little Nell and Samuel Pickwick
   (C) Adam Bede and Dorothea Brooke
   (D) Jean Valjean and Fantine

5. A cave wherein prisoners see only shadows cast by a fire is a central simile in a work by which of the following?
   (A) Plato
   (B) Aristotle
   (C) Spinoza
   (D) Descartes

6. Which of these poets is associated with Irish nationalism and Celtic mythology?
   (A) William Butler Yeats
   (B) John Dryden
   (C) Rudyard Kipling
   (D) Elizabeth Barrett Browning

7. "Of man's first disobedience, and the fruit / Of that
   forbidden tree" is the opening to
   (A) *The Fairie Queene* by Edmund Spenser.
   (B) *The Pilgrim's Progress* by John Bunyan.
   (C) *The Vision of Delight* by Ben Jonson.
   (D) *Paradise Lost* by John Milton.

8. Which of these characters does *not* appear in *David
   Copperfield?*
   (A) Uriah Heep
   (B) Mr. Micawber
   (C) Barkis
   (D) Pip

9. Gothic novels generally feature
   (A) romantic settings and happy endings.
   (B) gloomy settings and supernatural occurrences.
   (C) exotic settings and a young boy's coming-of-
       age.
   (D) historic settings and characters based on real
       people.

10. *Beowulf* is the oldest existing English
    (A) novel.
    (B) epic.
    (C) play.
    (D) historical document.

11. Who was Jorge Luis Borges?
    (A) A Spanish novelist of the sixteenth century
    (B) A Mexican poet and diplomat
    (C) An Argentine short-story writer
    (D) A Chilean playwright

12. The hero of *Gulliver's Travels*
    (A) visits a land of tiny people and a land of philosophers.
    (B) is shipwrecked on an island with only one inhabitant.
    (C) travels around the world in a hot-air balloon.
    (D) has a series of comical adventures in America.

13. Who wrote *The Rime of the Ancient Mariner* and *Kubla Khan?*
    (A) Edgar Allan Poe
    (B) Samuel Taylor Coleridge
    (C) Edward Fitzgerald
    (D) Robert Burns

14. Marcel Proust is famous for writing
    (A) a collection of poems called *The Flowers of Evil.*
    (B) a hymn to the joys of unconventionality and sexuality.
    (C) a seven-part novel about memory and time.
    (D) All of the above

15. What do Alfred, Lord Tennyson; T. H. White; and Sir Thomas Malory have in common?
    (A) They all wrote during the Victorian era.
    (B) They all left England to live in France.
    (C) They all wrote poetry on mythical subjects.
    (D) They all wrote about the Arthurian legend.

16. Which of these works is not by Samuel Beckett?
    (A) The novel *Malone Dies*
    (B) The play *Waiting for Godot*
    (C) The play *Endgame*
    (D) The play *The Maids*

17. Which of these plays are by Anton Chekhov?
    (A) *Ghosts, The Master Builder, When We Dead Awaken*
    (B) *The Sea Gull, Uncle Vanya, The Cherry Orchard*
    (C) *Miss Julie, The Dance of Death, The Father*
    (D) *Misalliance, Heartbreak House, Arms and the Man*

18. John Locke, Voltaire, and Jean Jacques Rousseau were
    (A) seventeenth- and eighteenth-century philosophers.
    (B) nineteenth-century politicians.
    (C) sixteenth- and seventeenth-century novelists.
    (D) eighteenth- and nineteenth-century poets.

19. Among the themes in Franz Kafka's work are
    (A) divine love and the achievement of mystical union with God.
    (B) war and hope expressed through the Earth's return to a natural state.
    (C) alienation and the impossibility of human interconnection.
    (D) sexual dependence and the role of women in society.

20. Which British poet is *not* matched correctly with his work?
    (A) William Blake, "To a Mouse"
    (B) George Gordon, Lord Byron, *Don Juan*
    (C) Percy Bysshe Shelley, "Ozymandias"
    (D) John Keats, "La Belle Dame sans Merci"

21. Who wrote *Heart of Darkness* and *Lord Jim*?
    (A) E. M. Forster
    (B) Rudyard Kipling
    (C) Joseph Conrad
    (D) Sir Walter Scott

22. Who was Victor Hugo?
    (A) A leader of the French Protestants in the sixteenth century
    (B) A leading playwright in Victorian England
    (C) The deformed hero of *The Hunchback of Notre Dame*
    (D) A key figure in the Romantic movement in France

23. Alan Paton, Nadine Gordimer, and Athol Fugard are
    (A) South African writers.
    (B) founders of the school of New Criticism.
    (C) twentieth-century African-American dramatists.
    (D) journalists who have received Pulitzer Prizes.

24. The Epic Theater of Bertolt Brecht attempts to
   (A) shock the audience and force them to react.
   (B) involve the audience intellectually rather than emotionally.
   (C) create a sustained illusion that arouses pity and terror.
   (D) convey the meaningless of existence through illogical dialogue.

25. Miguel de Cervantes's most important work was
   (A) *El Cid.*
   (B) *Life Is a Dream.*
   (C) "The Death of a Bullfighter."
   (D) *Don Quixote.*

26. What is the legend of Faust?
   (A) The story of a woman who unleashed a box full of evil on the world
   (B) The story of a king whose three daughters betray him
   (C) The story of a man who sells his soul to the devil in return for youth, knowledge, and power
   (D) The story of a deformed man whose love for a gypsy is set against the backdrop of medieval Paris

27. In what genre did the Brothers Grimm, Charles Perrault, and Hans Christian Anderson chiefly write?
   (A) Fairy tales
   (B) Novels of social protest
   (C) One-act plays
   (D) Sonnets

28. What happens in the play *Romeo and Juliet?*
    (A) A Moorish general kills his wife in the belief that she was his lieutenant's lover.
    (B) A leader of the state is murdered in a political conspiracy.
    (C) A troubled prince plots against the king to avenge his dead father.
    (D) A boy and girl from feuding families fall in love and die while trying to flee together.

29. Who is the author of *Hedda Gabler, A Doll's House,* and *The Wild Duck?*
    (A) Henrik Ibsen
    (B) Bertolt Brecht
    (C) Emile Zola
    (D) August Strindberg

30. Which siblings wrote *Jane Eyre* and *Wuthering Heights?*
    (A) William and Henry James
    (B) Edmond and Jules de Goncourt
    (C) Emily and Charlotte Brontë
    (D) Thomas and Heinrich Mann

31. Who created the characters of the Wife of Bath, the Prioress, and the Pardoner?
    (A) Geoffrey Chaucer
    (B) William Shakespeare
    (C) Chrétien de Troyes
    (D) Thomas Malory

32. Which of these novelists created the desperate, sentimental housewife, Madame Bovary?
    (A) Stendahl
    (B) Honoré de Balzac
    (C) Victor Hugo
    (D) Gustave Flaubert

33. A modern novelist for whom man's rediscovery of sexual vitality was the clue to his salvation is
    (A) D. H. Lawrence.
    (B) Thomas Mann.
    (C) E. M. Forster.
    (D) Günter Grass.

34. Who was the author of *Jude the Obscure, The Return of the Native,* and *The Mayor of Casterbridge?*
    (A) L. P. Hartley
    (B) Peter Handke
    (C) Thomas Hardy
    (D) Winifred Holtley

35. Who was George Eliot?
    (A) A novelist; she wrote *Middlemarch* and *Daniel Deronda*
    (B) A poet; he wrote "Gerontion" and *Old Possum's Book of Practical Cats*
    (C) A novelist; he wrote *Parktilden Village* and *Muriel*
    (D) A novelist; she wrote *Indiana* and *Consuelo*

36. Who wrote the story of Ulysses, a sailor who faced danger and adventure on his way home from the Trojan War?
    (A) Sophocles
    (B) Homer
    (C) James Joyce
    (D) Cicero

37. Who is the Nobel Prize–winning novelist who wrote *Buddenbrooks, The Magic Mountain,* and *Death in Venice?*
    (A) Thomas Mann
    (B) Anton Chekhov
    (C) Nikolai Gogol
    (D) Isak Dinesen

38. What happened to Robinson Crusoe?
    (A) He was orphaned and forced to steal for a living.
    (B) He fought for the freedom of the Jewish maiden, Rebecca.
    (C) He was shipwrecked on a deserted island.
    (D) He roamed the world, surviving misadventures, with Dr. Pangloss.

39. Jean-Paul Sartre, André Malraux, and Martin Buber are all
    (A) romantics.
    (B) existentialists.
    (C) expressionists.
    (D) illuminists.

40. Which characters were created by Henry Fielding?
    (A) Felix Krull and Gustav von Aschenbach
    (B) Roderick Random and Humphrey Clinker
    (C) Pamela Andrews and Clarissa Harlowe
    (D) Tom Jones and Joseph Andrews

41. For which novels is Jane Austen known?
    (A) *Villette* and *Shirley*
    (B) *Pride and Prejudice, Emma,* and *Persuasion*
    (C) *Felix Holt, Silas Marner,* and *Adam Bede*
    (D) *Cousin Bette* and *Lost Illusions*

42. Which Russian novelist wrote sweeping sagas of historical and moral crises?
    (A) Leo Tolstoy
    (B) Ivan Turgenev
    (C) Fyodor Dostoyevsky
    (D) Isaac Babel

43. A British novelist and critic who experimented with stream of consciousness and interior monologue was
    (A) Malcolm Lowry.
    (B) D. M. Thomas.
    (C) Virginia Woolf.
    (D) Lytton Strachey.

44. Which Renaissance poet wrote of a trip through Hell, Purgatory, and Heaven?
    (A) Geoffrey Chaucer
    (B) John Milton
    (C) Dante Alighieri
    (D) Giovanni Bocaccio

45. Of what is this poem an example?

> Snow, softly, slowly,
> settles at dusk in a dance
> of white butterflies.
> —Harry Behn

(A) A sonnet
(B) A haiku
(C) An epic
(D) A ballad

46. Which of these plays is *not* by August Strindberg?
(A) *A Dream Play*
(B) *Miss Julie*
(C) *The Dance of Death*
(D) *Six Characters in Search of an Author*

47. Which of these authors made the year 1984 famous?
(A) George Orwell
(B) Aldous Huxley
(C) H. G. Wells
(D) All of the above

48. Why was the writer Salman Rushdie forced into hiding?
(A) He was discovered to be a Nazi war criminal.
(B) He was wanted by the FBI as a spy and a traitor.
(C) He wrote a book that was deemed blasphemous by certain members of a religious group.
(D) He testified in court against mob boss John Gotti.

49. For what is Ovid primarily known?
    (A) His poetry and discourses on love and art
    (B) His tragic plays
    (C) His epic poem about Aeneas
    (D) His philosophy of government

50. Which of these plays is *not* a Greek tragedy?
    (A) *Oedipus the King*
    (B) *Electra*
    (C) *The Clouds*
    (D) *Antigone*

TEST 10:
Explanatory Answers

1. The correct answer is (C). Fyodor Mikhailovich Dostoevsky (1821–1881) had a career plagued by hostile reviews and mental imbalance. His father's murder by his serfs in 1844 may have precipitated Dostoevsky's preoccupation with murder and patricide, a theme that permeates his work. *Crime and Punishment* (1866) is the story of Raskolnikov, an impoverished student who kills an old pawnbroker. No sooner does he commit the crime than he begins to torment himself by uncovering his unconscious motives. *The Brothers Karamazov* (1880) has a complicated plot surrounding the death of a father and the evidence that implicates his four sons. The plot is perhaps secondary to the themes involving ethics and agnosticism.

2. The correct answer is (D). *Antony and Cleopatra* is a play by William Shakespeare. In 1899, Shaw (1856–1950) wrote a play based on a work by Plutarch and called it *Caesar and Cleopatra*. Shaw is known as an advocate of social reform as well as a writer of witty, satiric plays.

3. The correct answer is (B). One of the English Romantic poets, William Wordsworth (1770–1850) is remembered for his focus on natural scenes, simple people, and the mystical power of memory. His theory that the language of poetry should arise from

common speech was a turning point in English poetry. Such poems as "Lines Composed a Few Miles above Tintern Abbey" and "I Wandered Lonely as a Cloud" are prime examples of romanticism.

4. The correct answer is (A). Stephen Dedalus is the protagonist of *Portrait of the Artist as a Young Man* (1916) and a major character in *Ulysses* (1922), in which Molly Bloom figures as well. James Joyce (1882–1941), considered the finest English-language novelist of the twentieth century, experimented with a huge variety of narrative techniques and used symbols from such disparate sources as Greek mythology, Catholic theology, Irish history, and popular songs. The other characters listed are from works by Charles Dickens, George Eliot, and Victor Hugo.

5. The correct answer is (A). In his *Republic*, Plato (c. 428 B.C.E.—348 B.C.E.) discusses the question "What is philosophy?" He defines it as the "vision of truth" and sees those people with no philosophy as prisoners chained in a cave, with a fire behind them throwing shadows on the wall in front. The prisoners see only shadows, but since they know no other reality, they think of the shadows as real. Should a prisoner escape, see the outside world, and return to describe it to the others, that escapee will find that the shadows no longer seem clear to him or her. The escapee will find it difficult to convert the others, who still see the shadows clearly. Most of Plato's work is in the form of a dialogue between the philosopher Socrates and a pupil.

Other works include the *Apology, Phaedrus, Gorgias,* and *Symposium.*

6. The correct answer is (A). William Butler Yeats (1865–1939) was a central figure in the Irish Renaissance, a movement designed to restore Irish culture in the wake of a rise in nationalism. He helped to found the Abbey Theatre, which gained fame through production of controversial plays by Sean O'Casey, John Millington Synge, and Yeats himself. His plays, which include *The Countess Cathleen* (1891) and *The Herne's Egg* (1938), often mix Irish legend with Eastern mysticism. He is better known for his poetry, particularly such late works as "Sailing to Byzantium."

7. The correct answer is (D). *Paradise Lost* is a twelve-part epic by John Milton (1608–1674) about the expulsion of Satan from Heaven and Adam and Eve from the Garden of Eden. It is notable for its detailed characterization of biblical figures, its sustained tension, and its ringing, dramatic tone.

8. The correct answer is (D). Pip is the hero of *Great Expectations* (1861). *David Copperfield* (1850), like most of the novels by Charles Dickens (1812–1870), was originally serialized. It tells the tale of young David, who lives with his stepfather and whose only comfort in his childhood is his nurse, Clara Peggotty, who later marries Barkis. David is sent by his stepfather to London to fend for himself. He lives with the Micawbers and works in a warehouse before finding work with a

lawyer, whose clerk is Uriah Heep, an obsequious man who blackmails his employer. With the help of Mr. Micawber, David at long last removes the threat posed by Uriah Heep. Like most of Dickens's work, the book aims at raising social consciousness by exposing the cruelty of society to the poor and helpless. Unlike his other work, this book is supposed to be at least partly autobiographical.

9. The correct answer is (B). A gory book called *The Castle of Otranto* (1764) by Horace Walpole is probably the first English novel in the Gothic genre. Gothic novels were extremely popular and somewhat scandalous in their time—from the late eighteenth to the early nineteenth century. Other works in the genre include *The Mysteries of Udolpho* (1794) by Ann Radcliffe, *The Monk* (1795) by Matthew Lewis, and *Frankenstein or the Modern Prometheus* (1818) by Mary Wollstonecraft Shelley. Typical of Gothic novels were violent plots, supernatural occurrences, and medieval settings.

10. The correct answer is (B). *Beowulf* (c. 700) is a long epic poem in Old English about a Danish hero and his defeat of the monster Grendel. It is assumed to be based in part on Norse legend and in part on Danish history. Each of the more than 3,000 lines has four stressed syllables, at least two of which are alliterative (begin with the same sound).

11. The correct answer is (C). Jorge Luis Borges (1899–1986) wrote poetry and essays before turn-

ing to narrative fiction. His stories, some of which are translated in a collection called *Labyrinths* (1962), feature experimental structures and highly compressed symbolic patterns.

12. The correct answer is (A). In *Gulliver's Travels* (1726) the hero goes on four excursions. One takes him to the land of Lilliput, where the residents are extremely small. One takes him to the land of Brobdingnag, where the residents are giants. He also visits the land of Laputa, whose people are "wise" men and philosophers, and Houyhnhnmland, where horses keep Yahoos (who look suspiciously like humans) in servitude. The author, English satirist Jonathan Swift (1667–1745), used the novel to denounce human pettiness, self-styled philosophers, and European society in general.

13. The correct answer is (B). *The Rime of the Ancient Mariner* (1798) and *Kubla Khan* (1797) are among the most frequently quoted of all English poems. The latter was written in an opium-induced haze and was never finished. Samuel Taylor Coleridge (1772–1834) was a critical essayist of great importance and one of the leaders of the English romanticists. With Wordsworth, he published *Lyrical Ballads* (1798), which contained *The Rime of the Ancient Mariner* and a treatise by Wordsworth that set forth the credo of romantic literature. *The Rime of the Ancient Mariner* contains the often-misquoted lines: "Water, water, everywhere / Nor any drop to drink."

14. The correct answer is (C). *Remembrance of Things Past* (1913–1927) is the masterwork of French novelist Marcel Proust (1871–1922). The narrator's memory is involuntarily triggered by inanimate objects, and he also deliberately scrutinizes his past to make sense of experiences he had no way of understanding at the time. The author explores the disappointing nature of love, the hypocrisy behind the aristocratic façade, and the need to transcend time to find essential meaning. The other works alluded to are by Charles Baudelaire and André Gide.

15. The correct answer is (D). Arthur was probably a Celtic chieftain of the sixth century, but he may instead have been a Celtic deity from much earlier. The Arthurian legends were passed down in Wales and England for centuries before being collected and written down by Thomas Malory in *Morte d'Arthur* (c. 1469). In these eight tales, King Arthur is presented as the son of Uther Pendragon and the husband of Guinevere. Merlin the magician incorporates druidic rites into the legend as Arthur's teacher and aide. *Idylls of the King* (1859–1885), a series of poems by Alfred, Lord Tennyson, interprets the legend in a more Christian spirit, focusing on the introduction of sin into Camelot through the adultery of Guinevere. Terence Hanbury White wrote four epics based on the legend under the title *The Once and Future King* (1958). This version came to the stage as the musical *Camelot*.

16. The correct answer is (D). Samuel Beckett (1906–1989) is known for his plays about the overwhelming desire to communicate in the face of human disintegration. He has also written several novels, many using a stream-of-consciousness narrative. *Malone Dies* (1951) is told through the thoughts of a dying tramp. *Waiting for Godot* (1952) features two tramps, dependent on each other though despising each other, who wait endlessly for someone who never comes. *Endgame* (1957) focuses on a blind man, his parents who are imprisoned in ashcans, and his servant, from whom he derives all information about the disappearing outside world. *The Maids* (1948) is by French playwright Jean Genêt.

17. The correct answer is (B). Anton Pavlovich Chekhov (1860–1904) was a short-story writer as well as one of the greatest playwrights in any language. *The Sea Gull* (1896) tells of a writer and his love for Nina, a would-be actress. When she prefers a successful writer to him, he kills a sea gull and offers it to her as a symbol of his destroyed happiness. The successful writer leaves her, and Nina returns, but there is no hope of reconciliation. In *Uncle Vanya* (1899), Vanya gives up his own happiness to make his brother-in-law happy because he considers him a genius. When the brother-in-law proves to be less than Vanya imagines, Vanya unsuccessfully attempts to murder him and kills himself. *The Cherry Orchard* (1904) is about a family that is helpless in the face of bankruptcy and

the loss of their estate. Themes of despair, inability to communicate, and loss of idealism are mitigated by flashes of humor and Chekhov's deep understanding of human behavior. The other plays listed are by Henrik Ibsen, August Strindberg, and George Bernard Shaw.

18. The correct answer is (A). John Locke (1632–1704) was an English philosopher who wrote on the origin of ideas and knowledge in "An Essay Concerning Human Understanding." Locke's political theories are even more important; he was the father of modern liberalism, and his ideas are found in the constitutions of France and the United States, among others. François Marie Arouet (Voltaire) (1694–1778) helped bring Locke's ideas to France. He was a prolific writer of poems, dramas, allegories, essays, and histories, believing firmly that only a philosopher could write a history that was meaningful and thus creating a new way of looking at the past. Jean Jacques Rousseau (1712–1778) rejected the rationalism of both Locke and Voltaire and strove to create a climate in which people could respond to life through emotion rather than intellect. Nature and the individual were key elements of the school of thought that became romanticism.

19. The correct answer is (C). The Czech writer Franz Kafka (1883–1924) is known especially for his unfinished novels (*The Trial, The Castle,* and *Amerika*) and the story "Metamorphosis" (1915), in which the protagonist, Gregor Samsa, turns into a giant cock-

roach. His works feature strained and problematic relationships among guilt-ridden people and plots that range from hilarious to terrifying.

20. The correct answer is (A). "To a Mouse" is by the Scottish poet Robert Burns. Lord Byron (1788–1824), Percy Bysshe Shelley (1792–1822), and John Keats (1795–1821) were all English poets in the romantic tradition. *Don Juan* (1819–1824) features a thinly disguised Byron in the role of the Spanish profligate. "Ozymandias" (1818) is a sonnet by Shelley, and "La Belle Dame sans Merci" is a ballad by Keats, who is also known for his odes on melancholy, a nightingale, and a Grecian urn.

21. The correct answer is (C). Joseph Conrad (1857–1924) is remembered for his tales of adventure and moral dilemmas. *Heart of Darkness* (1902) tells of the exploitation perpetrated on the natives of the Belgian Congo by Kurtz, a white trader. The title character in *Lord Jim* abandons ship in his youth, leaving his passengers to die. They survive to tell the tale, and Jim spends the rest of his life trying to regain his lost honor. Both the short story and novel are narrated by Marlow, whose analysis of the events is as vital to the work as the events themselves.

22. The correct answer is (D). Victor Hugo (1802–1885) was one of the best-known poets in France and a leader of the Romantic movement, but English-speaking audiences know him for his novels. *The Hunchback of Notre Dame* (1831) and

Les Miserables (1862) feature sweeping, melodramatic plots.

23. The correct answer is (A). Alan Paton (1903–1988) is the author of *Cry, the Beloved Country* and other novels about racism. Nadine Gordimer (b. 1923) is also a novelist and short-story writer whose works have at times been banned in South Africa. Athol Fugard (b. 1932) is an actor and playwright, whose *Blood Knot* (1961) was the first play to be performed in his country with a mixed-race cast.

24. The correct answer is (B). Rather than telling one story from beginning to end, Epic Theater is generally episodic. The audience is alienated from the action via such unexpected effects as direct address by the actors and the use of placards and slides. By removing the possibility of emotional connection, Brecht (1898–1956) hoped to cause the audience to think and learn. The other techniques mentioned are typical of Artaud's Theater of Cruelty, the classical theory of tragedy espoused by Aristotle, and the Theater of the Absurd.

25. The correct answer is (D). *Don Quixote* (1615) is the story of a somewhat demented romantic who believes that he is a knight. He chooses the practical peasant, Sancho Panza, to be his squire, and the two travel abroad, with Don Quixote's vivid imagination providing endless adventures and misadventures. The work, by Miguel de Cervantes (1547–1616), marks a milestone in the history of the novel. The other items listed are a historic char-

acter whose exploits formed the basis for works by Pierre Corneille and Lope de Vega, a play by Pedro Calderón de la Barca, and a poem by Federico García Lorca.

26. The correct answer is (C). Based on the life of fifteenth-century magician Georg Faust, the legend of the man who sold his soul to the devil has been treated by many, including Christopher Marlowe in his play *The Tragical History of Dr. Faustus* (1588), Goethe in his play *Faust* (1808), and indirectly by Thomas Mann in his novel *Doktor Faustus* (1947).

27. The correct answer is (A). The brothers Grimm, Jacob (1785–1863) and Wilhelm (1786–1859), wrote and collected German legends and fairy tales, including "Rapunzel" and "Snow White and Rose Red." They were also known for their studies of the German language. Charles Perrault (1628–1703) was a French critic as well as a writer of fairy tales, including "Sleeping Beauty" and "Puss in Boots." Hans Christian Andersen (1805–1875) was a Dane who wrote novels, poetry, and plays as well as fairy tales, among which are "The Ugly Duckling," "The Little Mermaid," and "The Emperor's New Clothes."

28. The correct answer is (D). One of William Shakespeare's best-known tragedies, *Romeo and Juliet* (c. 1596) tells of the warring Montague and Capulet families of Verona, and how Romeo, a Montague, and Juliet, a Capulet, fall in love, are secretly married, and plot to flee Verona after

Romeo kills Juliet's cousin. A misunderstanding leads Romeo to believe that Juliet is dead; he kills himself, and on seeing his dead body, Juliet also kills herself. The other plots mentioned are those of *Othello, Julius Caesar,* and *Hamlet.*

29. The correct answer is (A). Henrik Ibsen (1828–1906) was a Norwegian playwright much of whose work focuses on the social problems of his time, such as the role of women, explored in *A Doll's House* (1879) and *Hedda Gabler* (1890), and the weakness of human idealism, treated in *The Wild Duck* (1884). Many of his plays were examples of realism, a style that presents life without idealization, but he also wrote fantasy plays such as Peer Gynt (1867) and highly symbolic dramas such as *When We Dead Awaken* (1900).

30. The correct answer is (C). Charlotte Brontë (1816–1855) and Emily Brontë (1818–1848) were sisters raised in Yorkshire, England. Charlotte Brontë's best-known novel is *Jane Eyre* (1847), the story of a poor governess and her domineering, obsessive employer. Emily Brontë's masterpiece, *Wuthering Heights* (1847), tells of the intense and unfulfilled love between Heathcliff and Catherine.

31. The correct answer is (A). Geoffrey Chaucer (1343–1400) was the author of *The Canterbury Tales.* It is the story of a group of pilgrims journeying to Canterbury, each of whom tells a tale. In the telling, the tales reveal much about the characters who are speaking and about Chaucer's time.

32. The correct answer is (D). Gustave Flaubert (1821–1880) was known for his detailed, precise style. *Madame Bovary* (1856), a masterpiece of craftsmanship, is the story of the life of a bourgeois woman and the despair that drives her to suicide.

33. The correct answer is (A). D. H. Lawrence (1885–1930) was the son of a miner, a profession on which he focuses in his early novel *Sons and Lovers* (1913). Other well-known novels are *The Rainbow* (1915), *Women in Love* (1920), *Aaron's Rod* (1922), and the controversial *Lady Chatterley's Lover,* which was censored in England until 1960.

34. The correct answer is (C). Thomas Hardy (1840–1928) was an English novelist in the naturalist tradition who wrote of characters trapped by fate and their environment in stories such as *The Return of the Native* (1878), *The Mayor of Casterbridge* (1886), and *Jude the Obscure* (1896).

35. The correct answer is (A). George Eliot is the pen name of Mary Ann Evans (1819–1880). One of the foremost Victorian novelists, she explored the moral and social problems of her era in novels such as *The Mill on the Floss* (1860), *Middlemarch* (1871), and *Daniel Deronda* (1874). The other writers mentioned are T. S. Eliot, George Elliot, and George Sand.

36. The correct answer is (B). Homer, supposed to have been a blind poet who lived in Greece in the ninth century B.C.E., may or may not have composed the

Odyssey, which is the story of Ulysses' journey from Troy to Ithaca, and the *Iliad,* which is the story of certain episodes during the Trojan War. The stories themselves were handed down orally before appearing in written form, and after their writing they were further edited and changed until the second century B.C.E.

37. The correct answer is (A). Thomas Mann (1875–1955) wrote novels, novellas, and short stories, many of which are explorations of the artistic temperament. His greatest novel, *The Magic Mountain* (1924), reflects his growing concern with the political state of Europe; in 1933 he was exiled from Germany by Hitler, and he became an American citizen in 1944.

38. The correct answer is (C). Daniel Defoe (1660–1731) wrote *Robinson Crusoe* when he was nearly sixty. The story is taken from the true story of Alexander Selkirk, who lived for five years on a deserted island. Defoe is also the author of *Moll Flanders* (1722) and *A Journal of the Plague Year* (1722). The other plot summaries are of *Oliver Twist* (1837), *Ivanhoe* (1819), and *Candide* (1759).

39. The correct answer is (B). The Existential movement was at its peak in France in the 1940s. Influenced by the philosophers Kierkegaard and Nietzsche, it postulated that existence precedes essence, that man is nothing but what he becomes by acting. Self-honesty is the key to moral life because no absolutes exist by which to make decisions or judgments.

40. The correct answer is (D). Henry Fielding's (1707–1754) best-known character is Tom Jones, the hero of his story about a foundling who grows into a headstrong young man and meets with many adventures before claiming his birthright. Fielding also wrote *Joseph Andrews* (1742), the tale of another young man, this one supposed to be the brother of Samuel Richardson's character, Pamela. The other characters mentioned are inventions of Thomas Mann, Tobias Smollett, and Samuel Richardson.

41. The correct answer is (B). Jane Austen (1775–1817) was the author of six complete novels: *Sense and Sensibility* (1811), *Pride and Prejudice* (1813), *Mansfield Park* (1814), *Emma* (1815), *Northanger Abbey,* and *Persuasion;* the last two were published in 1818 after her death. Her novels, which feature ordinary characters in ordinary surroundings, are brilliantly comic studies of human nature. The other novels mentioned are by Charlotte Brontë, George Eliot, and Honoré de Balzac.

42. The correct answer is (A). Count Leo Tolstoy (1828–1910) is best known for his immense historical novel *War and Peace* (1864), set during the Napoleonic Wars, and his story of an adulteress punished, *Anna Karenina* (1873). After writing *Anna Karenina,* Tolstoy underwent a religious conversion that resulted in his belief in passive resistance and his rejection of wealth and property. As well as novels and short stories, he wrote religious pieces and essays criticizing the czarist regime.

43. The correct answer is (C). Virginia Woolf (1882–1941) was the author of many novels and short stories, among which are *Mrs. Dalloway* (1922), *To the Lighthouse* (1927), and *The Waves* (1931). Her work incorporates experimental techniques and focuses on the psychological lives of her characters.

44. The correct answer is (C). *The Divine Comedy* (1321), Dante's masterwork, is an epic poem describing the author's journey, under the guidance of the Roman poet Virgil and the author's beloved, Beatrice, through Hell and Purgatory to Heaven. The poem is a condemnation of the corrupt Catholic church and a criticism of the Florentine political situation as well as a description of the state of human nature and an allegory of the movement of the soul toward God.

45. The correct answer is (B). A haiku is a Japanese poem of three lines, the first with five syllables, the second with seven syllables, and the third with five syllables. The poems usually contain figurative language to suggest aspects of nature.

46. The correct answer is (D). August Strindberg (1849–1912) was a Swedish playwright whose emotional life deeply influenced his work. Bitter because of an unhappy marriage and accusations of blasphemy for his short stories, he wrote *Miss Julie* (1888) and *The Dance of Death* (1901), plays detailing sexual and emotional torment between men and women. He suffered a nervous breakdown in 1896, and his later plays, including *A*

Dream Play (1902), are mystical in nature. He is often considered a forerunner of the Expressionist movement.

47. The correct answer is (A). George Orwell (1903–1950) was the author of the horrifying futuristic novel *1984* (1949), which looked toward a future in which life was controlled by an all-seeing Big Brother. He also wrote *Animal Farm* (1945), a novel in which farm animals revolt against the farmer who owns them. Both books are satires directed against the Communist regime in the Soviet Union under Joseph Stalin.

48. The correct answer is (C). In 1989, Salman Rushdie's fourth novel, *The Satanic Verses,* was published. A fantastical exploration of the Islamic faith, the book was declared blasphemic by the Ayatollah Khomeini of Iran, who put a bounty of $1 million on Rushdie ($2.6 million if the author were killed by an Iranian). Rushdie then went into hiding in England. His marriage fell apart, his freedom was curtailed, and he was forced to move from safe house to safe house. However, his situation did not prevent him from publishing; his novel *Haroun and the Sea of Stories* was published in 1991 to generally positive reviews.

49. The correct answer is (A). Ovid (43 B.C.E.–17 C.E.) was a Roman poet whose most famous work, *The Metamorphoses* (c. 8 C.E.), is a series of poems that tell of historical and legendary figures from the cre-

ation of the world to the time of Augustus. His *Art of Love,* when revived in the Middle Ages, became the basis of the medieval ideal of courtly love.

50. The correct answer is (C). *The Clouds* (423 B.C.E.) by Aristophanes is a comedy, the butt of which is Sophocles, whom the playwright mocks. *Oedipus the King* (c. 427 B.C.E.) and *Antigone* (413 B.C.E.) are tragedies by Sophocles; the first is about a man who, through misunderstanding and mistaken identity, kills his father and marries his mother. Antigone, Oedipus's daughter, sacrifices her own life to bury her brother. *Electra* (413 B.C.E.) is a tragedy by Euripides in which Electra seeks revenge on her mother, Clytemnestra, for the murder of her father, Agamemnon; she and her brother, Orestes, murder Clytemnestra, and Orestes goes mad.

TEST 11
THE BIRDS AND
THE BEES:
LIFE SCIENCE

> Beyond plants are animals,
> Beyond animals is man,
> Beyond man is the universe.
>
> —Jean Toomer

1. If a desert tortoise spends the summer or the dry season in a burrow, what is it doing?
   (A) Regenerating
   (B) Lactating
   (C) Hibernating
   (D) Estivating

2. Who was Gregor Mendel?
   (A) A British physician who discovered how blood circulates
   (B) An Austrian monk who pioneered the study of genetics
   (C) A Russian chemist who formulated the periodic table of elements
   (D) A Dutch scientist who classified members of the insect family

3. What does the theory of natural selection state?
   (A) A plant or animal can return to the characteristics of its ancestors.
   (B) A population of animals will move from one region to another.
   (C) Those organisms that are best adapted to the environment will survive.
   (D) All organisms are made up of cells.

4. Which of these pairs of animals can interbreed?
   (A) Cats and dogs
   (B) Horses and donkeys
   (C) Rats and mice
   (D) None of the above

5. What is the chemical change that produces alcohol in wine?
   (A) Fermentation
   (B) Distillation
   (C) Hydrolysis
   (D) Condensation

6. What is osmosis?
   (A) The removal of waste products
   (B) The movement of molecules of liquid through a membrane
   (C) The maintenance of a balanced environment
   (D) The clumping together of cells

7. If a man with pure dominant genes for six fingers on each hand and a woman with recessive genes for five fingers on each hand have a child, how many fingers will the child have on each hand?
   (A) Six
   (B) Five
   (C) Six on one hand, five on the other
   (D) Eleven

8. What is the best definition of a cell?
   (A) The site of protein synthesis
   (B) The material that makes up genes
   (C) The unit of structure and function of all living things
   (D) Any living plant or animal

9. What is the role of chromosomes?
   (A) They contain enzymes that release energy in respiration.
   (B) They propel organisms.
   (C) They control all of the functions of a cell.
   (D) They contain the genes that will determine the characteristics of an organism.

10. What is the difference between instinct and conditioning?
    (A) Instinct is a reaction of hunger; conditioning is a reaction of fear.
    (B) Instinct is innate behavior; conditioning is learned behavior.
    (C) Instinct is learning in early youth; conditioning is learning later in life.
    (D) Instinct is possessed by the higher animals; conditioning is possessed by lower animals.

11. What do the amoeba, the paramecium, and the *Euglena* have in common?
    (A) They are all sessile.
    (B) They are all one-celled organisms.
    (C) They are all types of algae.
    (D) They are all types of mold.

12. The thorns of the rose, the shape of the walking stick insect, and the coloration of the chameleon are examples of
    (A) adaptation.
    (B) mimicry.
    (C) metamorphosis.
    (D) substitution.

13. In what substance is nitrogen found?
    (A) Carbon dioxide
    (B) Water
    (C) Protein
    (D) Sugar

14. To what classes do salamanders and snakes belong?
    (A) Salamanders are reptiles and snakes are amphibians.
    (B) Snakes are reptiles and salamanders are amphibians.
    (C) Both are reptiles.
    (D) Both are amphibians.

15. In order, which animals are herbivores, carnivores, and omnivores?
    (A) Alligator, anteater, hedgehog
    (B) Skunk, elephant, pig
    (C) Dog, horse, eagle
    (D) Sheep, lion, human

16. An animal undergoing metamorphosis is
    (A) changing from cold-blooded to warm-blooded.
    (B) moving from one location to another.
    (C) changing from one developmental stage to the next.
    (D) mutating in a beneficial manner.

17. For what are James Watson and Francis Crick known?
    (A) Establishing the function and structure of DNA
    (B) Discovering how plants get nourishment
    (C) Recognizing the similarities between primates and humans
    (D) Discovering the function of gills in aquatic animals

18. Why do certain trees have needles instead of leaves?
    (A) The needles provide protection against bark-eating animals.
    (B) The needles do not taste good to predatory insects.
    (C) The needles contain the seeds that allow the trees to reproduce.
    (D) The needles allow the trees to exist in colder temperatures and with less water.

19. What is homeostasis?
    (A) The loss of water from a cell
    (B) The maintenance of a balanced internal environment
    (C) The process during which sex cells are formed
    (D) The sudden appearance of a new, inheritable trait

20. What was Charles Darwin's major contribution to the scientific world?
    (A) The refutation of the existence of God
    (B) The discovery of the age of the earth
    (C) The formulation of a viable theory of evolution
    (D) The invention of the microscope

21. Which of the following is *not* true of birds?
    (A) They are vertebrates.
    (B) They are warm-blooded.
    (C) They have a four-chambered heart.
    (D) They have functional teeth.

22. What is the correct order of stages in the life cycle of a butterfly?
    (A) Caterpillar → larva → butterfly
    (B) Egg → larva → pupa → imago
    (C) Egg → imago → caterpillar → butterfly
    (D) Larva → imago → pupa → butterfly

23. Why are identical twins studied to determine the effects of heredity and environment on personality?
    (A) Identical twins consist of a male and female.
    (B) Identical twins are usually treated the same way by parents.
    (C) Identical twins have identical genetic makeup.
    (D) Identical twins share the same environment in the womb.

24. In chemistry, what is a bond?
    (A) A tiny particle in the nucleus of an atom
    (B) The unit used to measure the amount of a substance
    (C) A molecule made up of only one atom
    (D) The force that holds atoms together to form molecules

25. Which of these animals are invertebrates?
    (A) Lobsters, crabs, and shrimp
    (B) Salmon, eels, and trout
    (C) Frogs, toads, and salamanders
    (D) Snakes, lizards, and turtles

26. The term *scientific method* refers to
    (A) a system in which numbers are expressed as products of a one-digit number and a power of 10.
    (B) the classification and labeling of organisms.
    (C) a process involving hypothesizing, collecting data, and testing the hypothesis.
    (D) the belief that science can explain social and cosmic disorders.

27. To be classified as a mammal, an animal must
    (A) live on land.
    (B) have hair and be warm-blooded.
    (C) have a three-chambered heart.
    (D) All of the above

28. How is aerobic respiration different from anaerobic respiration?
    (A) One is internal; one is external.
    (B) One involves oxygen; the other does not.
    (C) One is performed by animals; the other is performed by plants.
    (D) One applies to living matter; the other does not.

29. The process of germination involves
    (A) the beginning of growth in a plant embryo.
    (B) the dispersal of seeds by wind or water.
    (C) a variation in the genes of an organism.
    (D) the spread of contagion from one organism to another.

30. What is DNA?
    (A) A series of genes that determine a specific characteristic
    (B) A pair of chromosomes found in the nucleus of a cell
    (C) The product of the joining of a male and female gamete
    (D) A chain of nucleotides containing genetic information

31. When you refer to an organism's habitat, you mean
    (A) the behavior it exhibits.
    (B) the relationship between it and its environment.
    (C) the type of region in which it lives.
    (D) the population of its community.

32. Which list gives the correct order for the classification of living things?
    (A) Kingdom, phylum, class, order, family, genus, species
    (B) Kingdom, phylum, family, class, order, species, genus
    (C) Kingdom, class, phylum, order, genus, species, family
    (D) Kingdom, order, class, phylum, family, genus, species

33. Which statement about symmetry is not true?
    (A) Only animals with backbones are bilaterally symmetrical.
    (B) A hydra and a sea anemone are radially symmetrical.
    (C) An earthworm and a spider are bilaterally symmetrical.
    (D) Taxonomists use symmetry as a classifying trait.

34. An example of a food chain might be
    (A) Carbohydrate → protein → fat
    (B) Fungus → oak → robin
    (C) Algae → fish → heron
    (D) Salivary gland → stomach → small intestine

35. The reptiles known today as dinosaurs roamed the earth
    (A) about 1 million years ago.
    (B) at the same time as the first birds and mammals.
    (C) at the same time as Cro-Magnon man.
    (D) for about 5,000 years.

36. Meiosis and mitosis are both processes of
    (A) cell division.
    (B) human digestion.
    (C) phototropism.
    (D) liquid absorption.

37. What is an enzyme?
    (A) A kind of virus that attacks bacteria
    (B) The part of the red blood cell that carries oxygen
    (C) A protein that activates chemical conversions
    (D) A ductless gland found in mammals and birds

38. Which of these steps is *not* part of the carbon cycle?
    (A) Animals release carbon dioxide through respiration.
    (B) Plants use carbon dioxide in photosynthesis.
    (C) Microorganisms break down carbon compounds.
    (D) Incomplete combustion forms carbon monoxide.

39. What is a protein?
    (A) The nucleus of the hydrogen atom
    (B) The water and other cells in a living organism
    (C) Any of a certain class of single-celled organisms
    (D) A molecule made up of chains of amino acids

40. Which of the following is an example of a parasitic relationship?
    (A) Mistletoe growing on a cottonwood tree
    (B) Cellulose-digesting microorganisms in a deer's stomach
    (C) Wolves attacking a herd of caribou
    (D) A cattle egret eating insects stirred up by a cow

41. Which of these animals is likely to migrate?
    (A) Elk
    (B) Whale
    (C) Bald eagle
    (D) All of the above

42. Bacteria differ from most single-celled organisms in that
    (A) they lack a nuclear membrane.
    (B) they cause numerous diseases.
    (C) they have no means of locomotion.
    (D) they do not reproduce.

43. The primary cause of species extinction today is
    (A) destruction of habitat.
    (B) acid rain.
    (C) predation.
    (D) worldwide temperature fluctuations.

44. When a chemist refers to *synthesis,* he or she means
    (A) change that does not alter the chemical composition of a substance.
    (B) creation of a complex compound through combining of elements or simple compounds.
    (C) separation of combined liquids into individual liquids.
    (D) chemical decomposition of a substance into simpler substances.

45. Which of the following statements is *not* true of mutations?
    (A) They can be caused by radiation.
    (B) They are caused by a change in DNA.
    (C) They invariably are passed on to offspring.
    (D) They may be harmful or beneficial.

46. The reproductive organs of certain plants are contained in the
    (A) fruit.
    (B) flower.
    (C) stem.
    (D) root.

47. What is the difference between organic and inorganic chemistry?
    (A) Organic chemistry is concerned with physical properties of materials.
    (B) Inorganic chemistry is the study of energy; organic chemistry is the study of entropy.
    (C) Organic chemistry focuses on carbon compounds.
    (D) Inorganic chemistry deals with living organisms.

48. What takes place during photosynthesis?
    (A) Chlorophyll converts light energy into food.
    (B) Carbohydrates break down and release energy.
    (C) A new plant is formed from an existing plant part.
    (D) Roots respond to water in the soil by growing downward.

49. *Ecology* may best be defined as the study of
    (A) distribution of resources.
    (B) natural interrelationships.
    (C) technological advances.
    (D) toxic substances.

50. How is AIDS transmitted?
    (A) By contact between skin and skin
    (B) By exchange of body fluids
    (C) By bacterial infection
    (D) By an airborne virus

TEST 11:
Explanatory Answers

1. The correct answer is (D). When an animal estivates, as when it hibernates, its metabolism slows and its body temperature drops. Animals estivate or hibernate in response to extremes in temperature or lack of food or water. The difference is that hibernation takes place during the cold weather months, while estivation is a response to heat and lack of water.

2. The correct answer is (B). Mendel (1822–1884) was an Augustinian monk who conducted experiments on garden vegetables. His conclusions about pollination led to the development of the theories of heredity that make up the basis of genetics today. In particular, Mendel concluded that any inherited characteristic is the result of the combination of hereditary units from both parents. His conclusions were lost for thirty-five years; it was not until 1900 that they were rediscovered.

3. The correct answer is (C). Natural selection is a part of Darwin's theory of evolution. Because there is a struggle for existence among organisms, only those best suited to their environment will survive. Any favorable changes that develop—through mutation, for example—will be transmitted to offspring to aid further in survival.

4. The correct answer is (B). Horses and donkeys, although they are of different species, can interbreed, producing mules (the offspring of a male donkey and a female horse) and hinnies (the offspring of a female donkey and a male horse). Usually, these offspring are sterile. Deciding what determines a species is a point of scientific controversy. Speciation can be based on interbreeding, genetic makeup, shape and form, geographic location, and behavior. Usually, animals that can interbreed and produce viable offspring are said to be of the same species, but, as horses and donkeys illustrate, there are exceptions even to that rule.

5. The correct answer is (A). Fermentation, the breaking down of simple sugars, produces either lactic acid or ethyl alcohol and carbon dioxide. The fermentation of grapes or malt can result in an alcoholic beverage—wine or beer. In winemaking, the yeasts found on grape skins come into contact with fruit sugars when the grape is crushed and convert those sugars into alcohol.

6. The correct answer is (B). When a semipermeable membrane, such as a cell wall, divides two levels of a solvent, the molecules from the greater concentration of solvent will pass through the membrane until equilibrium is reached; this movement is called osmosis and helps to control the movement of liquids in and out of cells.

7. The correct answer is (A). In this purely theoretical speculation, the six-finger gene is dominant, and if

one partner has two six-finger genes and one has two five-finger genes, the child produced will have one dominant, six-finger gene and one recessive five-finger gene. Since the dominant gene determines the physical characteristic, the child will have six fingers on each hand.

8. The correct answer is (C). The Cell Theory, developed by scientists working in many countries, states that cells are the units of structure of all plants and animals, cells are the units of function of all plants and animals, and all living cells come only from other living cells. Cells carry out the essential processes that produce energy and sustain life.

9. The correct answer is (D). Chromosomes are found in the nuclei of cells. Each species has a specific number of chromosomes in all cells. Most chromosomes come in pairs, except for those found in sex cells, which have only half the usual number of chromosomes.

10. The correct answer is (B). Innate behavior is that which does not have to be learned; it includes biorhythms and instincts, which are not based on previous experience. Learned behavior includes conditioning, which occurs as a result of associating a response with a stimulus; imprinting, which is a type of learning that occurs early in life; and reasoning, which is finding solutions to problems not previously encountered.

11. The correct answer is (B). All life arose from a single-celled ancestor. Among the single-celled organisms

that are considered plants are algae and plankton. Protozoa, including amoebae and paramecia, are single-celled animals. Euglena is a single-celled organism that has characteristics of both plants and animals.

12. The correct answer is (A). Living things must adapt to survive in their environments. Adaptations are changes made by organisms to increase their chances of survival. The rose developed thorns for protection, the walking stick looks like a stick to blend in with its environment, and the chameleon changes its color for safety as its environment changes.

13. The correct answer is (C). Because organisms cannot use free nitrogen from the air, they must secure the element from compounds. Plants obtain nitrogen from nitrates that are dissolved in water in the soil. Animals obtain it from plant proteins or from other animals that have gotten nitrogen from plants. Decaying animals or animal waste in the soil are broken down by bacteria, replacing the soil's nitrogen. Other bacteria change the nitrogen to nitrates, and the nitrogen cycle goes on.

14. The correct answer is (B). Reptiles are animals that usually breathe through lungs, usually have a three-chambered heart, and lay eggs in leathery shells. Turtles, snakes, alligators, lizards, and crocodiles are reptiles. Amphibians are animals that breathe through gills in the larval stage and through lungs as adults; they undergo a complete

metamorphosis to reach adulthood. Frogs, salamanders, and newts are amphibians.

15. The correct answer is (D). Herbivores are animals
that eat only plants, such as many fish, cows, and
most rodents. Carnivores are flesh-eating animals,
such as seals, wolves, and cats. Omnivores eat both
plants and meat; humans are omnivores.

16. The correct answer is (C). Animals metamorphose
when they move from one state to the next in their
growth cycle. A frog, for instance, begins as an egg
that hatches into a gilled tadpole. It then develops
legs and lungs and absorbs its tail and finally
emerges as an adult frog.

17. The correct answer is (A). Francis Crick, born in
1916, and James Watson, born in 1928, are biolo-
gists who won the 1962 Nobel Prize in physiology
for discovering the double helix form of DNA, the
material that makes up genes.

18. The correct answer is (D). Most evergreens have
needlelike leaves that require less water than regular leaves and are more resistant to cold. Evergreens tend to keep their leaves all year, except for
the larch and a few other species. The sequoias,
evergreens that grow in California, are among the
oldest living things on Earth.

19. The correct answer is (B). Homeostasis can be
defined as the maintenance of equilibrium within
an internal environment. Such factors as osmosis,
temperature adjustment, and maintenance of constant pH values contribute to homeostasis.

20. The correct answer is (C). Charles Darwin (1809–1882) worked as a naturalist aboard the HMS *Beagle*. During his five-year voyage he observed nature intently, and his thoughts about animal development led to his theory of natural selection, which postulated that evolution occurs through the survival of the fittest individuals in a population.

21. The correct answer is (D). Birds, which are warm-blooded animals with feathers, grind their food in their gizzards to help digestion. They have small brains and a poor sense of smell, but their eyesight is very good. Not all birds can fly; penguins and ostriches are land-bound, and penguins are also able to swim.

22. The correct answer is (B). The metamorphosis of the butterfly occurs in several stages. An egg hatches into a larva, which is often a caterpillar. In the next stage, the larva pupates within a chrysalis, or cocoon. Finally, an imago, or full-grown butterfly, emerges.

23. The correct answer is (C). Deciding what personality traits are influenced by heredity and what traits are influenced by environment is very difficult and controversial. One way of determining which characteristics are genetic is to compare identical twins and fraternal twins in terms of a personality trait. If the trait is inherited, identical twins should be much more similar regarding the trait than fraternal twins. The study of identical twins who have

been separated since birth also provides much information about which traits are inherited and which are the result of environmental influences.

24. The correct answer is (D). A chemical bond is the union of atoms by the transfer or sharing of electrons. When electrons are shared, the bond is called covalent; when an electron is transferred from one atom to the other, the bond is called ionic.

25. The correct answer is (A). Invertebrates are animals that have no backbone or internal skeletons. They range from simple, one-celled protozoa to the complex insect. Arthropods such as the lobster, tick, and centipede are equipped with exoskeletons, or external skeletons.

26. The correct answer is (C). The scientific method is a label for a system in which a problem is formulated, a hypothetical answer is suggested, data about the problem are collected through observation or experimentation, and the hypothesis is tested and accepted or rejected.

27. The correct answer is (B). A mammal has a four-chambered heart, is warm-blooded, and has hair. Most female mammals bear live young, which they feed with milk produced in their mammary glands. Examples of mammals include dogs, humans, whales, and elephants.

28. The correct answer is (B). Both aerobic and anaerobic respiration are internal; that is, each takes place within a cell. In aerobic respiration, oxygen is used to break glucose into carbon dioxide and

water. In anaerobic respiration, yeast or bacteria may change glucose into ethanol and carbon dioxide in a process called *fermentation*. In animals a lack of oxygen may cause enzymes to break down glucose into lactic acid in the muscles. Energy is released with each change.

29. The correct answer is (A). The seed of a plant contains an embryo. Given the correct external conditions, growth begins in the embryo, and a new plant develops. Many seeds remain dormant in the ground until conditions involving heat and water are correct for germination.

30. The correct answer is (D). A nucleic acid is a chain of nucleotides, bonded chemically, which controls cellular activity. There are two kinds of nucleic acid: DNA and RNA. DNA is made up of nucleotides that contain deoxyribose, a sugar; phosphoric acid; and one of the following bases: adenine, guanine, cytosine, or thymine. The bases bond with bases in other nucleotides to form a structure called a *double helix*. Genes are made up of DNA. RNA is made by DNA and plays a role in the synthesis of protein.

31. The correct answer is (C). A habitat is the kind of place in which an organism lives. The term may refer to a large natural area such as a desert, rain forest, or tundra; or it may be more specific—a riverbed, hillside, or swamp may also be a habitat.

32. The correct answer is (A). *Taxonomy* is the term for the classification of living organisms according

to traits and relationships. When an organism is referred to by its "scientific name," that name is made up of the genus and species classifications. For example, human beings are *Homo sapiens*. The classifications for humans from kingdom down are as follows: kingdom—Animal; phylum—Chordata; subphylum—Vertebrata; class—Mammalia; order—Primates; family—Hominidae; genus—*Homo*; species—*sapiens*.

33. The correct answer is (A). Organisms that are radially symmetrical have similar parts arranged around a central axis, much like the spokes of a wheel. Organisms that are bilaterally symmetrical have similar parts arranged along a median axis, with one half more or less mirroring the other. All vertebrates and many invertebrates are bilaterally symmetrical.

34. The correct answer is (C). The term *food chain* refers to the sequence of energy transfer among organisms. Plants, which make up 90 percent of visible living organisms, get their food energy from sunlight. When they are eaten by herbivores (plant-eating animals) or omnivores (plant- or meat-eaters), they pass some of this energy on. Herbivores in turn pass on their energy to carnivores (meat-eaters) or omnivores. The energy from plants thus directly or indirectly sustains the remaining 10 percent of visible living things.

35. The correct answer is (B). Dinosaurs are classified as reptiles, although some appear to have been

warm-blooded. Fossil records indicate that they first appeared about 200 million years ago, perhaps around the same time that the first mammals appeared. They died out about 150 million years later, and smaller reptiles, birds, and mammals dominated the earth. Cro-Magnons did not show up for another 50 million years or so. Many theories exist as to why the dinosaurs vanished; the likeliest involves changes in climate and geography.

36. The correct answer is (A). Mitosis is the normal process of cell division in animals and plants. First the chromosomes in the nucleus double. A centriole divides in two, and each half leads one set of chromosomes to one side of the nucleus as the membrane of the nucleus disappears. A new membrane forms around each group of chromosomes, creating two identical nuclei where only one had been. The end product is two identical cells. In meiosis two divisions take place. First the chromosomes double, and the doubled chromosomes line up in pairs. The pairs then separate. Next the separated pairs line up and divide as in mitosis. The end product is four sex cells, each containing half the number of chromosomes of the original nucleus. When sex cells combine during reproduction, they create a new cell containing the normal number of chromosomes, half from one parent cell and half from the other.

37. The correct answer is (C). Enzymes are proteins that catalyze chemical reactions. They are produced by cells in animals, plants, and bacteria. Most enzymes are keyed to a single type of chemi-

cal reaction, which means that cells must make a
huge variety of enzymes. Some examples of human
enzymes are pepsin, which breaks down proteins to
produce peptides, and maltase, which breaks down
maltose to produce glucose. As with any protein,
an enzyme is made up of amino acids.

38. The correct answer is (D). Every living thing contains carbon. The movement of this element
between living things and the environment is called
the carbon cycle. Through photosynthesis plants
convert carbon into carbohydrates and other molecules. Through respiration they release the carbon
in the form of carbon dioxide and water. When
plants die, microorganisms break down the carbon
in them and release it. Animals gain carbon
through consumption of plants; they release it
through respiration and decay.

39. The correct answer is (D). Proteins perform a variety of tasks. For example, enzymes catalyze chemical changes, hemoglobin transports oxygen, hor-
mones regulate metabolism, and antibodies control
immunity. Each protein type is made up of a unique
sequence of amino acids, linked together by pep-
tide bonds to form long chains. DNA contains the
genetic information for the sequence of amino
acids for each protein. The information is first used
to make a molecule of messenger RNA from which
the protein sequence is derived.

40. The correct answer is (A). Living things survive
through complex interactions with their environ-

ment and with other living things. In a parasitic relationship, one organism lives off a host organism, occasionally destroying the host over time. The other relationships mentioned are examples of symbiosis or mutualism, in which both organisms benefit; predation, in which a free-living organism feeds on another; and commensalism, in which one organism benefits and the other is neither harmed nor helped.

41. The correct answer is (D). Animals migrate for a number of reasons, the primary one being the need to locate a place to breed. They may search for a better climate in winter or summer; for example, geese flying south and north. They may return to a particular area to spawn, as salmon do. Excessive population may force a migration, as with lemmings.

42. The correct answer is (A). Bacteria are neither plants nor animals. Each of the three main forms—rod-shaped, spiral, and round—is a single-celled organism. The organism houses DNA but has no separate nucleus to contain it. Some forms move by means of hair-like appendages called flagella; others are unable to propel themselves. Bacteria reproduce most commonly through binary fission (splitting). As is true of many single-celled organisms, some bacteria cause diseases. More important is their extraordinary variation and the fact that they may have been the first organisms on Earth.

43. The correct answer is (A). Approximately twenty years ago, the Earth lost about one species a day,

out of the perhaps 100 million species existing
(only 1.4 million of which are recognized and classified). Now the figure is closer to one species per
hour—nearly 10,000 per year—of *known species*.
Biodiversity studies examine the variety of species
on the planet with an eye toward conserving that
diversity, which is necessary for the functioning of
ecosystems on Earth. The major reason for the
increase in extinction rates is human expansion
into the habitats of other species. Only a little over
3 percent of the Earth's landmass is protected land.
Deforestation, flood control dams, inorganic fertil-
izers—nearly every human product meant to control land and water has an adverse effect on flora
and fauna. Scientists disagree about biodiversity
policy, but most agree that human population and
consumption must be controlled if extinction rates
of other species are to be slowed.

44. The correct answer is (B). When elements or simple
compounds are combined, forming a new complex
compound, the process is called synthesis. For
example, sodium (Na) and chlorine (Cl) can be
combined to form salt:

$$2Na + Cl_2 \longrightarrow 2NaCl$$

45. The correct answer is (C). A change in DNA,
brought on naturally or by chemical causes, neutron bombardment, or radiation, can spark a
change in an organism called a *mutation*. In higher
organisms, only mutations within sex cells may be

passed on to offspring. Skin cancer is an example of a mutation that takes place only within body cells and thus is not transmitted to offspring. Some mutations cause improvements; most are harmful.

46. The correct answer is (B). In flowering plants the flower is the center of reproductive activity. The stamen produces pollen, the male sex cells, in a sac called the anther. Pollen is carried to the pistil, which contains the eggs. Some plants self-pollinate, moving pollen to their own pistils. Others rely on animals or wind to move the pollen to a flower of the same species.

47. The correct answer is (C). Organic chemistry is the study of compounds formed from carbon; it thus incorporates the study of living matter. Inorganic chemistry deals mainly with minerals—elements and compounds that do not contain carbon.

48. The correct answer is (A). Photosynthesis is the process through which green plants manufacture food. Energy from direct sunlight is trapped by a substance called *chlorophyll*. The energy converts carbon dioxide and water into a complex compound, glucose, which is stored as food. The oxygen released as a by-product of this process is necessary for respiration in plants and animals.

49. The correct answer is (B). Ecologists study the interrelationships of organisms and their environments. An ecosystem is a community in which plants and animals coexist in a physical environment that sup-

plies the energy and water they require. An ecosystem that is truly self-perpetuating is a *climax community*. In general, ecosystems evolve over time.

50. The correct answer is (B). AIDS (Acquired Immune Deficiency Syndrome) is a group of symptoms caused by a virus that attacks the immune system, breaking it down and making its bearer susceptible to any and all diseases. The syndrome, or group of symptoms, is caused by a virus that attacks the immune system, breaking it down and making its bearer susceptible to any and all diseases. The HIV virus is transmitted through blood or semen. At first it primarily infected homosexual men, intravenous drug users, and hemophiliacs in this country, but heterosexual transmission is becoming increasingly common. The number of people living with HIV/AIDS in the United States as of the year 2000 was approximately 900,000, with another 300,000 who might be HIV positive but not know it. In the year 2000, the number of infected people worldwide was more than 36 million, with the largest number of new cases found in Sub-Saharan Africa. Pneumonia and a type of cancer called Kaposi's sarcoma are two common AIDS-caused diseases, but there are dozens of opportunistic diseases that may appear as a result of the infection.

TEST 12
A SWIFTLY TILTING PLANET: PHYSICAL SCIENCE

True science teaches us to doubt and to abstain from ignorance.

—CLAUDE BERNARD

1. What is a catalyst?
   (A) The smallest constituent of matter
   (B) A substance that controls the rate of a chemical reaction
   (C) A violent geological change
   (D) A substance that merges with an element to form a compound

2. The steady-state and big bang theories are associated with
   (A) the study of the creation and structure of the universe.
   (B) the initial construction of the hydrogen bomb.
   (C) the volatility of liquids such as ether and chloroform.
   (D) plate tectonics and the development of mountain ranges.

3. According to quantum theory,
    (A) energy is infinite.
    (B) forces that balance each other are in equilibrium.
    (C) force can be expressed as the acceleration it gives to an object.
    (D) energy is limited and discontinuous.

4. The Earth's atmosphere is
    (A) primarily nitrogen, with smaller amounts of oxygen and argon.
    (B) primarily oxygen, with traces of nitrogen and carbon.
    (C) primarily carbon dioxide, with some helium and ozone.
    (D) primarily ozone, with traces of oxygen and carbon dioxide.

5. Which of these concepts is *not* associated with Einstein's theory of relativity?
    (A) Nothing can move faster than the speed of light.
    (B) Energy and mass are equivalent.
    (C) Mass and time change with increases in velocity.
    (D) Although matter may alter in shape, it is never destroyed.

6. On the Celsius scale, the boiling point of water is
    (A) 100°
    (B) 212°
    (C) 373°
    (D) 0°

7. In a lunar eclipse,
   (A) the moon comes between the Earth and the sun.
   (B) the sun comes between the Earth and the moon.
   (C) the Earth comes between the sun and the moon.
   (D) None of the above

8. Both strong and weak nuclear forces have to do with
   (A) atoms.
   (B) electromagnetism.
   (C) gravity.
   (D) engines.

9. The three major classes of rocks are
   (A) granite, pumice, and quartzite.
   (B) stratified, molten, and sedimentary.
   (C) igneous, basalt, and clay.
   (D) metamorphic, sedimentary, and igneous.

10. What did Marie and Pierre Curie discover?
    (A) Radioactivity
    (B) Radium and polonium
    (C) Electrons
    (D) X rays

11. What is a vacuum?
    (A) A unit of measure of atmospheric pressure
    (B) Gaseous matter with a high concentration of ions
    (C) A device that operates through hydraulic pressure
    (D) Space from which all matter has been removed

12. You would be most likely to read a seismograph report in
    (A) a newspaper account of earthquake activity.
    (B) a *Scientific American* article on quarks.
    (C) a novel about life on other planets.
    (D) Einstein's early papers on inertia.

13. What is a molecule?
    (A) The smallest particle of matter
    (B) The smallest particle of an element or compound that has all the properties of that substance
    (C) A substance with the same atomic weight as a given element
    (D) A particle made up of a single nucleus and orbiting electrons in multiples of three or five

14. When an object is in equilibrium,
    (A) it is not being acted on by any forces.
    (B) it is resistant to gravitational forces.
    (C) it is being acted on by two or more balanced forces.
    (D) it is spherical or otherwise precisely symmetrical.

15. According to Newton's law of inertia,
    (A) a body at rest tends to remain at rest.
    (B) a body in motion tends to remain in motion.
    (C) an outside force can manipulate a body.
    (D) All of the above

16. To a physicist, conservation of energy means
    (A) use of natural resources must be controlled.
    (B) during a physical change, total energy remains constant.
    (C) a cautious approach to particle bombardment is recommended.
    (D) solid-state rather than electron materials are used.

17. Which of the following bodies is *not* a star?
    (A) Nova
    (B) White dwarf
    (C) Comet
    (D) Pulsar

18. If a bar magnet is allowed to swing freely,
    (A) it will attract any metallic object.
    (B) it will repel any metallic object.
    (C) it will point north and south.
    (D) it will display the properties of a pendulum.

19. The most amazing thing about a black hole is its ability to
    (A) attract.
    (B) expand.
    (C) navigate.
    (D) pulsate.

20. The half-life of an element is
    (A) equal to half of its atomic number.
    (B) the time it takes half of a given amount to decay.
    (C) half the number of years an atom takes to break down.
    (D) the number of electrons dispersed over a six-month period.

21. What results are expected from the depletion of ozone in the atmosphere?
    (A) An increase in skin cancer and cataracts and a reduction in crop yields
    (B) An increase in lung and heart disease
    (C) Melting of the polar ice caps and flooding of lowlying regions
    (D) An increase in acid rain and a depletion of forested areas

22. What is acceleration?
    (A) Speed in a straight line
    (B) The rate of increase in velocity
    (C) The rate at which motion occurs
    (D) The process of traveling from place to place

23. Which list gives the correct order of the planets in terms of average orbital distance from the sun?
    (A) Earth, Venus, Mars, Mercury, Saturn, Jupiter, Uranus, Neptune, Pluto
    (B) Mercury, Venus, Mars, Earth, Jupiter, Saturn, Neptune, Uranus, Pluto
    (C) Mercury, Venus, Earth, Mars, Saturn, Jupiter, Uranus, Pluto, Neptune
    (D) Mercury, Venus, Earth, Mars, Jupiter, Saturn, Uranus, Neptune, Pluto

24. In a nuclear chain reaction,
    (A) atoms explode, causing the air around them to explode.
    (B) neutrons split atoms, releasing neutrons that split other atoms.
    (C) electrons leap from atom to atom, destabilizing them.
    (D) the nucleus of a hydrogen atom enters an atom of uranium.

25. What is a light-year?
    (A) The amount of time it takes light from the sun to reach Earth
    (B) The length of time it takes Earth to revolve around the sun
    (C) The distance between the sun and the Earth
    (D) The distance light travels in one year

26. What is the difference between nuclear fission and nuclear fusion?
    (A) Fission produces an explosion; fusion produces safe energy.
    (B) In fission an atomic nucleus is split; in fusion two atomic nuclei are joined.
    (C) In a fission explosion only living things are killed; in a fusion explosion all objects are destroyed.
    (D) Much more energy is produced in fission than in fusion.

27. What is the difference between a solar system and a galaxy?
    (A) A solar system is a star and its family of planets and other bodies; a galaxy is a mass of stars, dust, and gases.
    (B) A solar system is a group of stars; a galaxy is a geographic location in the universe.
    (C) A solar system is a group of stars that form a pattern in the sky; a galaxy is a cluster of dust and gases.
    (D) There is no difference.

28. What is the study of thermodynamics?
    (A) The study of sound and its production and effects
    (B) The study of atomic nuclei and their properties and uses
    (C) The study of the properties and role of electrons
    (D) The study of heat and its conversion into other forms of energy

29. What does the law of gravitation state?
    (A) If an object is given momentum in one direction, another object will get an equal momentum in the other direction.
    (B) Molecules are in a continual state of rapid motion.
    (C) Any two bodies are attracted with a force inversely proportional to the square of their distance apart.
    (D) Force equals mass times acceleration.

30. What did Archimedes discover?
   (A) An object immersed in liquid appears to lose an amount of weight equal to the amount of water it displaces.
   (B) The volume of a confined gas at a constant temperature varies inversely with the temperature.
   (C) When a liquid flows through a horizontal tube, the amount of energy per kilo is unchanged.
   (D) Pressure applied to any part of an enclosed liquid is transmitted to every other part of the liquid.

31. What are the particles that make up an atom called?
   (A) Molecules
   (B) Protons, neutrons, and electrons
   (C) Mitochondria and vacuoles
   (D) Moles

32. What theory did Copernicus develop?
   (A) The first modern theory of heliocentric movement of the planets
   (B) The first modern theory explaining the phases of the moon
   (C) The theory that states that life can exist on other planets
   (D) The theory that states that stars move

33. What is a quark?
    (A) A type of mineral with the compound name
        SiO_2
    (B) A faint blue star-like object that is receding
        from our galaxy
    (C) A hypothetical particle with a fractional
        charge
    (D) An alkaloid isolated from a tree of the genus
        Cinchona

34. If a chemical solution is neutral, what is its pH?
    (A) 3
    (B) 7
    (C) 4.5
    (D) 14

35. If the barometric pressure fails abruptly, what will
    happen?
    (A) The sun will come out.
    (B) The temperature will rise.
    (C) There will be a storm.
    (D) It will be windy.

36. For what is Galileo known?
    (A) Discovering a comet and studying sunspots
        and satellites
    (B) Theorizing about motion, inventing a tele-
        scope, and discovering the composition of the
        Milky Way
    (C) Observing the planets, discovering a super-
        nova, and theorizing on the moon's motion
    (D) Describing the revolutions of planets and cal-
        culating the duration of planetary orbits

37. What are the layers of the Earth, from center to outer layer?
    (A) Liquid core, solid core, plate, rock
    (B) Crust, rock, sediment, mantle
    (C) Core, basin, sediment, crust
    (D) Solid core, liquid core, mantle, crust

38. What are the four states of matter?
    (A) Solid, liquid, gas, plasma
    (B) Atom, molecule, cell, organism
    (C) Acid, basic, alkaline, neutral
    (D) Terrestrial, solar, cosmic, universal

39. What does the Chaos Theory posit?
    (A) The universe was formed randomly.
    (B) There is no order in life.
    (C) Random behaviors can in fact be analyzed.
    (D) Global warming can change the predictability of nature and plunge the world into chaos.

40. What is an ion?
    (A) An atom with a positive or negative charge
    (B) An atom with a neutral charge
    (C) A particle possessing a positive electrical charge
    (D) An electron found in the outermost shell of an atom

41. What causes the "greenhouse effect"?
    (A) Clouds of pollution reflect the sun's rays.
    (B) A hole in the ozone layer allows infrared light to enter.
    (C) Gases keep infrared radiation from escaping into space.
    (D) No one yet knows.

42. To possess superconductivity, a substance must
    (A) surround a battery with an iron core.
    (B) lose all electrical resistance.
    (C) have a positive electrical charge.
    (D) be alkaline and contain hydrogen.

43. What makes isotopes of a given element different
    from each other?
    (A) The number of neutrons in the atom nucleus
    (B) The number of protons in the atom nucleus
    (C) The number of electrons in the atom nucleus
    (D) All elemental isotopes are the same.

44. What makes up the light spectrum?
    (A) Ultraviolet radiation, X rays, and gamma rays
    (B) Infrared radiation, microwaves, and radio
        waves
    (C) Transparent light, opaque light, and translu-
        cent light
    (D) White light diffracted into violet, indigo, blue,
        green, yellow, orange, and red

45. How is hail formed?
    (A) Raindrops pass through a layer of freezing
        rain and freeze partially.
    (B) Water vapor becomes solid crystal at tempera-
        tures below freezing.
    (C) Raindrops are blown up and down in a cloud,
        freezing and refreezing.
    (D) Drops of water form around large dust parti-
        cles and evaporate partially before hitting the
        ground.

46. What is the most important characteristic of X rays?
    (A) Their ability to produce heat
    (B) Their ability to produce an image by reflecting light
    (C) Their ability to magnify objects
    (D) Their ability to penetrate dense substances

47. What does the periodic table of elements show?
    (A) The geological periods during which the different elements were formed
    (B) Rows of elements by atomic number, with elements sharing similar properties grouped in columns
    (C) The atomic structure of the elements and their isotopes
    (D) Rows of elements, their symbols, atomic numbers, weight, melting point, and boiling point

48. What is a compound?
    (A) A liquid mixture that includes water
    (B) A liquid that produces gas bubbles
    (C) A substance that dissolves when added to water
    (D) A substance made of atoms of two or more elements

49. How do you calculate a wavelength?
    (A) Divide the speed of the wave motion by its frequency.
    (B) Measure the number of vibrations in a wave motion.
    (C) Measure the distance between the top and the middle of a wave.
    (D) Calculate the pitch of the sound the wave produces.

50. What is the identifying characteristic of crystal?
    (A) It does not have a definite form.
    (B) It conducts heat and electricity.
    (C) It has a regular repeating arrangement of atoms.
    (D) Its molecules can move about with no force holding them together.

TEST 12:
Explanatory Answers

1. The correct answer is (B). A catalyst changes the amount of energy needed for a reaction to take place, thus affecting the rate of the reaction. A catalyst that slows down a reaction is an inhibitor. Enzymes are organic catalysts.

2. The correct answer is (A). Cosmology is the study of the universe. Hubble's law (1929) implied that the universe is expanding uniformly. This law led to the big bang theory, which states that an explosion created the expanding universe from a compact lump of energy and matter. The steady-state theory accepted the idea of an expanding universe but claimed that the universe has always existed and that new matter is created to fill the empty space left by receding galaxies.

3. The correct answer is (D). Max Planck (1858–1947) solved the problem of infinite energy by deciding that particles could only radiate at certain limited energy levels. These levels could be expressed as the frequency, λ, times Planck's constant, h. In other words, energy is not produced continuously and without limit; the energy can exist only as whole-number multiples of h l, discrete parcels of energy called *quanta*. Albert Einstein (1879–1955) applied this theory to light, proving that light does not truly travel in waves but

in separated particles, which we now call photons. The correct answer is (Newton was actually the first to talk about particles of light; the quantum theory merged his theory with wave theory.) Niels Bohr (1885–1962) applied the quantum theory to the atom, creating a model that described the limited number of possible orbits for electrons and thus explained the relative stability of the atom.

4. The correct answer is (A). Nitrogen makes up over 78 percent of the Earth's atmosphere, the gaseous mass surrounding the planet. Oxygen makes up a little over 20 percent, and argon and carbon dioxide make up less than 1 percent each. Trace amounts of helium, hydrogen, krypton, methane, neon, ozone, and xenon also exist. Water vapor and various pollutants also appear in the atmosphere.

5. The correct answer is (D). Choice (D) is the law of conservation of matter. Einstein's theory was a direct descendant of many Newtonian principles and an attempt to solve problems that they did not illuminate. The primary assumption in relativity is that the speed of light is constant no matter how fast the observer moves or where the light originates. From that, Einstein determined that nothing could move faster than light. He posited that events that seemed simultaneous to one observer would not necessarily appear that way to an observer with another frame of reference—that time was relative to the observer's location in the space-time continuum. "$E = mc^2$" is perhaps the most famous equa-

tion of all time. Translated, it says that "energy equals mass times the speed of light squared," or "if an object radiates energy E, its mass decreases by E divided by the speed of light squared." It thus implies that mass and energy are equivalent. Substituting real numbers for the variables proves that huge amounts of energy can be radiated by objects of minute mass—atoms, for example. Einstein also determined that as an object's velocity approaches the speed of light, time and the object's mass are altered.

6. The correct answer is (A). The Celsius scale is a centigrade scale; that is, the interval between freezing and boiling is divided into one hundred degrees. On the scale, 0°C is the freezing point of water, and 100°C is the boiling point. The other two measures given are the boiling point of water on the Fahrenheit scale (212°F) and the boiling point of water on the Absolute scale.

7. The correct answer is (C). During an eclipse, light falling on a body in space is blocked by another body. In a lunar eclipse, no light reaches the moon because the Earth stands in the way. In a solar eclipse, no light reaches the Earth because the moon stands in the way. Eclipses can be partial, in which case some light still reaches the body, or they may be total, in which case the body is entirely dark.

8. The correct answer is (A). There are four forces of nature: gravity, electromagnetism, strong nuclear force, and weak nuclear force. The strong nuclear

force is the force that holds the nucleus of an atom together. It is the strongest force in nature; not only does it hold neutrons and protons in the nucleus, but it also is responsible for particle creation when atoms meet in high-energy collisions. The weak nuclear force is an interaction that may lead to particle decay and emission or absorption of neutrinos.

9. The correct answer is (D). Rocks are classified according to their formation. Rocks that undergo a change inside the Earth due to heat or pressure are called metamorphic rocks. Marble and slate are two examples. Rocks that are formed through erosion of older rocks and deposit of sediment from that erosion are sedimentary rocks. Clay and limestone are sedimentary. Rocks that were originally molten matter inside the earth are called igneous rocks. Basalt and pumice are two such rocks.

10. The correct answer is (B). Radioactivity is the tendency of an atomic nucleus to decay through the emission of particles. Three things may be emitted: alpha particles (each one being two protons and two neutrons), beta particles (each one being an electron or a positron), and gamma radiation. Antoine Becquerel (1852–1908) discovered radioactivity occurring naturally in uranium in 1896. Marie Curie (1867–1934) began to study uranium, and with Pierre Curie (1859–1906), she discovered the new elements polonium and radium, which also proved naturally radioactive. The Curies shared the Nobel Prize in physics with Becquerel in 1903 for work on radioactivity. After Pierre's death Marie won the

Nobel Prize in chemistry in 1911 for the discovery of the two new elements. Radioactivity may be induced artificially in more stable elements through high-energy collisions.

11. The correct answer is (D). There is no such thing as a perfect vacuum, but if there were, it would be empty of matter. Space from which a high percentage of matter has been removed is known as a *high vacuum.*

12. The correct answer is (A). A seismograph is an instrument that measures the motion of the Earth. Seismographs are used to locate oil, to determine ocean depth, and to detect and measure earthquakes.

13. The correct answer is (B). A molecule is made up of atoms. The atoms may be all of one type: O_2 is the smallest particle of oxygen that can exist by itself; it contains two oxygen atoms. The atoms may be of different types: H_2O is a molecule of water; it is made up of two hydrogen atoms and one oxygen atom.

14. The correct answer is (C). An object in equilibrium is acted on by forces with no result; the forces themselves are in a state of balance, and the object remains at rest.

15. The correct answer is (D). Isaac Newton (1642–1727), probably the greatest physicist the world has ever known, was the first to express the relationship between force and motion. His first law of motion is the law of inertia. It states that

bodies at rest or in motion tend to remain that way unless acted on by outside forces. The other two laws of motion state that the acceleration of a mass by a force is inversely proportional to the mass and directly proportional to the force and that for every action there is an equal and opposite reaction.

16. The correct answer is (B). The major conservation laws state that the values of mass, momentum, charge, and energy remain constant during a physical process. For example, if energy disappears in one form, it must reappear in another form. With the equivalence of mass and energy implied by Einstein's relativity theory, it becomes possible for mass to disappear and reappear as energy.

17. The correct answer is (C). A comet is a condensed body of gases and particles that is believed to originate in a great cloud of material orbiting the solar system. A star is primarily hydrogen. It has a strong gravitational force, and the light and heat it emits come from nuclear energy. A nova is a star that suddenly bursts forth with a huge increase in light radiation and then fades again. A white dwarf is a very small star, about the size of Earth. A pulsar is a very dense star that emits pulses of radio waves.

18. The correct answer is (C). In ancient times, the Greeks observed that certain kinds of iron attracted other material containing iron. Lodestones, natural magnets made of iron ore, were found to attract iron to opposite sides of the magnet. There proved to be an invisible field surround-

ing the magnet; a similar field also surrounds Earth. Just as Earth has two poles, so does any magnet. The north pole of a magnet is attracted in the direction of Earth's north pole. A compass uses this aspect of a magnet as a navigational tool. Somewhat confusingly, the so-called north pole of a magnet is repelled by the north pole of another magnet and attracted to the south pole of the other magnet. If a magnet is broken in half, each half has a north and south pole. The implication is that the atoms themselves are magnets.

19. The correct answer is (A). A black hole is probably the dense matter left after the collapse of a star. Because of its density it has a gravitational pull strong enough to attract everything around, including light and all other radiation. Black holes would appear to astronomers as dark patches in space.

20. The correct answer is (B). The nuclei of radioactive elements break down over time, emitting particles and radiation as they do so. The time it takes half of a given amount of a substance to decay is called the substance's *half-life*. The half-life is used to identify elements, and geologists and archaeologists use it to compute the age of minerals.

21. The correct answer is (A). Ozone is a gas that absorbs the sun's ultraviolet radiation, protecting Earth from its damaging effects. In 1985, a hole in the ozone layer was discovered above Antarctica; another hole was later found over the northern United States, Canada, Europe, and Russia. The

results expected from this ozone depletion include increases in skin cancers and cataracts, decreases in crop production and in production of oceanic phytoplankton and krill, and possibly a change in humans' immune response to disease.

22. The correct answer is (B). Acceleration can be expressed in this way:

$$\frac{\text{increase in velocity}}{\text{time}}$$

The other definitions listed as choices are of velocity, speed, and motion.

23. The correct answer is (D). The approximate distance from the sun for each planet is:

Planet	Distance from Sun
Mercury	36,000,000 miles
Venus	67,000,000 miles
Earth	93,000,000 miles
Mars	141,000,000 miles
Jupiter	480,000,000 miles
Saturn	900,000,000 miles
Uranus	1,800,000,000 miles
Neptune	2,800,000,000 miles
Pluto	3,600,000,000 miles

These figures show the average distance from the sun. In fact, some planets' orbits are extremely eccentric. Pluto, for example, is currently closer to the sun than Neptune is, and it will remain that way until the turn of the century.

24. The correct answer is (B). During nuclear fission, neutrons split the nuclei of atoms, and the neutrons that are produced go on to split other nuclei in a self-perpetuating reaction. The nuclear chain reaction is the power behind fission bombs and nuclear reactors.

25. The correct answer is (D). A light-year is one unit of measure of distance in space. It measures the distance light travels in one Earth year and equals 5,870,000,000,000 miles. For technical reasons astronomers often use the *parsec* as a unit of measure. The parsec equals 3.258 light-years.

26. The correct answer is (B). When an atom is split into two or more nuclei by the absorption of a neutron, a huge amount of energy is released. This is called fission; it is the basis of the atomic bomb and the nuclear reactor. In fusion, two atoms are joined. The amount of energy given off is several times that of fission. A temperature of 1 million degrees centigrade must be reached to initiate fusion.

27. The correct answer is (A). *Solar system* is a phrase usually used only to describe our sun and its attendant planets, asteroids, meteors, and comets. A galaxy is a huge mass of millions of stars, dust, and gases. There are millions of galaxies, which are

separated from one another by vast distances. Our galaxy is called the Milky Way.

28. The correct answer is (D). Thermodynamics is the study of heat and energy. The terms used to calculate heat are *calorie* (the quantity of heat required to raise one gram of water one degree centigrade) and *Btu* (the quantity of heat required to raise one pound of water one degree Fahrenheit). Thermodynamics explores the transfer of heat by conduction, convection, and radiation. The other sciences mentioned are acoustics, nuclear physics, and electronics.

29. The correct answer is (C). Postulated by Newton, the law of gravitation explains why the planets move as they do. It can be expressed as a formula:

$$F = \frac{Gm_1 m_2}{d_2}$$

where F is the force of attraction, m_1 and m_2 are the two masses, and d_2 is their distance apart. G is a constant that equals 0.000000000033, which makes the force between the Earth and the moon 15 million trillion tons. The other laws mentioned are Newton's third law of motion, the kinetic theory of matter, and the law of force.

30. The correct answer is (A). Archimedes' principle, purportedly discovered as its author sat in a bathtub, governs the forces of buoyancy and flotation. Archimedes (287 B.C.E.–212 B.C.E.) was a Greek physicist, mathematician, and inventor who calculated the value of pi, proved the law of the lever, and invented the

Archimedes screw as well as developing the principle of buoyancy. The other laws mentioned are Boyle's law, Bernoulli's principle, and Pascal's law.

31. The correct answer is (B). An atom is the smallest unit of a chemical element that possesses the properties of that element. The nucleus of an atom consists of protons, which are positively charged particles, and neutrons, which are uncharged particles. Electrons, negatively charged particles, exist outside the nucleus: the number of electrons and protons in an atom is equal in a neutral atom. The number of protons in an atom determines its atomic number and its chemical nature; the total number of protons and neutrons makes up its atomic weight.

32. The correct answer is (A). Nicholas Copernicus (1473–1543) was a Polish astronomer who developed a shocking idea: that the planets move around the sun. According to the Egyptian scientist Ptolemy, the Earth was the center of movement. Though Copernicus did not have the laws of gravity to back him up, he revolutionized astronomy—and the religious world, which believed, as the Bible said, that the solar system revolved around the Earth—with his theory of the planets moving around the sun.

33. The correct answer is (C). Quarks are hypothetical particles that make up particles called *hadrons*, which are members of the baryon class of particles, a class that includes protons and neutrons. In 1964, Murray Gell-Mann explained the properties

of hadrons, which are only one of perhaps eighty varieties of particles. The name *quark,* which means "nothing" in German, comes from James Joyce's *Finnegan's Wake.*

34. The correct answer is (B). A chemical solution, or a liquid that consists of a solute dissolved in a solvent, has a pH value that tells whether the solution is acidic or alkaline. The pH value is based on the concentration of hydrogen ions and ranges from less than 0 to 14, with a lower pH being more acidic; 7 is neutral, and a higher pH is more alkaline.

35. The correct answer is (C). Atmospheric pressure is the pressure exerted by the atmosphere, which exists in several layers out to about forty thousand miles from the Earth's surface. A barometer measures the pressure, usually using mercury. In weather forecasting, falling barometric pressure indicates foul weather is coming, and rising barometric pressure indicates fair weather is on the way.

36. The correct answer is (B). Galileo Galilei (1564–1642) was an Italian astronomer whose theories of motion prepared the way for Isaac Newton's studies. He built the first astronomical telescope and with it discovered that the Milky Way is composed of stars. In 1633, he was brought before the Inquisition for heresy, based on his theories about the movement of the planets, and forced to renounce his astronomical beliefs.

37. The correct answer is (D). The Earth's crust, consisting of continents and ocean basins, varies from five to

twenty miles in thickness. Temperatures can reach 1600° Fahrenheit. The mantle is a solid layer of rock that goes down about another eighteen hundred miles and increases in temperature to 4000° Fahrenheit. The outer core is about fourteen hundred miles thick and consists of iron and nickel; it can rise to nearly 9000° Fahrenheit. The center of the inner core, solid iron and nickel, lies four thousand miles below the surface and can be as hot as 9000° Fahrenheit.

38. The correct answer is (A). Matter in its physical states has mass, and it cannot be destroyed or manufactured, only changed. Some compounds, such as water, can be found in several states: liquid, solid (as ice), and gas (as steam). Plasma exists in the interior of stars and in stellar gas; because it is an electrical conductor, it is important in the manufacture of nuclear energy.

39. The correct answer is (C). The idea behind the Chaos Theory, which is still hotly debated by scientists, was first introduced in the nineteenth century by Henri Poincare, who wondered if the solar system was truly stable. He calculated that when a third body is added to the Newtonian orbitary equations of two bodies, orbits can become chaotic—that is, irregular or random. The Chaos Theory helps us understand that complex random behaviors can in fact be analyzed. Specialists have found applications of the theory in astronomy, chemistry (when certain chemicals react chaotically), meteorology (meteorologists feel that

atmospheric chaos makes long-term predictions impossible), politics, economics, and physiology.

40. The correct answer is (A). An ion can be charged positively or negatively, depending on whether it gains or loses electrons. If it gains electrons, it has a negative charge and is called an anion. If it loses electrons, it has a positive charge and is called a cation.

41. The correct answer is (C). The greenhouse gases include water vapor, CO_2, methane, nitrous oxide, and ozone. Ordinarily, these gases trap and hold a certain amount of infrared—if they did not, our planet would be frigid at all times. Human pollution is causing the gases to build up faster than before, and new gases, such as chlorofluorocarbons, have been added to the mixture. This increase in production has unbalanced the chemistry of the atmosphere, escalating the greenhouse effect and causing many scientists to predict a global warming. Figures from the Natural Resources Defense Council and *Science* magazine indicate that the 1980s were significantly hotter worldwide than any previous decade in recorded history. Predicted effects include the erosion of shorelines and disappearance of islands as global sea levels rise, and the extermination of temperature-sensitive species.

42. The correct answer is (B). When certain substances, such as zinc, magnesium, and lead sulfite, are cooled to absolute zero, they lose all electrical resistance and become what are called superconductors. This property is important because, if a way could be

found to eliminate the need for very cold temperatures, superconductors could be the basis for a whole new generation of super-efficient electrical equipment. Recently scientists have discovered that certain ceramic compounds possess superconductivity at temperatures well above absolute zero.

43. The correct answer is (A). Atoms of a given chemical element must contain the same number of protons but can contain different numbers of neutrons, giving them different masses. These atoms are called *isotopes*. Chlorine atoms, for example, have seventeen electrons and seventeen protons, but can have either eighteen or twenty neutrons. Most chemical elements have more than one isotope.

44. The correct answer is (D). The visible spectrum consists of white light, or colorless sunlight, refracted into colors. Newton's experiments on light proved this, showing that color depends on wavelength. Beyond the visible spectrum lie electromagnetic waves: gamma rays; X rays; ultraviolet radiation at wavelengths shorter than those of visible light; and infrared radiation, microwaves, and radio waves at wavelengths longer than those of visible light.

45. The correct answer is (C). Hail can occur at any time during the year. When raindrops are blown upward to the coldest part of a cloud, they freeze, then sink and are coated with more water, blown up and refrozen, and so on until they are heavy enough to drop.

46. The correct answer is (D). Because X rays, electromagnetic waves that are invisible and very short, can

penetrate thick material, they are useful in medicine. The rays in an X-ray machine are produced by heating a filament to provide a stream of electrons that bombard an anode. Bone absorbs more X rays than does muscle or skin; that is why X-ray machines can take pictures of the skeletal structure.

47. The correct answer is (B). The periodic table arranges elements (substances that cannot be decomposed chemically) in horizontal rows called periods, by their atomic number, or number of protons. The elements form vertical columns that reflect the periodic recurrence of chemical or physical properties.

48. The correct answer is (D). A compound contains two or more elements in a constant proportion. Chemical bonds hold the elements together. Compounds can be given formula names: H_2O is the formula for the compound water, and CO_2 is the formula for the compound carbon dioxide.

49. The correct answer is (A). Waves are the transfer of energy by vibration. A wavelength, the distance between a point on one wave and the same point on another, is measured by dividing the speed of the waves by their frequency.

50. The correct answer is (C). Crystals are solid substances with a regular geometric shape that reflect the arrangements of atoms within. They are formed by the solidification of an element, compound, or mixture and are often used, according to their physical characteristics, in various sectors of industry or as jewelry.

TEST 13
THE WAVE
OF THE FUTURE:
TECHNOLOGY

Technology . . . the knack of so arranging the
world that we don't have to experience it.

—MAX FRISCH

1. A battery works by
   (A) connecting to an outside source of electricity.
   (B) converting chemical energy into electrical energy.
   (C) warming up a wire to the point that it generates heat.
   (D) changing neutrons into electrons.

2. What does a laser do?
   (A) It focuses heat rays.
   (B) It blocks the visible spectrum.
   (C) It amplifies a beam of light.
   (D) It converts electrons into light.

3. You would be likely to use Mach numbers if you were a
   (A) test pilot.
   (B) electrician.
   (C) nutrition expert.
   (D) anthropologist.

4. Orville and Wilbur Wright
    (A) designed a motorized aircraft that flew in 1903.
    (B) piloted a successful glider in 1896.
    (C) started the first commercial airline in 1925.
    (D) flew the first transatlantic flight in 1927.

5. Microwaves that are used in cooking work by
    (A) radiating infrared waves (heat).
    (B) causing molecules to vibrate and generate heat.
    (C) bouncing heat rays off the metallic sides of the oven.
    (D) amplifying waves of light to produce heat.

6. Cyrus McCormick and John Deere contributed inventions that improved the working life of the
    (A) housewife.
    (B) athlete.
    (C) driver.
    (D) farmer.

7. A semiconductor is material that
    (A) conducts electricity better than most metals.
    (B) insulates better than most minerals.
    (C) does not conduct electricity.
    (D) has limited conductivity at room temperature.

8. What does a television transmitter transmit?
    (A) Radio waves
    (B) Television waves
    (C) Light waves
    (D) Sound waves

9. Johann Gutenberg was probably the first European to use
   (A) explosives.
   (B) carbon dating.
   (C) movable type.
   (D) hydroelectric power.

10. What is the difference between a ballistic missile and a guided missile?
    (A) The former carries nuclear warheads
    (B) The latter can be redirected in flight
    (C) The former is designed as an antiaircraft weapon
    (D) The latter is launched from an aircraft

11. Some people involved with the invention of the telegraph include
    (A) Savery, Newcomen, and Watt.
    (B) Oersted, Henry, and Morse.
    (C) Benz, Daimler, and Diesel.
    (D) Daguerre, Herschel, and Land.

12. An electrode is the same as a
    (A) terminal.
    (B) battery.
    (C) electron.
    (D) circuit.

13. What did George Eastman invent?
    (A) Motion pictures
    (B) The Kodak camera
    (C) The telescope
    (D) Magnifying lenses

14. A photoelectric cell is stimulated by
    (A) heat.
    (B) chemical change.
    (C) neutrons.
    (D) light.

15. In an assembly line,
    (A) each worker assembles a single product.
    (B) more than one product is assembled.
    (C) a product is assembled in steps.
    (D) each worker oversees a variety of processes.

16. The hardware in a computer system
    (A) controls the operation of the system.
    (B) may include programs for filing and storage.
    (C) may include keyboard and printer.
    (D) contains sequential instructions.

17. Thomas Edison is known for his inventions dealing
    with
    (A) sound and electricity.
    (B) flight and motion.
    (C) food production and storage.
    (D) light and weather.

18. A silicon chip is part of a
    (A) floppy disk.
    (B) microcomputer.
    (C) cassette.
    (D) teleprinter.

19. You would use a particle accelerator to
    (A) detect radiation leakage.
    (B) increase the rate at which an engine revs.
    (C) bombard atoms with parts of other atoms.
    (D) model theoretical changes in an environment.

20. Alexander Graham Bell's major invention involved
    (A) sending a code via electric circuits.
    (B) recording sound on two or more microphones.
    (C) recording information on strips of tape.
    (D) transmitting speech on waves of electricity.

21. Robert Fulton is known as the inventor of which of
    the following?
    (A) Steamboat
    (B) Cotton gin
    (C) Elevator .
    (D) Revolver

22. Which of these is a lever?
    (A) Ice tongs
    (B) Crowbar
    (C) Balance scale
    (D) All of the above

23. What is the job of a sensor?
    (A) It locates and maps a radioactive source.
    (B) It tests the depth and bottom conditions of
        oceans or rivers.
    (C) It translates external conditions into signals.
    (D) It takes X rays in sequential patterns.

24. What is the path of visual signals in a television
    broadcast?
    (A) camera → transmitter → antenna → antenna
        → receiver → cathode-ray tube
    (B) camera → videotape → antenna → cathode-
        ray tube → receiver
    (C) antenna → camera → transmitter → receiver
        → cathode-ray tube
    (D) microphone → transmitter → receiver →
        speaker → cathode-ray tube

25. An integrated circuit
    (A) is made of copper tubes.
    (B) does not contain wires.
    (C) is microscopic in size.
    (D) All of the above

26. How does a CD work?
    (A) Sound is transferred from a tape to a disc.
    (B) Audio frequencies are digitally encoded on a disc.
    (C) Audio frequencies are pressed onto a disc by
        computer.
    (D) Sound is recorded live, stored in a computer,
        and transferred onto a computer disc by laser.

27. How does a nuclear reactor work?
    (A) Atomic nuclei are split, producing a self-perpetuating chain reaction.
    (B) Alpha, beta, or gamma rays cause a discharge that produces a nuclear reaction.
    (C) Coal is heated to such intensity that atomic nuclei fuse together.
    (D) An atom absorbs energy and then emits a photon, causing intense heat.

28. What is the difference between radar and sonar?
    (A) Radar is used to record sounds; sonar is used to make sounds.
    (B) Radar records sounds at very high frequencies; sonar records very low-frequency sounds.
    (C) Radar uses electromagnetic waves; sonar uses sound waves.
    (D) Radar absorbs echoes; sonar produces echoes.

29. Which of these devices use cathode-ray tubes?
    (A) Semiconductors, generators, and transformers
    (B) Microphones, cameras, and holographs
    (C) Anemometers, teleprinters, and microwave ovens
    (D) Television, radar, and computer terminals

30. What can a receiver produce?
    (A) Sound waves and pictures
    (B) Microwaves and audio frequencies
    (C) Holograms and infrared waves
    (D) All of the above

31. How does a fax machine work?
    (A) Printed material is scanned and converted into electronic signals, which are reconverted and printed.
    (B) It sends out sound impulses, which bounce off a satellite that converts them to light waves.
    (C) A computer translates an image into modified Morse Code, and a second computer converts the code to print.
    (D) A lens refracts an image, and a laser-light pen copies the refracted image.

32. For what is Guglielmo Marconi best known?
    (A) The invention of the steam engine
    (B) The development of the incandescent lamp
    (C) The invention of the telephone
    (D) The development of wireless telegraphy

33. What is the usual method for toxic waste disposal?
    (A) Burning
    (B) Sealing in metal drums and burying
    (C) Processing and dumping at sea
    (D) Recycling

34. What do these things have in common: coal, gas, oil, the sun, plutonium, water, and wind?
    (A) They are all potential pollutants.
    (B) They all provide safe, inexpensive heat.
    (C) They all provide methods of combustion.
    (D) They are all sources of energy.

35. What is a watt?
    (A) A unit of power
    (B) A degree of brightness
    (C) A charge of electricity
    (D) An open circuit

36. How does a turbine work?
    (A) Steam moves a piston to and fro in a cylinder.
    (B) A heavy wheel rotates, storing kinetic energy.
    (C) A stream of fluid or air turns a shaft that drives machinery.
    (D) A bar turns around a pivot.

37. Where would you be most likely to find a main-frame computer?
    (A) A home
    (B) A bank
    (C) A college English department
    (D) A high school

38. How does hydraulic machinery work?
    (A) Through liquid that expands and contracts
    (B) Through pressure exerted by heat
    (C) Through the movement of levers
    (D) Through pressure exerted on liquid

39. What did Anton van Leeuwenhoek invent?
    (A) The thermometer
    (B) The microscope
    (C) The bifocal lens
    (D) The telescope

40. How does a VCR record from a television?
    (A) Electrical signals from the television are trans-
        mitted to magnetic tape.
    (B) Sound and picture are transformed into
        printed messages on the television.
    (C) Glass fibers pick up radio wave transmissions
        and record them on tape.
    (D) A disk in the television reacts directly with
        magnetic tape, producing a recording.

41. How does a telescope work?
    (A) Light is magnified.
    (B) Objects are photographed and enlarged.
    (C) Light is refracted or reflected and focused.
    (D) Light is bounced back and forth between mir-
        rors.

42. Why was the space shuttle an important technolog-
    ical advance?
    (A) It could go farther than any other spacecraft.
    (B) It was reusable.
    (C) It could fly unmanned with great precision.
    (D) All of the above

43. What is a robot?
    (A) A machine in the shape of a human
    (B) A machine controlled from a distance
    (C) A machine that can think
    (D) A machine that senses and then reacts

44. The best descriptor for CD-ROM might be
    (A) auditory.
    (B) multimedia.
    (C) visual.
    (D) olfactory.

45. Where might you find an internal combustion engine?
    (A) In a jet
    (B) In a hovercraft
    (C) In an automobile
    (D) In a steamship

46. Where can computer data be stored?
    (A) On a hard disk
    (B) On a floppy disk
    (C) On a CD-ROM
    (D) All of the above

47. What is the purpose of isotope scanning, ultrasound, and electrocardiographs?
    (A) Diagnosis and control of disease
    (B) Cure of heart disease
    (C) Maintenance of a healthy fetus
    (D) Reduction of the size of a tumor

48. Which of these are satellites?
    (A) Sputnik I
    (B) The moon
    (C) Ganymede
    (D) All of the above

49. What is a hologram?
    (A) A colorized picture of an object
    (B) A three-dimensional image of an object
    (C) A photograph that develops automatically
    (D) A photograph taken from the moon

50. For what inventions is Benjamin Franklin known?
    (A) The lightning rod and bifocals
    (B) The marine torpedo and the steamship
    (C) The calculating machine and the hydraulic
        press
    (D) The phonograph and the wax record

TEST 13:
Explanatory Answers

1. The correct answer is (B). Batteries come in many varieties, but all are made up three things: a positive electrode, a negative electrode, and a chemical solution called an *electrolyte*. The positive and negative electrodes are placed in the solution and connected externally with a wire. Positive ions from the solution travel to the negative electrode, and electrons travel from the negative electrode through the wire and into the positive electrode, creating a circuit.

2. The correct answer is (C). Just as a nuclear pile sets up a chain reaction with neutrons, so does a laser set up a chain reaction with photons, the particles that make up light. The laser stimulates atoms so that a majority of them are at a higher energy level than usual. The difference in energy between high-energy atoms and normal atoms may be matched by the frequency of a photon. If that photon hits the excited atom, it causes the atom to release a photon of the same frequency as the first and return to a normal level of energy. The released photon then moves in the same direction as the first photon, and both continue to hit high-energy atoms as they travel. The result is a burst of radiation, which is reflected back and forth between the silvered ends of the laser. When the radiation is

intense enough, it passes through one end of the laser. The light emitted is all one wavelength and is extremely intense. *Laser* is an acronym for light amplification by stimulated emission of radiation.

3. The correct answer is (A). A Mach number measures the ratio of an object's speed to the speed of sound. When the Mach number exceeds 1, the object is supersonic; it exceeds the speed of sound.

4. The correct answer is (A). The Wright brothers owned a bicycle shop, and they used bicycle parts to make the first successful motorized airplane. A biplane, it had two propellers and was powered by a gasoline engine. It made a sustained flight near Kitty Hawk, North Carolina, on December 17, 1903.

5. The correct answer is (B). Microwaves are radio waves with wavelengths between 300 mm and 1 mm, placing them between infrared and radio short waves on the electromagnetic spectrum. They are used in radar and certain communications devices as well as in ovens. In ovens the waves penetrate food, causing molecules of moisture to vibrate and produce heat. A substance containing no moisture will not be affected.

6. The correct answer is (D). Cyrus McCormick (1809–1884) invented a reaper in 1831 that mechanized the harvest for the first time. John Deere (1804–1886) invented the first steel plow and created the farm implement company that bore his name. These inventions revolutionized farming by

making it possible for fewer people to cultivate more acreage.

7. The correct answer is (D). A conductor allows electricity to flow through it. An insulator prevents the flow of electricity. A semiconductor has conducting properties between the two. At high temperatures it conducts well; at low temperatures, it insulates. Impurities that add electrons to or take electrons away from a semiconductor can increase its conductivity. In a negative (*n*-type) semiconductor, electricity is carried by the electrons. In a positive (*p*-type) semiconductor, it is carried via the "holes" where electrons were removed.

8. The correct answer is (A). All waves have amplitude (height), length, and frequency (number of waves that pass a point in a given amount of time). In radio or television, sound or images are converted into electrical signals by a microphone or camera, and these signals are used to modulate (vary) the amplitude or frequency of radio waves produced by a transmitter.

9. The correct answer is (C). Movable type was used in printing presses in Korea in the fourteenth century. Johann Gutenberg (c. 1397–1468) was probably the first European to use the technique. His most important work was the Mazarin Bible, usually called the Gutenberg Bible, completed in Mainz, Germany, in 1455. It was the first complete book printed in Europe. Gutenberg's press was a hand press. Letters were placed by hand in a form,

and ink was rolled over them. The form was then pressed against a sheet of paper.

10. The correct answer is (B). Ballistic missiles follow a parabolic path once launched, and they fall freely after reaching the apex of their ascent. Guided missiles may have self-contained controls, or they may be controlled from the ground by radio. By these means, their paths may be altered as they fly.

11. The correct answer is (B). In 1819, the Danish physicist Hans Christian Oersted accidentally discovered that a current flowing through a wire makes the wire act like a magnet. His discovery led to William Sturgeon's construction of the first electromagnet. In 1831, Joseph Henry demonstrated that an electromagnet could gain and lose magnetism almost instantly even though the switch that completed and broke the circuit was a mile away. However, it took Samuel F. B. Morse to develop this notion into a practical telegraph (1844). In his telegraph, an electromagnet in the receiver was activated when a circuit was completed by pressing a key in the transmitter. The intermittent current was received as audible clicks. The other inventors listed were involved with the steam engine, the internal-combustion engine, and photography.

12. The correct answer is (A). In an electric circuit, current passes between metallic and nonmetallic conductors. An electrode, or terminal, makes the connection between the two kinds of conductors. A negative electrode is called a *cathode*; current passes

through it on its way from a nonmetallic to a metallic conductor. A positive electrode is called an *anode;* current passes through it on its way from a metallic to a nonmetallic conductor. Most electrodes are made of metal, copper being one example.

13. The correct answer is (B). George Eastman (1854–1932) invented a new process of photography that led to his chief invention, the Kodak camera, in 1888. The dry-plate process allowed him to replace bulky photographic plates with roll film, another Eastman invention. In 1892, Eastman founded a company to mass-produce the camera, paving the way for photography to become an affordable hobby. In 1928, he invented a process for color photography.

14. The correct answer is (D). The cathode or the semiconductor of a photoelectric cell is coated with a material that is sensitive to light. When light hits the material, electrons are emitted. This either completes a circuit, allowing current to flow, or it increases a current that is already flowing due to a battery hookup. The amount of current depends on the intensity of the light.

15. The correct answer is (C). The Industrial Revolution mechanized industry, enabling the owners of companies to increase profit by increasing the productivity of the labor force. The development of the assembly line led to even greater profit. Each worker on an assembly line has a specific task. Machines and workers are assigned to stations

TEST 13

along the line, and a product proceeds from station to station until it is completed. Henry Ford (1863–1947) first applied the process to automobile manufacturing, and his venture was certainly one of the most profitable early attempts at mass production.

16. The correct answer is (C). The hardware in a system includes the physical system itself, which may be made up of a keyboard, a central processing unit (CPU), a monitor, speakers, and a printer. The other features mentioned belong to software, the information that controls the computer's functioning.

17. The correct answer is (A). Among the inventions of Thomas Edison (1847–1931), in order of their invention, were the carbon microphone (1877), the record player (1878), the lightbulb (1879), and the kinetoscope (1889), an early motion-picture machine. He worked with teams of researchers in one of the largest laboratories of the time, a precursor of today's gigantic industrial research laboratories.

18. The correct answer is (B). An integrated circuit does not use wires to complete the circuit; instead, it is constructed from one piece of semiconductor material. A chip contains a tiny integrated circuit. In a silicon chip, silicon is the semiconductor material used.

19. The correct answer is (C). The most common kind of particle accelerator is the cyclotron, for which Ernest Lawrence won the Nobel Prize in physics in 1939. The accelerator directs beams of atomic par-

ticles against a target, accelerating the particles through the use of electric fields, or electromagnetic waves. Early accelerators were very long straight lines, and those are still the most efficient. The cyclotron bends the beam in an arc, enabling acceleration to take place in a smaller space.

20. The correct answer is (D). Alexander Graham Bell (1847–1922) worked with deaf students before designing the first telephone in 1876. In a telephone, vibrations in one microphone vary the flow of current into a circuit. When the current reaches a second microphone, it causes identical vibrations in it, vibrations that translate into sound waves. Bell used the money and influence he gained from his invention to help found the magazine *Science* and to support other scientists.

21. The correct answer is (A). Robert Fulton (1765–1815) stole John Fitch's thunder and received credit for producing the first steamboat in 1807, more than twenty years after Fitch's ship was built. Fulton's ship, the *Clermont,* traveled amid much publicity from New York City to Albany in record time. Although Eli Whitney invented one kind of cotton gin, the idea probably originated with a black slave in the mid-1700s. The other two inventions listed belong to Elisha Otis and Samuel Colt.

22. The correct answer is (D). A lever is one of the five types of simple machines, the others being the pulley, inclined plane, screw, and wheel and axle. A lever is a bar supported by a stationary fulcrum.

Force is applied to a point along the lever to overcome resistance (lift a load) at another point. The locations of the fulcrum, resistance, and force determine the kind of lever. A balance has a fulcrum in the center. A crowbar and tongs have the fulcrum at the end. With the crowbar, force is applied at one end of the lever to lift a resistance in the center. With the tongs, force is applied in the middle of the lever to lift a resistance at the opposite end from the fulcrum.

23. The correct answer is (C). A sensor detects an external condition such as light, heat, movement, or pressure. It evaluates the condition and emits a signal (usually electrical) based on the amount of the condition it senses. Sensors are found in some elevator buttons, photographic light meters, and car alarms.

24. The correct answer is (A). Images are converted into electrical signals by a camera, and these signals are used to modulate radio waves produced by a transmitter. These waves are sent out via an antenna, and some of them are picked up by antennas that are hooked up to receivers. The receiver converts the waves back to electrical signals, and in the cathode-ray tube, electrons are projected onto a screen to re-form the image.

25. The correct answer is (B). The fact that an integrated circuit is formed entirely of one semiconductor material and contains no wires means that it is more reliable than an ordinary circuit: there is little chance of a short circuit or loose connections.

26. The correct answer is (B). In the late 1970s electronics companies began developing the compact disc, on which audio frequencies are digitally encoded and stored for scanning by laser. This technique produced better sound quality than records or tapes, and CDs were found to be harder to bootleg. In 1978, Sony and Phillips jointly decided on a 4.72-inch (12-cm) disc. The new product was introduced in 1983, and in just a few years it was obvious that CDs would soon take the place of LPs and cassettes in the market. While in 1983 over 295 million LPs were shipped, by 1991 only 4.8 million were produced, as compared to 333 million CDs.

27. The correct answer is (A). In a nuclear reactor, fuel, which is usually uranium or plutonium, is treated to cause the fission of atomic nuclei, setting up a chain reaction that is controlled by a substance such as graphite or cadmium metal. Heat is emitted and used to heat water and to provide steam. Fusion reactors are still in the experimental stage, since extremely high temperatures are needed to initiate the reaction.

28. The correct answer is (C). Radar (*r*adio *d*etecting *a*nd *r*anging) calculates the distance of an object by bouncing electromagnetic waves off the object and timing their return. Sonar (*so*und *na*vigation *r*anging) detects objects underwater by bouncing a high-frequency sound wave off them and timing its return.

29. The correct answer is (D). Cathode-ray tubes are vacuum tubes in which electrons, accelerated by

high voltages, are focused into a beam and projected onto a screen. Among their uses are the production of images on television screens, computer terminals, and radar screens.

30. The correct answer is (A). A receiver picks up electromagnetic waves and converts them into either sound waves, as in a radio, or pictures, as in a television, using a device that vibrates with varying electric current.

31. The correct answer is (A). Fax technology has been around since the nineteenth century. By 1910, a photoelectric scanning system developed by a German inventor named Korn allowed the transmission of photographs between Berlin and other European cities, and the first transatlantic transmission took place in 1922. Early uses of the system included the transmission of news photos, weather maps, and telegrams. When direct-dial telephones achieved widespread use in the 1960s, nationwide faxing became possible. Today, fax machines use a digital scanning process to encode information in terms of the density of each dot on the page of text, convert that information into electronic impulses, send the impulses over phone lines, and reconvert the signals at the other end.

32. The correct answer is (D). The Italian physicist Marconi (1874–1937) won the 1909 Nobel Prize for developing long-wave wireless telegraphy. This paved the way for the invention of radio and television, which convert electromagnetic waves into

sound and/or pictures. The other inventions listed are by James Watt, Thomas Edison, and Alexander Graham Bell.

33. The correct answer is (B). Toxic waste, which consists of chemicals such as heavy metals, hydrocarbons, and poisonous solvents, is usually disposed of by sealing it in metal cans and burying it. Often the drums corrode, leaking toxic waste into the environment. The other waste disposal methods are used on solid wastes.

34. The correct answer is (D). Each of these sources of energy has its drawbacks. Coal, gas, and oil are not renewable and contribute to pollution. Plutonium, used in nuclear reactors, is dangerous, and the waste it produces is difficult to dispose of. Water, wind, and solar energy are nonpolluting, but they are often unavailable when they are most needed, and we do not yet possess the necessary technology to use these resources to their full potential.

35. The correct answer is (A). A watt is a unit of power equal to the rate of work represented by a current of one ampere under a pressure of one volt. An ampere is the unit of electrical current, and a volt is the unit of electrical potential. An ohm, another important term in electricity, is the unit of electrical resistance.

36. The correct answer is (C). A turbine engine uses a continuous stream of gas or liquid to turn a shaft. The other devices mentioned are a steam engine, a flywheel, and a lever.

37. The correct answer is (B). A mainframe computer is a general-purpose computing platform that is usually used to operate a network of other computers. It is most often used in big businesses; 60 percent of corporate data is now stored in mainframe computers. However, as the workforce that knows how to operate these large computers ages and retires, many mainframes are being replaced with smaller Windows- or Unix-based systems.

38. The correct answer is (D). Hydraulic machinery operates under the aegis of Pascal's law, which states that pressure applied to any part of an enclosed liquid moves without diminishing to all parts of the liquid.

39. The correct answer is (B). Anton van Leeuwenhoek (1632–1723) was a Dutch scientist interested in natural history. He made microscopes that magnified organisms more than two hundred times. This allowed him to observe and describe one-celled organisms and bacteria. The thermometer and the telescope were invented by Galileo; the bifocal lens, by Benjamin Franklin.

40. The correct answer is (A). A VCR (videocassette recorder) records the electrical signals from television onto magnetic tape. There are tracks on the tape for audio and for video and a device to match the sound and picture so that they can be played back simultaneously.

41. The correct answer is (C). There are three kinds of telescope: the refracting telescope, which bends

light through a lens so that it converges to a point; the reflecting telescope, which reflects and focuses light in a mirror; and the catadioptric telescope, which focuses light using both lenses and mirrors.

42. The correct answer is (B). The first operational space shuttle flight took place in 1982, and flights continued until the explosion of the *Challenger* shuttle in 1986. The shuttle, a reusable spacecraft, lifts off like a rocket and lands like an airplane. It is used for scientific investigation and launching and repair of satellites. From 1986 to 1988, the shuttle program was closely evaluated, and in October of 1988, the program was restarted with the launch of the shuttle *Discovery*.

43. The correct answer is (D). A robot is a machine that can sense its environment—through vision, touch, or another sense—and act on it. Usually, robots are controlled by computers, and they are often used today in assembly-line production.

44. The correct answer is (B). CD-ROM technology gives computers audio and video capability, making them multimedia machines with interactive potential. Examples of uses include the new electronic books, which allow a user with a handheld Sony Data Discman to skim a bestseller onscreen while a narrator reads aloud; Ecodisc, which gives users a visual and auditory walk through the woods, allowing them to choose the path and see the landscape from any angle they choose; and language dictionaries that include oral pronunciation.

A single 3.14-inch CD-ROM disc can hold 100,000 pages of text, about one-third that many pages of graphics, or six hours of sound.

45. The correct answer is (C). In an internal combustion engine, chemical energy is converted into heat energy and then into mechanical energy by burning a mixture of fuel and air. In an automobile, fuel and air are mixed by the carburetor and drain into the cylinder as the piston strokes downward. As the piston rises, the compressed fuel and air are ignited by a spark: the hot gases drive the piston down, rotating the crankshaft, which drives the car.

46. The correct answer is (D). Computers store information in memory that is permanent, semipermanent, or temporary. Permanent storage places information on ROM (read-only memory) chips and CD-ROMS. Semipermanent storage places information on a floppy disk that can be overwritten. Temporary storage places information on RAM memory chips, which must have a continuous source of power to retain their memory.

47. The correct answer is (A). Isotope scanning shows where diseased tissue lies because this tissue takes up large amounts of compounds that contain radioactive isotopes. Ultrasound can identify problems in soft tissue by reflecting sound vibrations off the tissue. Ultrasound is also used to heal and to watch the movement of blood. The electrocardiograph picks up voltages from the heart and graphs

them, allowing an observer to see whether the heart is contracting normally.

48. The correct answer is (D). A satellite is a body that orbits a planet. Natural satellites are often referred to as moons. Ganymede, for example, is one of Jupiter's moons. Artificial satellites are launched by rockets and can be used for communications, navigation, weather forecasting, military reconnaissance, and scientific investigation.

49. The correct answer is (B). Holography uses lasers to record an image on a photographic plate. Two beams are used: One is diffracted by the object being recorded and falls on the plate; the other falls directly onto the plate. The patterns produced are then recorded, and when the plate is illuminated by light of the same frequency, a three-dimensional image is viewed.

50. The correct answer is (A). Benjamin Franklin (1706–1790) was an inventor, printer, statesman, and scientist. He published *Poor Richard's Almanack*; set up a fire company, a hospital, and a library; invented bifocals and the Franklin stove; and experimented with electricity. He also signed the Declaration of Independence and helped negotiate the peace treaty of 1783 with England. The other inventions mentioned are by Robert Fulton, Blaise Pascal, and Thomas Edison.

TEST 14
THE QUEEN OF THE SCIENCES AND THE DISMAL SCIENCE: MATHEMATICS AND ECONOMICS

The pulse of modern life is economic.

—Ch'en Tu-hsiu

1. Which of these could be considered an asset?
   (A) Income tax
   (B) A checking account
   (C) Interest payments paid to a creditor
   (D) A car that is rented or leased

2. Which of these figures is three-dimensional?
   (A) A point
   (B) A line
   (C) A square
   (D) A cylinder

3. What is the Dow Jones Composite Average?
   (A) The average of the closing prices of sixty-five stocks on the New York Stock Exchange
   (B) The average of the closing prices of all the stocks on the New York Stock Exchange
   (C) The average of the midday prices of all government bonds
   (D) The average interest rates offered by banks

4. In the following graph, which country listed has the fewest nuclear reactors?

   (A) The United States
   (B) West Germany
   (C) France
   (D) Great Britain

5. What is the primary job of the Federal Reserve Board?
   (A) To oversee loans to foreign nations
   (B) To regulate the federal budget
   (C) To regulate money supply and interest rates
   (D) To monitor the nation's store of gold

6. What is this number in Arabic numerals: MDC-CLXVII?
   (A) 1972
   (B) 1552
   (C) 1066
   (D) 1767

7. In economics, what is a market?
   (A) Any context in which the sale and purchase of goods and services occurs
   (B) A place where edible goods are sold
   (C) An economic system that depends on price fluctuations
   (D) Activities associated with the sales and distribution of products

8. Who was Euclid?
   (A) A Greek mathematician who calculated the value of pi
   (B) A French philosopher who developed analytic geometry
   (C) A Greek mathematician who developed the study of plane geometry
   (D) A Greek mathematician who developed a formula for computing the area of a triangle

9. What was Thomas Malthus's conclusion about population growth?
   (A) That population can be controlled by genocide
   (B) That population will grow faster than food supply, leading to poverty
   (C) That population will grow faster among lower classes than among upper classes
   (D) That population will eventually decrease in wealthy European countries

10. 3 to the sixth power, or 3^6, equals
    (A) 18
    (B) 9
    (C) 81
    (D) 729

11. How is the gross national product measured?
    (A) By monitoring investment in foreign markets
    (B) By counting the money spent to buy, or received for producing, goods and services
    (C) By measuring the change in the value of the dollar over time
    (D) By measuring the gap between national consumption and national production

12. What is the size of ∠A?

  (A) 90°
  (B) 180°
  (C) 45°
  (D) 10°

13. Under what circumstances might bankruptcy be
    declared?
    (A) If a person does not pay his creditors on a
        timely basis
    (B) If a bank is robbed at gunpoint
    (C) If the New York Stock Exchange is closed
    (D) If a war or national emergency is declared by
        federal authorities

14. What is required to make mass production cost-
    effective?
    (A) Many factories producing the same item
    (B) A large number of units being produced
    (C) A city-dwelling workforce
    (D) A growing population

15. What does the Pythagorean theorem state?
    (A) The area of an equilateral triangle is one-fourth the square of a side multiplied by the square root of 3.
    (B) The diagonal of any square is equal to the length of a side multiplied by the square root of 2.
    (C) In any triangle the sum of the three angles is equal to 180°.
    (D) In a right triangle the square of the hypotenuse is equal to the sum of the squares of the legs.

16. Which of these situations illustrates the laws of supply and demand?
    (A) Prices of beef rise, and the demand for beef lessens.
    (B) A large quantity of potatoes hits the market; the price of potatoes drops.
    (C) As the price of wheat rises, suppliers bring more wheat to the market.
    (D) All of the above

17. What is inflation?
    (A) High interest rates on government securities
    (B) An overall trend toward rising prices, occurring for reasons about which economists disagree
    (C) Economic stagnation caused by unemployment
    (D) An overall trend toward rising wages, caused either by a shortage of workers or by the influence of trade unions

18. Why was the FDIC formed?
    (A) To regulate the levels of income taxation
    (B) To protect citizens against strikes by government employees
    (C) To protect bank depositors from the effects of a depression
    (D) To protect consumers against monopolization

19. How many inches are there in a yard?
    (A) 12
    (B) 24
    (C) 36
    (D) 8

20. Why might a country practice protectionism?
    (A) Because of high unemployment and large trade deficits
    (B) Because of efficient labor practices and low income taxes
    (C) Because of high foreign oil prices and a stable dollar
    (D) Because of inflation and high interest rates

21. What is the purpose of a mortgage?
    (A) To protect the lender against nonpayment by the homeowner
    (B) To protect the homeowner against property damage
    (C) To pay for home improvements
    (D) To enable homeowners to make down payments

22. Why does a corporation consider an initial public offering?
    - (A) To avoid a takeover by a larger corporation
    - (B) To export goods through new joint ventures
    - (C) To raise capital
    - (D) To legalize business practices with its board of directors

23. What kind of income tax do Americans pay?
    - (A) Proportional income tax
    - (B) Progressive income tax
    - (C) Regressive income tax
    - (D) Value added income tax

24. When does a federal deficit exist?
    - (A) When the amount of taxes exceeds the amount of income
    - (B) When government salaries exceed government expenditures
    - (C) When government spending exceeds government revenues
    - (D) When actual income exceeds projected income

25. When is a stock market *bullish?*
    - (A) When recession threatens
    - (B) When stock prices are fluctuating
    - (C) When stock prices are rising and investment is up
    - (D) When trading is heavy

26. An interest rate can be
    (A) a percentage of an amount of money bor-
        rowed.
    (B) a tax on overseas investments.
    (C) a proportion of income paid to the federal
        government.
    (D) payment made after an initial down payment.

27. According to Keynesian economics,
    (A) government action can raise the level of
        national income.
    (B) productive labor includes service jobs as well
        as manufacturing.
    (C) population increases faster than resources.
    (D) the division of labor is necessary to produc-
        tion.

28. If your company's profit is $5 billion, that is the
    same as
    (A) five million million dollars.
    (B) fifty thousand million dollars.
    (C) five hundred million dollars.
    (D) five thousand million dollars.

29. Which of these is generally not considered an eco-
    nomic resource?
    (A) Land
    (B) Tools
    (C) Labor
    (D) Money

30. The average height of three people is always
    (A) the height of the one who is neither tallest nor shortest.
    (B) their height in inches divided by 12.
    (C) the sum of their heights divided by 3.
    (D) the height of the shortest plus the height of the tallest.

31. The consumer price index shows
    (A) the price of a meal in various parts of the United States.
    (B) changes in costs of various essential goods and commodities.
    (C) the average wages of an American worker.
    (D) the percentage of wages spent on food and clothing.

32. If a country's imports exceed its exports, it
    (A) takes in more in sales than it loses in production.
    (B) imposes heavy tariffs on goods entering from overseas.
    (C) spends more on foreign goods than it makes selling its own goods abroad.
    (D) buys more foreign goods than other countries do.

33. Pi is the ratio of
    (A) the total cost to the number of units.
    (B) a circle's circumference to its diameter.
    (C) the length of a triangle's hypotenuse to the length of the side opposite the hypotenuse.
    (D) All of the above

34. Where a monopoly exists, there is no possibility of
    (A) profit.
    (B) productivity.
    (C) increased demand.
    (D) competition.

35. The graph above shows
    (A) a dramatic increase in population over time.
    (B) a dramatic decrease in population over time.
    (C) a decrease followed by a tapering off.
    (D) a steady increase followed by a downswing.

36. A depression and a recession are both periods of
    (A) high spending.
    (B) low business activity.
    (C) high prices.
    (D) increased production.

37. Why was the economic situation in the United States in the early 1990s termed a recession?
    (A) Consumer spending was down, unemployment was up, and growth was slow.
    (B) Interest rates and inflation rose sharply.
    (C) The stock market plunged dramatically.
    (D) Income taxes increased, profits rose slowly, and the deficit soared.

38. The term *credit* refers to a promise
    (A) to pay in the future for goods or services received now.
    (B) to add a percentage to every base price on every purchase.
    (C) to supply collateral on demand to a bank or credit union.
    (D) to deliver goods or services within a specified period of time.

39. The most common kind of tariff is
    (A) a form of income tax.
    (B) a price agreed on by two or more countries.
    (C) a tax on imports.
    (D) money paid to cover shipping costs.

40. According to Adam Smith, the force of greed is counterbalanced in the economy by
    (A) social conscience.
    (B) competition.
    (C) church dogma.
    (D) regressive taxation.

41. William Haywood, John L. Lewis, and Samuel Gompers founded
    (A) Standard Oil.
    (B) U.S. Steel.
    (C) labor federations.
    (D) the Federal Reserve.

42. If a pole is 2 meters tall, it is
    (A) less than 2 feet tall.
    (B) about 3 feet tall.
    (C) about 4 feet tall.
    (D) over 6 feet tall.

43. In a purely capitalist economy,
    (A) individuals are free to own property and the means of production.
    (B) government restrictions are limited.
    (C) individuals compete to provide goods and services for profit.
    (D) All of the above

44. Which shape is matched incorrectly to its number of sides?
    (A) heptagon—six
    (B) decagon—ten
    (C) octagon—eight
    (D) pentagon—five

45. Among the duties of the Federal Trade Commission is
    (A) insuring people's savings in private loan associations.
    (B) licensing and regulating small businesses.
    (C) preventing unfair pricing or advertising.
    (D) administering disability insurance.

46. What is a federal subsidy?
    (A) Assistance to an unprofitable service that benefits the public
    (B) A tax added to a product to raise revenue for the state
    (C) A business under the control of the federal government
    (D) A division of the welfare system designed to aid families

47. If a baseball team's win-loss ratio is 4 to 1, the team
    (A) must have played five games in all.
    (B) won four times as many games as they lost.
    (C) won three times as many games as they lost.
    (D) None of the above

48. The cost-of-living index measures the change in
    (A) housing costs over a period of ten years.
    (B) prices of items needed to maintain a given standard of living.
    (C) cost of nonessential goods and services over time.
    (D) average wages from one year to the next.

49. Which statement about lines is entirely true?
    (A) Parallel lines never meet; perpendicular lines
        intersect once.
    (B) Parallel lines never meet; perpendicular lines
        cross twice.
    (C) Parallel lines intersect at a point; perpendicu-
        lar lines form right angles.
    (D) Parallel lines are perpendicular lines that never
        intersect.

50. Social security programs in the United States
    include
    (A) maximum work hours, minimum wages, and
        child labor laws.
    (B) job placement for veterans and farm workers.
    (C) unemployment compensation, retirement insur-
        ance, and Medicare.
    (D) the Job Corps, VISTA, and neighborhood
        Youth Corps.

TEST 14:
Explanatory Answers

1. The correct answer is (B). Assets are everything owned by an individual, a partnership, a corporation, or an estate and can include a sum of money, a piece of equipment, real estate, a claim on another, or even a patent.

2. The correct answer is (D). Two-dimensional figures have length and width. A three-dimensional figure takes up space as well; other examples are a cube, a pyramid, a sphere, and a cone. The study of two-dimensional figures is called plane geometry; the study of three-dimensional figures is solid geometry.

3. The correct answer is (A). The Dow Jones Composite Average is the mean of closing prices of thirty industrial stocks, fifteen public utility stocks, and twenty transportation stocks. These means are averaged together at the end of each day on the New York Stock Exchange to produce the Dow Jones Composite Average. The Dow Jones Industrial Average, consisting of the thirty industrial stocks, is more often reported than the Composite Average.

4. The correct answer is (B). A bar graph is a chart used to compare quantities. It uses rectangular lengths to represent the size of the quantities compared.

5. The correct answer is (C). The Federal Reserve Board, established in 1913, distributes currency to banks and oversees the sales and purchases of government securities. All national banks and certain state banks belong to the Federal Reserve System, which is regulated by the Board; many of these banks are "banker's banks," acting for banks as smaller banks do for individuals.

6. The correct answer is (D). In Roman numerals, M = 1000, D = 500, C = 100, L = 50, X = 10, V = 5, and I = 1. Certain numbers are more complicated to write; 9, for example, is written IX, and 19 is XIX.

7. The correct answer is (A). A market does not have to have a physical entity; it is any context in which goods or services are bought and sold. For instance, telecommunications networks over which stocks are sold can be considered markets.

8. The correct answer is (C). Euclid, who lived about 300 B.C.E., developed the system of deductive proofs that is the basis of plane geometry. He wrote his theories in a series of thirteen books called the *Elements*. The other mathematicians mentioned are Archimedes, Descartes, and Hero.

9. The correct answer is (B). Thomas Malthus (1766–1834) was an English economist whose *Essay on the Principle of Population* stated that population increases in a geometric ratio while the means of subsistence increases arithmetically, leading to poverty. He claimed that disease, war, famine,

and moral restraint act as checks on population growth.

10. The correct answer is (D). When a number is multiplied by itself, the result is the second power, or square, of the base number. A base number to the sixth power is multiplied by itself, and the result multiplied by the base, and so on three more times.

$$3^2 = 9, 3^3 = 27, 3^4 = 81, 3^5 = 243, \text{ and } 3^6 = 729.$$

11. The correct answer is (B). The gross national product is the flow of production over a given period of time, usually a year. You can measure the GNP in two ways; by measuring the money spent on the output of goods and services, called the flow-of-product method, or by measuring the money received for producing the goods and services, called the earnings or income method. The GNP aids economists in forecasting the movement of the economy.

12. The correct answer is (C). The measurement of angles was developed by the Babylonians, who divided circles into 360 parts and named the parts degrees. Therefore, a straight angle is 180°, a right angle is 90°, and an angle with half the measurement of a right angle would be 45°.

13. The correct answer is (A). When a person or business is insolvent, meaning that its liabilities exceed its assets and it cannot pay debts, bankruptcy may be declared. Bankruptcy can free the bankrupt's assets for equal distribution among creditors and often releases the bankrupt from liability.

14. The correct answer is (B). The phenomenon of increasing returns to scale is applied to mass production. When all inputs, such as labor and machinery, are increased by a certain amount, the amount of output will be increased still more. However, this phenomenon exists only when input is on a large scale—when organization is elaborate and the labor force is large.

15. The correct answer is (D). Pythagoras (c. 582–507 B.C.E.) was a Greek philosopher and mathematician whose followers considered him a god. They were among the first to postulate that the Earth is a sphere; they believed that the essence of all things is numbers and that all concepts could be expressed numerically.

16. The correct answer is (D). The laws of supply and demand run the marketplace. Demand can be graphed in a downward slope: its law states that when the price of a good rises, less of it is demanded; or when a large quantity of a good is on the market, its price will fall. The law of supply, when graphed, slopes upward, and states that as the price of a good rises, suppliers will put more of it on the market. Where these two graphs intersect is the price and quantity of that good at which market equilibrium is reached.

17. The correct answer is (B). In classical economic theory, inflation is said to be either *demand-pull* (when the nation's aggregate demand for goods and services outruns supply) or *cost-push* (when

prices rise due to higher labor costs, producer cartels, or other factors). In addition, the *monetarist* school of economists blames inflation on increases in the nation's supply of money. For recent bouts of inflation, such as the one in the mid-1970s, it is difficult to pinpoint a single cause.

18. The correct answer is (C). Before and during the Great Depression of the 1930s, banks failed regularly, losing depositors millions of dollars. In 1933, the FDIC (Federal Deposit Insurance Corporation) was formed to insure bank deposits up to a certain amount in the event of bank failure.

19. The correct answer is (C). A yard, equal to 0.9144 meter, is 3 feet, or 36 inches. Inches, feet, yards, and miles are English measurements of length. Much of the rest of the world uses metric measurement.

20. The correct answer is (A). Protectionism is the method of protecting national goods and services by placing tariffs or quotas on imports. The desire to lower trade deficits, provide revenues, raise wages, and equalize the costs of national and international production are some reasons given for tariffs, reasons many economists call fallacious. Tariffs can work in the short run to equalize prices and provide jobs, as well as to aid underdeveloped nations and help struggling businesses, but long-term or prohibitive tariffs draw resources away from their best use, diminish trade freedom, and lessen the chance for raising the standard of living.

21. The correct answer is (A). A mortgage is a contract between a lending association and a homeowner. Most homebuyers must take out a loan to pay for a house. The mortgage is repaid on a monthly schedule that can be spread over as much as thirty years. For a fixed-rate mortgage, payments are level over the life of the mortgage, although in the first several years, these payments consist primarily of interest, not principal payments. If the homeowner does not keep up with the mortgage payments, the lender can foreclose or force a sale of the house to pay off the loan.

22. The correct answer is (C). When a corporation needs to raise large amounts of capital, common stock can be issued and sold in part to outside investors. The corporation can borrow short-term funds from a commercial bank or in the commercial paper market and can also issue bonds. Bonds are long-term securities that promise a certain amount in interest until the time they mature, when the bond's principal is paid off. Most bonds carry credit ratings from national rating agencies. Preferred stock can be sold, too; this is less risky for buyers than common stock but riskier than bonds.

23. The correct answer is (B). Proportional income taxes take the same percentage of income from each taxpayer. Progressive income taxes take a larger percentage from those who earn more. Regressive income taxes take a smaller percentage from those who earn more. Although recent tax reforms move our system closer to the propor-

tional, and loopholes tend to move it closer to the regressive, the personal income tax system is still progressive.

24. The correct answer is (C). The federal deficit is the difference between the amount the government receives in revenues and the amount it spends. Through 1992, the budget deficit increased steadily, but it began to decrease in 1993, and continued to go down until 1998, when there was a surplus of over $69 billion. The surplus continued to grow for three years, but in 2002 the government announced a projected deficit of $165 billion. The trade deficit, another national problem, is calculated by finding the difference between the money value of imports and the money value of exports, when imports are greater.

25. The correct answer is (C). A bullish market is one in which stock averages are rising because of heavy investment and positive economic expectations for the future. A bearish market occurs when the market lacks conviction, stock prices are falling, and a recession threatens.

26. The correct answer is (A). When one person's money is used by another, the first usually calculates a percentage of the amount of money borrowed and charges the borrower accordingly. The interest rate is that percentage. It can either be fixed for the life of the loan or floating. A prime rate is the floating-rate percentage banks charge their best customers. The prime rate in the United States

soared above 20 percent in 1981, but it has not reached that level since.

27. The correct answer is (A). John Maynard Keynes (1883–1946) redefined equilibrium in the economy by showing that capitalists would provide jobs in proportion to their anticipated sales, so unemployed workers could not necessarily accept lower wages and thus become employed. In other words, because sales depend on the income of buyers, more sales cannot be anticipated by capitalists who are paying lower wages; therefore, they will not tend to hire additional workers, even at those lower wages. Adjustments, Keynes felt, were only possible through a long-range plan on the part of a government. Keynes supported public-works programs as a means for providing income and stimulating buying. The other ideas mentioned are from theories attributed to John Stuart Mill, Thomas Malthus, and Adam Smith.

28. The correct answer is (D). In the United States, 1 billion is represented as 1 followed by nine zeros. This makes it equivalent to $1,000 \times 1,000,000$, or one thousand million. In Great Britain, 1 billion is 1 followed by twelve zeros, or a million million.

29. The correct answer is (D). An economic resource is considered to be anything that goes into the production of goods and services. This includes natural resources such as land and minerals; human resources such as labor; buildings; and real capital—machinery and tools that aid in production.

Money capital is not considered an economic resource because it is not directly productive.

30. The correct answer is (C). The average of a set of values equals the sum of the values divided by the number of values. The average height of three people whose heights are 67 inches, 69 inches, and 74 inches equals:

$$\frac{67 + 69 + 74}{3} = \frac{210}{3} = 70 \text{ inches}$$

31. The correct answer is (B). An index is a figure that shows a change in value compared to a base value. The consumer price index figures the change in cost over time of a set of goods and services considered essential for an urban American family. The index shows change due to inflation and is used to determine the cost of living, which in turn is used to determine wages and social security benefits.

32. The correct answer is (C). An export is merchandise sold abroad: an import is merchandise received from abroad. A country whose imports exceed its exports is buying more from other nations than it is selling to them. Such a discrepancy over a period of time is called an "unfavorable balance of trade."

33. The correct answer is (B). Pi is a Greek letter used to represent a number equal to about 3.14. The number is the ratio of the circumference, or distance around, any circle to that circle's diameter, or longest possible distance across:

$$\pi = \frac{C}{d}$$

Pi is an irrational number; that is, it is expressed as an infinite decimal with no repetition of sets of digits. Computers have enabled mathematicians to calculate the value of pi to thousands of decimal places.

34. The correct answer is (D). The aim of the monopoly and the competitive business is the same: to maximize profits. If a business is a monopoly, it controls the supply of a product, thereby controlling the rate of its release. Most large businesses in the world today are not monopolies: government regulations see to that. They are, however, oligopolies; that is, a very few businesses control most of the release of a given product. Although a hundred businesses may create a given product, a mere two or three may control as much as 75 percent of the market.

35. The correct answer is (D). A line graph is often used to show how data change over time. This particular graph shows the population of New York State according to ten-year censuses from 1900 to 1980. The population increased through 1970, whereupon it started to decline.

36. The correct answer is (B). A recession is a mild depression. Both situations involve low prices, high unemployment, and a slowdown in business activity. Both are major parts of the business cycle, a sequence that moves from prosperity to decline to

recovery. Recession occurs more commonly today because of government controls and supports that keep many economies afloat despite conditions that would normally lead to depression.

37. The correct answer is (A). Economists usually define a recession as two quarters of declining growth, but the National Bureau of Economic Research, which officially declares recessions, often disagrees with this definition. The NBER looks at unemployment, housing, consumer spending, and other factors. Slow growth in the early 1990s, linked with rising unemployment, less spending, a drop in profits, and meager business investments led many experts to declare a recession.

38. The correct answer is (A). Credit is a promise of future payment to be made for a present purchase or loan. An individual may charge an item on a credit card, or a nation may borrow from another nation; both involve credit. Some people believe that the business cycle depends on the control of bank credit; that easy credit causes inflation and tight credit causes deflation.

39. The correct answer is (C). Tariffs may be imposed to protect domestic industry or to raise money for a government. Tariffs may discriminate against a given country; if country A charges country B twice as much as country C for the same goods, it has imposed a discriminatory tariff. They may be retaliatory; if country A objects to country B's tariffs or

trade restrictions, it may charge country B a huge tariff on any goods country B ships over.

40. The correct answer is (B). It was clear to Adam Smith (1723–1790) that self-interest motivates society. According to Smith, the greed of individuals was controlled through the market system of competition. No one who demands more money for labor or goods and services than the going rate will succeed. As demand increases, supply will increase to meet it; as demand decreases, supply decreases. Thus, individual greed is thwarted by the public will. Smith's belief that the market would regulate itself as if by an "invisible hand" led to the policy of laissez-faire economics—economic systems without government interference or control. Two hundred years and one Industrial Revolution later, this is still the policy of choice for many conservative economists.

41. The correct answer is (C). The Industrial Workers of the World was an amalgam of forty-three small labor unions joined in 1905 in Chicago under the leadership of Eugene V. Debs, Daniel De Leon, and Big Bill Haywood (1869–1928). The new union advocated direct confrontation as opposed to arbitration. Like many European unions at the time, the IWW considered the union itself the basic social unit and favored the control of the means of production by an organized working class. It reached its peak of power just before World War I. With the outbreak of war, the union leaders were jailed and accused of sedition, and the union was essentially

broken. The American Federation of Labor was formed in 1886 with Samuel Gompers (1850–1924) as president. A central conflict emerged between factions who preferred to organize around industrial units (steelworkers, autoworkers, etc.) and those who favored organization by skill (mechanics, painters, etc.). This led to a split in the federation in 1935, with John L. Lewis (1880–1969) leading the industrial faction and forming the Congress of Industrial Organizations. Lewis later pulled his United Mine Workers out of the CIO. In 1955 the CIO merged again with the AFL, forming an international amalgam now known as the AFL-CIO.

42. The correct answer is (D). A meter is the basic unit of length in the metric system. One meter is approximately equal to 3.28 feet. Two meters, therefore, is about 6.56 feet.

43. The correct answer is (D). Pure capitalism is an economic system in which private ownership and individual profit are the mainstays. The state plays a very small role in the economic system; it protects the rights of the individual by maintaining order and preventing abuses. Capitalism is also known as free enterprise, since everyone is theoretically free to compete in the market. Many things keep pure capitalism from being realized: Antitrust laws regulate growth, labor laws affect profit, corporate power minimizes the ability of smaller corporations to compete, and the evolution of a world economy that assigns corporations and nations the

rights of individuals redefines many of the terms that make up the capitalist credo.

44. The correct answer is (A). A heptagon has seven sides. In order from three sides to ten, the names of the shapes are triangle, quadrilateral, pentagon, hexagon, heptagon, octagon, nonagon, decagon. The first two are from the Latin; *triangle* means "three angles," and *quadrilateral* means "four sides." *Gon* is a Greek root meaning "angles."

45. The correct answer is (C). The Federal Trade Commission was created in 1914 to prevent illegal price-fixing agreements and other monopolistic behavior on the part of businesses. It also has a mandate to seek out and eliminate unfair or deceptive advertising and to issue cease-and-desist orders to businesses that conspire to restrain interstate trade. The other duties listed belong to the Federal Savings and Loan Insurance Corporation, the Small Business Administration, and the Social Security Administration.

46. The correct answer is (A). A subsidy may be paid in money or in property to assist a business that is considered essential to the public welfare. It may also be paid to a manufacturer or producer (such as farmers in the United States) to keep prices from being raised.

47. The correct answer is (B). A baseball team with a 4-to-1 win-loss ratio may have played five games, but it may just as easily have played ten. A ratio is a way of comparing two numbers. The team in ques-

tion won four games for every one that it lost. There is no telling from the information given how many games it played. If it played five games, it won four and lost one. If it played ten games, it won eight and lost two. If it played twenty games, it won sixteen and lost four. Ratios may be expressed in many ways. This one may be written

$$4:1, 4 \text{ to } 1, \text{ or } \frac{4}{1}.$$

48. The correct answer is (B). A standard of living is generally based on per capita income and gross national product. It states the minimum level of consumption of goods and services to which a group aspires or is accustomed, and it may involve such things as educational opportunities and luxury items. The cost of living is the cost of maintaining that standard. In the United States, the cost-of-living index has been used to determine wages, pensions, and social security benefits.

49. The correct answer is (A). A line has no endpoints; it continues infinitely. Two lines in the same plane that do not intersect are parallel. Two lines that intersect to form right angles are perpendicular.

50. The correct answer is (C). Many countries have some form of social security; in 1888, Germany was the first European country to establish a system of health insurance for workers. Some systems provide benefits from a fund paid into by workers; socialist countries require no such direct contribution. In the United States, the Social Security

Administration administers old-age, survivor's, and disability insurance, Medicare, Medicaid, and Supplemental Security Income for the disabled. Since retired people live on the money contributed by working people, as the population ages, the system faces serious deficits. The other programs mentioned are part of the Fair Labor Standards Act, the U.S. Employment Service, and the Office of Economic Opportunity.

ANSWER SHEET

TEST 1

1. Ⓐ Ⓑ Ⓒ Ⓓ   2. Ⓐ Ⓑ Ⓒ Ⓓ   3. Ⓐ Ⓑ Ⓒ Ⓓ   4. Ⓐ Ⓑ Ⓒ Ⓓ   5. Ⓐ Ⓑ Ⓒ Ⓓ
6. Ⓐ Ⓑ Ⓒ Ⓓ   7. Ⓐ Ⓑ Ⓒ Ⓓ   8. Ⓐ Ⓑ Ⓒ Ⓓ   9. Ⓐ Ⓑ Ⓒ Ⓓ   10. Ⓐ Ⓑ Ⓒ Ⓓ
11. Ⓐ Ⓑ Ⓒ Ⓓ   12. Ⓐ Ⓑ Ⓒ Ⓓ   13. Ⓐ Ⓑ Ⓒ Ⓓ   14. Ⓐ Ⓑ Ⓒ Ⓓ   15. Ⓐ Ⓑ Ⓒ Ⓓ
16. Ⓐ Ⓑ Ⓒ Ⓓ   17. Ⓐ Ⓑ Ⓒ Ⓓ   18. Ⓐ Ⓑ Ⓒ Ⓓ   19. Ⓐ Ⓑ Ⓒ Ⓓ   20. Ⓐ Ⓑ Ⓒ Ⓓ
21. Ⓐ Ⓑ Ⓒ Ⓓ   22. Ⓐ Ⓑ Ⓒ Ⓓ   23. Ⓐ Ⓑ Ⓒ Ⓓ   24. Ⓐ Ⓑ Ⓒ Ⓓ   25. Ⓐ Ⓑ Ⓒ Ⓓ
26. Ⓐ Ⓑ Ⓒ Ⓓ   27. Ⓐ Ⓑ Ⓒ Ⓓ   28. Ⓐ Ⓑ Ⓒ Ⓓ   29. Ⓐ Ⓑ Ⓒ Ⓓ   30. Ⓐ Ⓑ Ⓒ Ⓓ
31. Ⓐ Ⓑ Ⓒ Ⓓ   32. Ⓐ Ⓑ Ⓒ Ⓓ   33. Ⓐ Ⓑ Ⓒ Ⓓ   34. Ⓐ Ⓑ Ⓒ Ⓓ   35. Ⓐ Ⓑ Ⓒ Ⓓ
36. Ⓐ Ⓑ Ⓒ Ⓓ   37. Ⓐ Ⓑ Ⓒ Ⓓ   38. Ⓐ Ⓑ Ⓒ Ⓓ   39. Ⓐ Ⓑ Ⓒ Ⓓ   40. Ⓐ Ⓑ Ⓒ Ⓓ
41. Ⓐ Ⓑ Ⓒ Ⓓ   42. Ⓐ Ⓑ Ⓒ Ⓓ   43. Ⓐ Ⓑ Ⓒ Ⓓ   44. Ⓐ Ⓑ Ⓒ Ⓓ   45. Ⓐ Ⓑ Ⓒ Ⓓ
46. Ⓐ Ⓑ Ⓒ Ⓓ   47. Ⓐ Ⓑ Ⓒ Ⓓ   48. Ⓐ Ⓑ Ⓒ Ⓓ   49. Ⓐ Ⓑ Ⓒ Ⓓ   50. Ⓐ Ⓑ Ⓒ Ⓓ

ANSWER SHEET

TEST 2

1. Ⓐ Ⓑ Ⓒ Ⓓ   2. Ⓐ Ⓑ Ⓒ Ⓓ   3. Ⓐ Ⓑ Ⓒ Ⓓ   4. Ⓐ Ⓑ Ⓒ Ⓓ   5. Ⓐ Ⓑ Ⓒ Ⓓ
6. Ⓐ Ⓑ Ⓒ Ⓓ   7. Ⓐ Ⓑ Ⓒ Ⓓ   8. Ⓐ Ⓑ Ⓒ Ⓓ   9. Ⓐ Ⓑ Ⓒ Ⓓ   10. Ⓐ Ⓑ Ⓒ Ⓓ
11. Ⓐ Ⓑ Ⓒ Ⓓ   12. Ⓐ Ⓑ Ⓒ Ⓓ   13. Ⓐ Ⓑ Ⓒ Ⓓ   14. Ⓐ Ⓑ Ⓒ Ⓓ   15. Ⓐ Ⓑ Ⓒ Ⓓ
16. Ⓐ Ⓑ Ⓒ Ⓓ   17. Ⓐ Ⓑ Ⓒ Ⓓ   18. Ⓐ Ⓑ Ⓒ Ⓓ   19. Ⓐ Ⓑ Ⓒ Ⓓ   20. Ⓐ Ⓑ Ⓒ Ⓓ
21. Ⓐ Ⓑ Ⓒ Ⓓ   22. Ⓐ Ⓑ Ⓒ Ⓓ   23. Ⓐ Ⓑ Ⓒ Ⓓ   24. Ⓐ Ⓑ Ⓒ Ⓓ   25. Ⓐ Ⓑ Ⓒ Ⓓ
26. Ⓐ Ⓑ Ⓒ Ⓓ   27. Ⓐ Ⓑ Ⓒ Ⓓ   28. Ⓐ Ⓑ Ⓒ Ⓓ   29. Ⓐ Ⓑ Ⓒ Ⓓ   30. Ⓐ Ⓑ Ⓒ Ⓓ
31. Ⓐ Ⓑ Ⓒ Ⓓ   32. Ⓐ Ⓑ Ⓒ Ⓓ   33. Ⓐ Ⓑ Ⓒ Ⓓ   34. Ⓐ Ⓑ Ⓒ Ⓓ   35. Ⓐ Ⓑ Ⓒ Ⓓ
36. Ⓐ Ⓑ Ⓒ Ⓓ   37. Ⓐ Ⓑ Ⓒ Ⓓ   38. Ⓐ Ⓑ Ⓒ Ⓓ   39. Ⓐ Ⓑ Ⓒ Ⓓ   40. Ⓐ Ⓑ Ⓒ Ⓓ
41. Ⓐ Ⓑ Ⓒ Ⓓ   42. Ⓐ Ⓑ Ⓒ Ⓓ   43. Ⓐ Ⓑ Ⓒ Ⓓ   44. Ⓐ Ⓑ Ⓒ Ⓓ   45. Ⓐ Ⓑ Ⓒ Ⓓ
46. Ⓐ Ⓑ Ⓒ Ⓓ   47. Ⓐ Ⓑ Ⓒ Ⓓ   48. Ⓐ Ⓑ Ⓒ Ⓓ   49. Ⓐ Ⓑ Ⓒ Ⓓ   50. Ⓐ Ⓑ Ⓒ Ⓓ

ANSWER SHEET

TEST 3

1. Ⓐ Ⓑ Ⓒ Ⓓ 2. Ⓐ Ⓑ Ⓒ Ⓓ 3. Ⓐ Ⓑ Ⓒ Ⓓ 4. Ⓐ Ⓑ Ⓒ Ⓓ 5. Ⓐ Ⓑ Ⓒ Ⓓ
6. Ⓐ Ⓑ Ⓒ Ⓓ 7. Ⓐ Ⓑ Ⓒ Ⓓ 8. Ⓐ Ⓑ Ⓒ Ⓓ 9. Ⓐ Ⓑ Ⓒ Ⓓ 10. Ⓐ Ⓑ Ⓒ Ⓓ
11. Ⓐ Ⓑ Ⓒ Ⓓ 12. Ⓐ Ⓑ Ⓒ Ⓓ 13. Ⓐ Ⓑ Ⓒ Ⓓ 14. Ⓐ Ⓑ Ⓒ Ⓓ 15. Ⓐ Ⓑ Ⓒ Ⓓ
16. Ⓐ Ⓑ Ⓒ Ⓓ 17. Ⓐ Ⓑ Ⓒ Ⓓ 18. Ⓐ Ⓑ Ⓒ Ⓓ 19. Ⓐ Ⓑ Ⓒ Ⓓ 20. Ⓐ Ⓑ Ⓒ Ⓓ
21. Ⓐ Ⓑ Ⓒ Ⓓ 22. Ⓐ Ⓑ Ⓒ Ⓓ 23. Ⓐ Ⓑ Ⓒ Ⓓ 24. Ⓐ Ⓑ Ⓒ Ⓓ 25. Ⓐ Ⓑ Ⓒ Ⓓ
26. Ⓐ Ⓑ Ⓒ Ⓓ 27. Ⓐ Ⓑ Ⓒ Ⓓ 28. Ⓐ Ⓑ Ⓒ Ⓓ 29. Ⓐ Ⓑ Ⓒ Ⓓ 30. Ⓐ Ⓑ Ⓒ Ⓓ
31. Ⓐ Ⓑ Ⓒ Ⓓ 32. Ⓐ Ⓑ Ⓒ Ⓓ 33. Ⓐ Ⓑ Ⓒ Ⓓ 34. Ⓐ Ⓑ Ⓒ Ⓓ 35. Ⓐ Ⓑ Ⓒ Ⓓ
36. Ⓐ Ⓑ Ⓒ Ⓓ 37. Ⓐ Ⓑ Ⓒ Ⓓ 38. Ⓐ Ⓑ Ⓒ Ⓓ 39. Ⓐ Ⓑ Ⓒ Ⓓ 40. Ⓐ Ⓑ Ⓒ Ⓓ
41. Ⓐ Ⓑ Ⓒ Ⓓ 42. Ⓐ Ⓑ Ⓒ Ⓓ 43. Ⓐ Ⓑ Ⓒ Ⓓ 44. Ⓐ Ⓑ Ⓒ Ⓓ 45. Ⓐ Ⓑ Ⓒ Ⓓ
46. Ⓐ Ⓑ Ⓒ Ⓓ 47. Ⓐ Ⓑ Ⓒ Ⓓ 48. Ⓐ Ⓑ Ⓒ Ⓓ 49. Ⓐ Ⓑ Ⓒ Ⓓ 50. Ⓐ Ⓑ Ⓒ Ⓓ

ANSWER SHEET

TEST 4

1. Ⓐ Ⓑ Ⓒ Ⓓ 2. Ⓐ Ⓑ Ⓒ Ⓓ 3. Ⓐ Ⓑ Ⓒ Ⓓ 4. Ⓐ Ⓑ Ⓒ Ⓓ 5. Ⓐ Ⓑ Ⓒ Ⓓ
6. Ⓐ Ⓑ Ⓒ Ⓓ 7. Ⓐ Ⓑ Ⓒ Ⓓ 8. Ⓐ Ⓑ Ⓒ Ⓓ 9. Ⓐ Ⓑ Ⓒ Ⓓ 10. Ⓐ Ⓑ Ⓒ Ⓓ
11. Ⓐ Ⓑ Ⓒ Ⓓ 12. Ⓐ Ⓑ Ⓒ Ⓓ 13. Ⓐ Ⓑ Ⓒ Ⓓ 14. Ⓐ Ⓑ Ⓒ Ⓓ 15. Ⓐ Ⓑ Ⓒ Ⓓ
16. Ⓐ Ⓑ Ⓒ Ⓓ 17. Ⓐ Ⓑ Ⓒ Ⓓ 18. Ⓐ Ⓑ Ⓒ Ⓓ 19. Ⓐ Ⓑ Ⓒ Ⓓ 20. Ⓐ Ⓑ Ⓒ Ⓓ
21. Ⓐ Ⓑ Ⓒ Ⓓ 22. Ⓐ Ⓑ Ⓒ Ⓓ 23. Ⓐ Ⓑ Ⓒ Ⓓ 24. Ⓐ Ⓑ Ⓒ Ⓓ 25. Ⓐ Ⓑ Ⓒ Ⓓ
26. Ⓐ Ⓑ Ⓒ Ⓓ 27. Ⓐ Ⓑ Ⓒ Ⓓ 28. Ⓐ Ⓑ Ⓒ Ⓓ 29. Ⓐ Ⓑ Ⓒ Ⓓ 30. Ⓐ Ⓑ Ⓒ Ⓓ
31. Ⓐ Ⓑ Ⓒ Ⓓ 32. Ⓐ Ⓑ Ⓒ Ⓓ 33. Ⓐ Ⓑ Ⓒ Ⓓ 34. Ⓐ Ⓑ Ⓒ Ⓓ 35. Ⓐ Ⓑ Ⓒ Ⓓ
36. Ⓐ Ⓑ Ⓒ Ⓓ 37. Ⓐ Ⓑ Ⓒ Ⓓ 38. Ⓐ Ⓑ Ⓒ Ⓓ 39. Ⓐ Ⓑ Ⓒ Ⓓ 40. Ⓐ Ⓑ Ⓒ Ⓓ
41. Ⓐ Ⓑ Ⓒ Ⓓ 42. Ⓐ Ⓑ Ⓒ Ⓓ 43. Ⓐ Ⓑ Ⓒ Ⓓ 44. Ⓐ Ⓑ Ⓒ Ⓓ 45. Ⓐ Ⓑ Ⓒ Ⓓ
46. Ⓐ Ⓑ Ⓒ Ⓓ 47. Ⓐ Ⓑ Ⓒ Ⓓ 48. Ⓐ Ⓑ Ⓒ Ⓓ 49. Ⓐ Ⓑ Ⓒ Ⓓ 50. Ⓐ Ⓑ Ⓒ Ⓓ

ANSWER SHEET

TEST 5

1. Ⓐ Ⓑ Ⓒ Ⓓ 2. Ⓐ Ⓑ Ⓒ Ⓓ 3. Ⓐ Ⓑ Ⓒ Ⓓ 4. Ⓐ Ⓑ Ⓒ Ⓓ 5. Ⓐ Ⓑ Ⓒ Ⓓ
6. Ⓐ Ⓑ Ⓒ Ⓓ 7. Ⓐ Ⓑ Ⓒ Ⓓ 8. Ⓐ Ⓑ Ⓒ Ⓓ 9. Ⓐ Ⓑ Ⓒ Ⓓ 10. Ⓐ Ⓑ Ⓒ Ⓓ
11. Ⓐ Ⓑ Ⓒ Ⓓ 12. Ⓐ Ⓑ Ⓒ Ⓓ 13. Ⓐ Ⓑ Ⓒ Ⓓ 14. Ⓐ Ⓑ Ⓒ Ⓓ 15. Ⓐ Ⓑ Ⓒ Ⓓ
16. Ⓐ Ⓑ Ⓒ Ⓓ 17. Ⓐ Ⓑ Ⓒ Ⓓ 18. Ⓐ Ⓑ Ⓒ Ⓓ 19. Ⓐ Ⓑ Ⓒ Ⓓ 20. Ⓐ Ⓑ Ⓒ Ⓓ
21. Ⓐ Ⓑ Ⓒ Ⓓ 22. Ⓐ Ⓑ Ⓒ Ⓓ 23. Ⓐ Ⓑ Ⓒ Ⓓ 24. Ⓐ Ⓑ Ⓒ Ⓓ 25. Ⓐ Ⓑ Ⓒ Ⓓ
26. Ⓐ Ⓑ Ⓒ Ⓓ 27. Ⓐ Ⓑ Ⓒ Ⓓ 28. Ⓐ Ⓑ Ⓒ Ⓓ 29. Ⓐ Ⓑ Ⓒ Ⓓ 30. Ⓐ Ⓑ Ⓒ Ⓓ
31. Ⓐ Ⓑ Ⓒ Ⓓ 32. Ⓐ Ⓑ Ⓒ Ⓓ 33. Ⓐ Ⓑ Ⓒ Ⓓ 34. Ⓐ Ⓑ Ⓒ Ⓓ 35. Ⓐ Ⓑ Ⓒ Ⓓ
36. Ⓐ Ⓑ Ⓒ Ⓓ 37. Ⓐ Ⓑ Ⓒ Ⓓ 38. Ⓐ Ⓑ Ⓒ Ⓓ 39. Ⓐ Ⓑ Ⓒ Ⓓ 40. Ⓐ Ⓑ Ⓒ Ⓓ
41. Ⓐ Ⓑ Ⓒ Ⓓ 42. Ⓐ Ⓑ Ⓒ Ⓓ 43. Ⓐ Ⓑ Ⓒ Ⓓ 44. Ⓐ Ⓑ Ⓒ Ⓓ 45. Ⓐ Ⓑ Ⓒ Ⓓ
46. Ⓐ Ⓑ Ⓒ Ⓓ 47. Ⓐ Ⓑ Ⓒ Ⓓ 48. Ⓐ Ⓑ Ⓒ Ⓓ 49. Ⓐ Ⓑ Ⓒ Ⓓ 50. Ⓐ Ⓑ Ⓒ Ⓓ

ANSWER SHEET

TEST 6

1. Ⓐ Ⓑ Ⓒ Ⓓ 2. Ⓐ Ⓑ Ⓒ Ⓓ 3. Ⓐ Ⓑ Ⓒ Ⓓ 4. Ⓐ Ⓑ Ⓒ Ⓓ 5. Ⓐ Ⓑ Ⓒ Ⓓ
6. Ⓐ Ⓑ Ⓒ Ⓓ 7. Ⓐ Ⓑ Ⓒ Ⓓ 8. Ⓐ Ⓑ Ⓒ Ⓓ 9. Ⓐ Ⓑ Ⓒ Ⓓ 10. Ⓐ Ⓑ Ⓒ Ⓓ
11. Ⓐ Ⓑ Ⓒ Ⓓ 12. Ⓐ Ⓑ Ⓒ Ⓓ 13. Ⓐ Ⓑ Ⓒ Ⓓ 14. Ⓐ Ⓑ Ⓒ Ⓓ 15. Ⓐ Ⓑ Ⓒ Ⓓ
16. Ⓐ Ⓑ Ⓒ Ⓓ 17. Ⓐ Ⓑ Ⓒ Ⓓ 18. Ⓐ Ⓑ Ⓒ Ⓓ 19. Ⓐ Ⓑ Ⓒ Ⓓ 20. Ⓐ Ⓑ Ⓒ Ⓓ
21. Ⓐ Ⓑ Ⓒ Ⓓ 22. Ⓐ Ⓑ Ⓒ Ⓓ 23. Ⓐ Ⓑ Ⓒ Ⓓ 24. Ⓐ Ⓑ Ⓒ Ⓓ 25. Ⓐ Ⓑ Ⓒ Ⓓ
26. Ⓐ Ⓑ Ⓒ Ⓓ 27. Ⓐ Ⓑ Ⓒ Ⓓ 28. Ⓐ Ⓑ Ⓒ Ⓓ 29. Ⓐ Ⓑ Ⓒ Ⓓ 30. Ⓐ Ⓑ Ⓒ Ⓓ
31. Ⓐ Ⓑ Ⓒ Ⓓ 32. Ⓐ Ⓑ Ⓒ Ⓓ 33. Ⓐ Ⓑ Ⓒ Ⓓ 34. Ⓐ Ⓑ Ⓒ Ⓓ 35. Ⓐ Ⓑ Ⓒ Ⓓ
36. Ⓐ Ⓑ Ⓒ Ⓓ 37. Ⓐ Ⓑ Ⓒ Ⓓ 38. Ⓐ Ⓑ Ⓒ Ⓓ 39. Ⓐ Ⓑ Ⓒ Ⓓ 40. Ⓐ Ⓑ Ⓒ Ⓓ
41. Ⓐ Ⓑ Ⓒ Ⓓ 42. Ⓐ Ⓑ Ⓒ Ⓓ 43. Ⓐ Ⓑ Ⓒ Ⓓ 44. Ⓐ Ⓑ Ⓒ Ⓓ 45. Ⓐ Ⓑ Ⓒ Ⓓ
46. Ⓐ Ⓑ Ⓒ Ⓓ 47. Ⓐ Ⓑ Ⓒ Ⓓ 48. Ⓐ Ⓑ Ⓒ Ⓓ 49. Ⓐ Ⓑ Ⓒ Ⓓ 50. Ⓐ Ⓑ Ⓒ Ⓓ

ANSWER SHEET

TEST 7

1. Ⓐ Ⓑ Ⓒ Ⓓ 2. Ⓐ Ⓑ Ⓒ Ⓓ 3. Ⓐ Ⓑ Ⓒ Ⓓ 4. Ⓐ Ⓑ Ⓒ Ⓓ 5. Ⓐ Ⓑ Ⓒ Ⓓ
6. Ⓐ Ⓑ Ⓒ Ⓓ 7. Ⓐ Ⓑ Ⓒ Ⓓ 8. Ⓐ Ⓑ Ⓒ Ⓓ 9. Ⓐ Ⓑ Ⓒ Ⓓ 10. Ⓐ Ⓑ Ⓒ Ⓓ
11. Ⓐ Ⓑ Ⓒ Ⓓ 12. Ⓐ Ⓑ Ⓒ Ⓓ 13. Ⓐ Ⓑ Ⓒ Ⓓ 14. Ⓐ Ⓑ Ⓒ Ⓓ 15. Ⓐ Ⓑ Ⓒ Ⓓ
16. Ⓐ Ⓑ Ⓒ Ⓓ 17. Ⓐ Ⓑ Ⓒ Ⓓ 18. Ⓐ Ⓑ Ⓒ Ⓓ 19. Ⓐ Ⓑ Ⓒ Ⓓ 20. Ⓐ Ⓑ Ⓒ Ⓓ
21. Ⓐ Ⓑ Ⓒ Ⓓ 22. Ⓐ Ⓑ Ⓒ Ⓓ 23. Ⓐ Ⓑ Ⓒ Ⓓ 24. Ⓐ Ⓑ Ⓒ Ⓓ 25. Ⓐ Ⓑ Ⓒ Ⓓ
26. Ⓐ Ⓑ Ⓒ Ⓓ 27. Ⓐ Ⓑ Ⓒ Ⓓ 28. Ⓐ Ⓑ Ⓒ Ⓓ 29. Ⓐ Ⓑ Ⓒ Ⓓ 30. Ⓐ Ⓑ Ⓒ Ⓓ
31. Ⓐ Ⓑ Ⓒ Ⓓ 32. Ⓐ Ⓑ Ⓒ Ⓓ 33. Ⓐ Ⓑ Ⓒ Ⓓ 34. Ⓐ Ⓑ Ⓒ Ⓓ 35. Ⓐ Ⓑ Ⓒ Ⓓ
36. Ⓐ Ⓑ Ⓒ Ⓓ 37. Ⓐ Ⓑ Ⓒ Ⓓ 38. Ⓐ Ⓑ Ⓒ Ⓓ 39. Ⓐ Ⓑ Ⓒ Ⓓ 40. Ⓐ Ⓑ Ⓒ Ⓓ
41. Ⓐ Ⓑ Ⓒ Ⓓ 42. Ⓐ Ⓑ Ⓒ Ⓓ 43. Ⓐ Ⓑ Ⓒ Ⓓ 44. Ⓐ Ⓑ Ⓒ Ⓓ 45. Ⓐ Ⓑ Ⓒ Ⓓ
46. Ⓐ Ⓑ Ⓒ Ⓓ 47. Ⓐ Ⓑ Ⓒ Ⓓ 48. Ⓐ Ⓑ Ⓒ Ⓓ 49. Ⓐ Ⓑ Ⓒ Ⓓ 50. Ⓐ Ⓑ Ⓒ Ⓓ

ANSWER SHEET

TEST 8

1. Ⓐ Ⓑ Ⓒ Ⓓ 2. Ⓐ Ⓑ Ⓒ Ⓓ 3. Ⓐ Ⓑ Ⓒ Ⓓ 4. Ⓐ Ⓑ Ⓒ Ⓓ 5. Ⓐ Ⓑ Ⓒ Ⓓ
6. Ⓐ Ⓑ Ⓒ Ⓓ 7. Ⓐ Ⓑ Ⓒ Ⓓ 8. Ⓐ Ⓑ Ⓒ Ⓓ 9. Ⓐ Ⓑ Ⓒ Ⓓ 10. Ⓐ Ⓑ Ⓒ Ⓓ
11. Ⓐ Ⓑ Ⓒ Ⓓ 12. Ⓐ Ⓑ Ⓒ Ⓓ 13. Ⓐ Ⓑ Ⓒ Ⓓ 14. Ⓐ Ⓑ Ⓒ Ⓓ 15. Ⓐ Ⓑ Ⓒ Ⓓ
16. Ⓐ Ⓑ Ⓒ Ⓓ 17. Ⓐ Ⓑ Ⓒ Ⓓ 18. Ⓐ Ⓑ Ⓒ Ⓓ 19. Ⓐ Ⓑ Ⓒ Ⓓ 20. Ⓐ Ⓑ Ⓒ Ⓓ
21. Ⓐ Ⓑ Ⓒ Ⓓ 22. Ⓐ Ⓑ Ⓒ Ⓓ 23. Ⓐ Ⓑ Ⓒ Ⓓ 24. Ⓐ Ⓑ Ⓒ Ⓓ 25. Ⓐ Ⓑ Ⓒ Ⓓ
26. Ⓐ Ⓑ Ⓒ Ⓓ 27. Ⓐ Ⓑ Ⓒ Ⓓ 28. Ⓐ Ⓑ Ⓒ Ⓓ 29. Ⓐ Ⓑ Ⓒ Ⓓ 30. Ⓐ Ⓑ Ⓒ Ⓓ
31. Ⓐ Ⓑ Ⓒ Ⓓ 32. Ⓐ Ⓑ Ⓒ Ⓓ 33. Ⓐ Ⓑ Ⓒ Ⓓ 34. Ⓐ Ⓑ Ⓒ Ⓓ 35. Ⓐ Ⓑ Ⓒ Ⓓ
36. Ⓐ Ⓑ Ⓒ Ⓓ 37. Ⓐ Ⓑ Ⓒ Ⓓ 38. Ⓐ Ⓑ Ⓒ Ⓓ 39. Ⓐ Ⓑ Ⓒ Ⓓ 40. Ⓐ Ⓑ Ⓒ Ⓓ
41. Ⓐ Ⓑ Ⓒ Ⓓ 42. Ⓐ Ⓑ Ⓒ Ⓓ 43. Ⓐ Ⓑ Ⓒ Ⓓ 44. Ⓐ Ⓑ Ⓒ Ⓓ 45. Ⓐ Ⓑ Ⓒ Ⓓ
46. Ⓐ Ⓑ Ⓒ Ⓓ 47. Ⓐ Ⓑ Ⓒ Ⓓ 48. Ⓐ Ⓑ Ⓒ Ⓓ 49. Ⓐ Ⓑ Ⓒ Ⓓ 50. Ⓐ Ⓑ Ⓒ Ⓓ

ANSWER SHEET

TEST 9

1.Ⓐ Ⓑ Ⓒ Ⓓ	2.Ⓐ Ⓑ Ⓒ Ⓓ	3.Ⓐ Ⓑ Ⓒ Ⓓ	4.Ⓐ Ⓑ Ⓒ Ⓓ	5.Ⓐ Ⓑ Ⓒ Ⓓ
6.Ⓐ Ⓑ Ⓒ Ⓓ	7.Ⓐ Ⓑ Ⓒ Ⓓ	8.Ⓐ Ⓑ Ⓒ Ⓓ	9.Ⓐ Ⓑ Ⓒ Ⓓ	10.Ⓐ Ⓑ Ⓒ Ⓓ
11.Ⓐ Ⓑ Ⓒ Ⓓ	12.Ⓐ Ⓑ Ⓒ Ⓓ	13.Ⓐ Ⓑ Ⓒ Ⓓ	14.Ⓐ Ⓑ Ⓒ Ⓓ	15.Ⓐ Ⓑ Ⓒ Ⓓ
16.Ⓐ Ⓑ Ⓒ Ⓓ	17.Ⓐ Ⓑ Ⓒ Ⓓ	18.Ⓐ Ⓑ Ⓒ Ⓓ	19.Ⓐ Ⓑ Ⓒ Ⓓ	20.Ⓐ Ⓑ Ⓒ Ⓓ
21.Ⓐ Ⓑ Ⓒ Ⓓ	22.Ⓐ Ⓑ Ⓒ Ⓓ	23.Ⓐ Ⓑ Ⓒ Ⓓ	24.Ⓐ Ⓑ Ⓒ Ⓓ	25.Ⓐ Ⓑ Ⓒ Ⓓ
26.Ⓐ Ⓑ Ⓒ Ⓓ	27.Ⓐ Ⓑ Ⓒ Ⓓ	28.Ⓐ Ⓑ Ⓒ Ⓓ	29.Ⓐ Ⓑ Ⓒ Ⓓ	30.Ⓐ Ⓑ Ⓒ Ⓓ
31.Ⓐ Ⓑ Ⓒ Ⓓ	32.Ⓐ Ⓑ Ⓒ Ⓓ	33.Ⓐ Ⓑ Ⓒ Ⓓ	34.Ⓐ Ⓑ Ⓒ Ⓓ	35.Ⓐ Ⓑ Ⓒ Ⓓ
36.Ⓐ Ⓑ Ⓒ Ⓓ	37.Ⓐ Ⓑ Ⓒ Ⓓ	38.Ⓐ Ⓑ Ⓒ Ⓓ	39.Ⓐ Ⓑ Ⓒ Ⓓ	40.Ⓐ Ⓑ Ⓒ Ⓓ
41.Ⓐ Ⓑ Ⓒ Ⓓ	42.Ⓐ Ⓑ Ⓒ Ⓓ	43.Ⓐ Ⓑ Ⓒ Ⓓ	44.Ⓐ Ⓑ Ⓒ Ⓓ	45.Ⓐ Ⓑ Ⓒ Ⓓ
46.Ⓐ Ⓑ Ⓒ Ⓓ	47.Ⓐ Ⓑ Ⓒ Ⓓ	48.Ⓐ Ⓑ Ⓒ Ⓓ	49.Ⓐ Ⓑ Ⓒ Ⓓ	50.Ⓐ Ⓑ Ⓒ Ⓓ

ANSWER SHEET

TEST 10

1.Ⓐ Ⓑ Ⓒ Ⓓ	2.Ⓐ Ⓑ Ⓒ Ⓓ	3.Ⓐ Ⓑ Ⓒ Ⓓ	4.Ⓐ Ⓑ Ⓒ Ⓓ	5.Ⓐ Ⓑ Ⓒ Ⓓ
6.Ⓐ Ⓑ Ⓒ Ⓓ	7.Ⓐ Ⓑ Ⓒ Ⓓ	8.Ⓐ Ⓑ Ⓒ Ⓓ	9.Ⓐ Ⓑ Ⓒ Ⓓ	10.Ⓐ Ⓑ Ⓒ Ⓓ
11.Ⓐ Ⓑ Ⓒ Ⓓ	12.Ⓐ Ⓑ Ⓒ Ⓓ	13.Ⓐ Ⓑ Ⓒ Ⓓ	14.Ⓐ Ⓑ Ⓒ Ⓓ	15.Ⓐ Ⓑ Ⓒ Ⓓ
16.Ⓐ Ⓑ Ⓒ Ⓓ	17.Ⓐ Ⓑ Ⓒ Ⓓ	18.Ⓐ Ⓑ Ⓒ Ⓓ	19.Ⓐ Ⓑ Ⓒ Ⓓ	20.Ⓐ Ⓑ Ⓒ Ⓓ
21.Ⓐ Ⓑ Ⓒ Ⓓ	22.Ⓐ Ⓑ Ⓒ Ⓓ	23.Ⓐ Ⓑ Ⓒ Ⓓ	24.Ⓐ Ⓑ Ⓒ Ⓓ	25.Ⓐ Ⓑ Ⓒ Ⓓ
26.Ⓐ Ⓑ Ⓒ Ⓓ	27.Ⓐ Ⓑ Ⓒ Ⓓ	28.Ⓐ Ⓑ Ⓒ Ⓓ	29.Ⓐ Ⓑ Ⓒ Ⓓ	30.Ⓐ Ⓑ Ⓒ Ⓓ
31.Ⓐ Ⓑ Ⓒ Ⓓ	32.Ⓐ Ⓑ Ⓒ Ⓓ	33.Ⓐ Ⓑ Ⓒ Ⓓ	34.Ⓐ Ⓑ Ⓒ Ⓓ	35.Ⓐ Ⓑ Ⓒ Ⓓ
36.Ⓐ Ⓑ Ⓒ Ⓓ	37.Ⓐ Ⓑ Ⓒ Ⓓ	38.Ⓐ Ⓑ Ⓒ Ⓓ	39.Ⓐ Ⓑ Ⓒ Ⓓ	40.Ⓐ Ⓑ Ⓒ Ⓓ
41.Ⓐ Ⓑ Ⓒ Ⓓ	42.Ⓐ Ⓑ Ⓒ Ⓓ	43.Ⓐ Ⓑ Ⓒ Ⓓ	44.Ⓐ Ⓑ Ⓒ Ⓓ	45.Ⓐ Ⓑ Ⓒ Ⓓ
46.Ⓐ Ⓑ Ⓒ Ⓓ	47.Ⓐ Ⓑ Ⓒ Ⓓ	48.Ⓐ Ⓑ Ⓒ Ⓓ	49.Ⓐ Ⓑ Ⓒ Ⓓ	50.Ⓐ Ⓑ Ⓒ Ⓓ

ANSWER SHEET

TEST 11

1. Ⓐ Ⓑ Ⓒ Ⓓ   2. Ⓐ Ⓑ Ⓒ Ⓓ   3. Ⓐ Ⓑ Ⓒ Ⓓ   4. Ⓐ Ⓑ Ⓒ Ⓓ   5. Ⓐ Ⓑ Ⓒ Ⓓ
6. Ⓐ Ⓑ Ⓒ Ⓓ   7. Ⓐ Ⓑ Ⓒ Ⓓ   8. Ⓐ Ⓑ Ⓒ Ⓓ   9. Ⓐ Ⓑ Ⓒ Ⓓ   10. Ⓐ Ⓑ Ⓒ Ⓓ
11. Ⓐ Ⓑ Ⓒ Ⓓ   12. Ⓐ Ⓑ Ⓒ Ⓓ   13. Ⓐ Ⓑ Ⓒ Ⓓ   14. Ⓐ Ⓑ Ⓒ Ⓓ   15. Ⓐ Ⓑ Ⓒ Ⓓ
16. Ⓐ Ⓑ Ⓒ Ⓓ   17. Ⓐ Ⓑ Ⓒ Ⓓ   18. Ⓐ Ⓑ Ⓒ Ⓓ   19. Ⓐ Ⓑ Ⓒ Ⓓ   20. Ⓐ Ⓑ Ⓒ Ⓓ
21. Ⓐ Ⓑ Ⓒ Ⓓ   22. Ⓐ Ⓑ Ⓒ Ⓓ   23. Ⓐ Ⓑ Ⓒ Ⓓ   24. Ⓐ Ⓑ Ⓒ Ⓓ   25. Ⓐ Ⓑ Ⓒ Ⓓ
26. Ⓐ Ⓑ Ⓒ Ⓓ   27. Ⓐ Ⓑ Ⓒ Ⓓ   28. Ⓐ Ⓑ Ⓒ Ⓓ   29. Ⓐ Ⓑ Ⓒ Ⓓ   30. Ⓐ Ⓑ Ⓒ Ⓓ
31. Ⓐ Ⓑ Ⓒ Ⓓ   32. Ⓐ Ⓑ Ⓒ Ⓓ   33. Ⓐ Ⓑ Ⓒ Ⓓ   34. Ⓐ Ⓑ Ⓒ Ⓓ   35. Ⓐ Ⓑ Ⓒ Ⓓ
36. Ⓐ Ⓑ Ⓒ Ⓓ   37. Ⓐ Ⓑ Ⓒ Ⓓ   38. Ⓐ Ⓑ Ⓒ Ⓓ   39. Ⓐ Ⓑ Ⓒ Ⓓ   40. Ⓐ Ⓑ Ⓒ Ⓓ
41. Ⓐ Ⓑ Ⓒ Ⓓ   42. Ⓐ Ⓑ Ⓒ Ⓓ   43. Ⓐ Ⓑ Ⓒ Ⓓ   44. Ⓐ Ⓑ Ⓒ Ⓓ   45. Ⓐ Ⓑ Ⓒ Ⓓ
46. Ⓐ Ⓑ Ⓒ Ⓓ   47. Ⓐ Ⓑ Ⓒ Ⓓ   48. Ⓐ Ⓑ Ⓒ Ⓓ   49. Ⓐ Ⓑ Ⓒ Ⓓ   50. Ⓐ Ⓑ Ⓒ Ⓓ

ANSWER SHEET

TEST 12

1. Ⓐ Ⓑ Ⓒ Ⓓ   2. Ⓐ Ⓑ Ⓒ Ⓓ   3. Ⓐ Ⓑ Ⓒ Ⓓ   4. Ⓐ Ⓑ Ⓒ Ⓓ   5. Ⓐ Ⓑ Ⓒ Ⓓ
6. Ⓐ Ⓑ Ⓒ Ⓓ   7. Ⓐ Ⓑ Ⓒ Ⓓ   8. Ⓐ Ⓑ Ⓒ Ⓓ   9. Ⓐ Ⓑ Ⓒ Ⓓ   10. Ⓐ Ⓑ Ⓒ Ⓓ
11. Ⓐ Ⓑ Ⓒ Ⓓ   12. Ⓐ Ⓑ Ⓒ Ⓓ   13. Ⓐ Ⓑ Ⓒ Ⓓ   14. Ⓐ Ⓑ Ⓒ Ⓓ   15. Ⓐ Ⓑ Ⓒ Ⓓ
16. Ⓐ Ⓑ Ⓒ Ⓓ   17. Ⓐ Ⓑ Ⓒ Ⓓ   18. Ⓐ Ⓑ Ⓒ Ⓓ   19. Ⓐ Ⓑ Ⓒ Ⓓ   20. Ⓐ Ⓑ Ⓒ Ⓓ
21. Ⓐ Ⓑ Ⓒ Ⓓ   22. Ⓐ Ⓑ Ⓒ Ⓓ   23. Ⓐ Ⓑ Ⓒ Ⓓ   24. Ⓐ Ⓑ Ⓒ Ⓓ   25. Ⓐ Ⓑ Ⓒ Ⓓ
26. Ⓐ Ⓑ Ⓒ Ⓓ   27. Ⓐ Ⓑ Ⓒ Ⓓ   28. Ⓐ Ⓑ Ⓒ Ⓓ   29. Ⓐ Ⓑ Ⓒ Ⓓ   30. Ⓐ Ⓑ Ⓒ Ⓓ
31. Ⓐ Ⓑ Ⓒ Ⓓ   32. Ⓐ Ⓑ Ⓒ Ⓓ   33. Ⓐ Ⓑ Ⓒ Ⓓ   34. Ⓐ Ⓑ Ⓒ Ⓓ   35. Ⓐ Ⓑ Ⓒ Ⓓ
36. Ⓐ Ⓑ Ⓒ Ⓓ   37. Ⓐ Ⓑ Ⓒ Ⓓ   38. Ⓐ Ⓑ Ⓒ Ⓓ   39. Ⓐ Ⓑ Ⓒ Ⓓ   40. Ⓐ Ⓑ Ⓒ Ⓓ
41. Ⓐ Ⓑ Ⓒ Ⓓ   42. Ⓐ Ⓑ Ⓒ Ⓓ   43. Ⓐ Ⓑ Ⓒ Ⓓ   44. Ⓐ Ⓑ Ⓒ Ⓓ   45. Ⓐ Ⓑ Ⓒ Ⓓ
46. Ⓐ Ⓑ Ⓒ Ⓓ   47. Ⓐ Ⓑ Ⓒ Ⓓ   48. Ⓐ Ⓑ Ⓒ Ⓓ   49. Ⓐ Ⓑ Ⓒ Ⓓ   50. Ⓐ Ⓑ Ⓒ Ⓓ

ANSWER SHEET

TEST 13

1. Ⓐ Ⓑ Ⓒ Ⓓ   2. Ⓐ Ⓑ Ⓒ Ⓓ   3. Ⓐ Ⓑ Ⓒ Ⓓ   4. Ⓐ Ⓑ Ⓒ Ⓓ   5. Ⓐ Ⓑ Ⓒ Ⓓ
6. Ⓐ Ⓑ Ⓒ Ⓓ   7. Ⓐ Ⓑ Ⓒ Ⓓ   8. Ⓐ Ⓑ Ⓒ Ⓓ   9. Ⓐ Ⓑ Ⓒ Ⓓ   10. Ⓐ Ⓑ Ⓒ Ⓓ
11. Ⓐ Ⓑ Ⓒ Ⓓ   12. Ⓐ Ⓑ Ⓒ Ⓓ   13. Ⓐ Ⓑ Ⓒ Ⓓ   14. Ⓐ Ⓑ Ⓒ Ⓓ   15. Ⓐ Ⓑ Ⓒ Ⓓ
16. Ⓐ Ⓑ Ⓒ Ⓓ   17. Ⓐ Ⓑ Ⓒ Ⓓ   18. Ⓐ Ⓑ Ⓒ Ⓓ   19. Ⓐ Ⓑ Ⓒ Ⓓ   20. Ⓐ Ⓑ Ⓒ Ⓓ
21. Ⓐ Ⓑ Ⓒ Ⓓ   22. Ⓐ Ⓑ Ⓒ Ⓓ   23. Ⓐ Ⓑ Ⓒ Ⓓ   24. Ⓐ Ⓑ Ⓒ Ⓓ   25. Ⓐ Ⓑ Ⓒ Ⓓ
26. Ⓐ Ⓑ Ⓒ Ⓓ   27. Ⓐ Ⓑ Ⓒ Ⓓ   28. Ⓐ Ⓑ Ⓒ Ⓓ   29. Ⓐ Ⓑ Ⓒ Ⓓ   30. Ⓐ Ⓑ Ⓒ Ⓓ
31. Ⓐ Ⓑ Ⓒ Ⓓ   32. Ⓐ Ⓑ Ⓒ Ⓓ   33. Ⓐ Ⓑ Ⓒ Ⓓ   34. Ⓐ Ⓑ Ⓒ Ⓓ   35. Ⓐ Ⓑ Ⓒ Ⓓ
36. Ⓐ Ⓑ Ⓒ Ⓓ   37. Ⓐ Ⓑ Ⓒ Ⓓ   38. Ⓐ Ⓑ Ⓒ Ⓓ   39. Ⓐ Ⓑ Ⓒ Ⓓ   40. Ⓐ Ⓑ Ⓒ Ⓓ
41. Ⓐ Ⓑ Ⓒ Ⓓ   42. Ⓐ Ⓑ Ⓒ Ⓓ   43. Ⓐ Ⓑ Ⓒ Ⓓ   44. Ⓐ Ⓑ Ⓒ Ⓓ   45. Ⓐ Ⓑ Ⓒ Ⓓ
46. Ⓐ Ⓑ Ⓒ Ⓓ   47. Ⓐ Ⓑ Ⓒ Ⓓ   48. Ⓐ Ⓑ Ⓒ Ⓓ   49. Ⓐ Ⓑ Ⓒ Ⓓ   50. Ⓐ Ⓑ Ⓒ Ⓓ

ANSWER SHEET

TEST 14

1. Ⓐ Ⓑ Ⓒ Ⓓ   2. Ⓐ Ⓑ Ⓒ Ⓓ   3. Ⓐ Ⓑ Ⓒ Ⓓ   4. Ⓐ Ⓑ Ⓒ Ⓓ   5. Ⓐ Ⓑ Ⓒ Ⓓ
6. Ⓐ Ⓑ Ⓒ Ⓓ   7. Ⓐ Ⓑ Ⓒ Ⓓ   8. Ⓐ Ⓑ Ⓒ Ⓓ   9. Ⓐ Ⓑ Ⓒ Ⓓ   10. Ⓐ Ⓑ Ⓒ Ⓓ
11. Ⓐ Ⓑ Ⓒ Ⓓ   12. Ⓐ Ⓑ Ⓒ Ⓓ   13. Ⓐ Ⓑ Ⓒ Ⓓ   14. Ⓐ Ⓑ Ⓒ Ⓓ   15. Ⓐ Ⓑ Ⓒ Ⓓ
16. Ⓐ Ⓑ Ⓒ Ⓓ   17. Ⓐ Ⓑ Ⓒ Ⓓ   18. Ⓐ Ⓑ Ⓒ Ⓓ   19. Ⓐ Ⓑ Ⓒ Ⓓ   20. Ⓐ Ⓑ Ⓒ Ⓓ
21. Ⓐ Ⓑ Ⓒ Ⓓ   22. Ⓐ Ⓑ Ⓒ Ⓓ   23. Ⓐ Ⓑ Ⓒ Ⓓ   24. Ⓐ Ⓑ Ⓒ Ⓓ   25. Ⓐ Ⓑ Ⓒ Ⓓ
26. Ⓐ Ⓑ Ⓒ Ⓓ   27. Ⓐ Ⓑ Ⓒ Ⓓ   28. Ⓐ Ⓑ Ⓒ Ⓓ   29. Ⓐ Ⓑ Ⓒ Ⓓ   30. Ⓐ Ⓑ Ⓒ Ⓓ
31. Ⓐ Ⓑ Ⓒ Ⓓ   32. Ⓐ Ⓑ Ⓒ Ⓓ   33. Ⓐ Ⓑ Ⓒ Ⓓ   34. Ⓐ Ⓑ Ⓒ Ⓓ   35. Ⓐ Ⓑ Ⓒ Ⓓ
36. Ⓐ Ⓑ Ⓒ Ⓓ   37. Ⓐ Ⓑ Ⓒ Ⓓ   38. Ⓐ Ⓑ Ⓒ Ⓓ   39. Ⓐ Ⓑ Ⓒ Ⓓ   40. Ⓐ Ⓑ Ⓒ Ⓓ
41. Ⓐ Ⓑ Ⓒ Ⓓ   42. Ⓐ Ⓑ Ⓒ Ⓓ   43. Ⓐ Ⓑ Ⓒ Ⓓ   44. Ⓐ Ⓑ Ⓒ Ⓓ   45. Ⓐ Ⓑ Ⓒ Ⓓ
46. Ⓐ Ⓑ Ⓒ Ⓓ   47. Ⓐ Ⓑ Ⓒ Ⓓ   48. Ⓐ Ⓑ Ⓒ Ⓓ   49. Ⓐ Ⓑ Ⓒ Ⓓ   50. Ⓐ Ⓑ Ⓒ Ⓓ

SUGGESTED READING

The following is a list of reference books that can help expand your general knowledge in each of the fifteen categories tested. It is not intended as a complete compendium of available books on the subject but instead offers a basic collection of introductory volumes that are available in most public libraries and bookstores.

TEST 1: AMERICAN HISTORY

Adler, Mortimer, ed. *The Annals of America.* Chicago: Encyclopaedia Britannica, Inc., 1986. A nineteen-volume history of the United States from 1492 to 1986.

Andrews, Charles M. *The Colonial Period of American History.* New Haven: Yale University Press, 1964. A four-volume Pulitzer Prize–winning history of colonial America.

Foner, Philip. *The History of Black Americans: From Africa to the Emergence of the Cotton Kingdom (Contributions in American History).* Westport, CT: Greenwood Press, 1975. A history of the roles of blacks in America from their roots in Africa to the Civil War.

Leitch, Barbara, ed. *A Concise Dictionary of Indian Tribes of North America.* Algonac, MI: Reference Publications, 2003. Descriptions of Indian tribes from the Inuit in the North to the Tonkawa in the South.

Morris, Richard, ed. *Encyclopedia of American History.* New York: HarperCollins, 1996. Alphabetized entries on the history of the United States.

Peirce, Neal R., and Hagstrom, Jerry. *The Book of America: Inside Fifty States.* New York: W. W. Norton, 1984. Descriptions of states' characters and histories.

TEST 2: WORLD HISTORY

Alpher, Joseph, ed. *Encyclopedia of Jewish History.* New York: Facts on File, 1987. Jewish history from biblical times to the present.

The Cambridge Ancient History. Cambridge, England: Cambridge University Press. A twelve-volume history of the ancient world from prehistory to the Roman Empire.

Cary, M., ed. *The Oxford Classical Dictionary.* London: Oxford University Press, Inc., 1996. A dictionary of classical names, places, and terms.

Dunan, Marcel, ed. *The Larousse Encyclopedia of Modern History.* New York: Crown Publishing Group, 1987. A history of the world from 1500 to the twentieth century.

Durant, Will, and Durant, Ariel. *The Story of Civilization.* New York: Fine Communications, 1997. A history of the world from Egyptian civilization to the age of Napoleon.

Fossier, Robert, ed. *The Cambridge Illustrated History of the Middle Ages.* Cambridge, England: Cambridge University Press, 1986. A three-volume, lavishly illustrated history of Western Europe and Byzantium from 350 to 1520.

Gron, Bernard, ed. *The Timetables of History.* New York: Touchstone Books, 1991. Includes time lines that link people and events through history.

Holt, P. M., ed. *The Cambridge History of Islam.* Cambridge, England: Cambridge University Press, 1980. A two-volume history of the Islamic world.

Tuchman, Barbara. *The March of Folly.* New York: Random House, Inc., 1985. Records the pursuits of governments that have been contrary to their own best interests.

TEST 3: CIVICS

Corwin, Edward S., ed. *The Constitution and What It Means Today.* Princeton, NJ: Princeton University Press, 1990. An explanation of Constitutional imperatives and cases that challenge and define the Constitution.

De Conde, Alexander, ed. *Encyclopedia of American Foreign Policy.* New York: Charles Scribner's Publishing, 2001. Essays exploring themes and doctrines of American foreign policy.

Elliott, Stephen, ed. *A Reference Guide to the United States Supreme Court.* New York: Facts on File, 1986. A concise description of the role of the Supreme Court.

Safire, William. *Safire's Political Dictionary.* New York: Ballantine Books, 1987. A dictionary of political terms.

Schlesinger, Arthur M., Jr., ed. *History of American Presidential Elections, 1789–1984.* New York: Chelsea House Publications, 1986. Descriptions of and speeches from presidential elections to Reagan's second term.

Stineman, Esther. *American Political Women.* Littleton, CO: Libraries Unlimited, 1980. Biographical sketches of women in politics, including Bella Abzug, Barbara Jordan, and Geraldine Ferraro.

TEST 4: GEOGRAPHY

The International Geographic Encyclopedia and Atlas. Boston: Houghton Mifflin, 1979. Entries on locations from Aachen to Zyradow, plus maps and charts.

Kurian, George. *Encyclopedia of the Third World.* New York: Facts on File, 1992. Maps, facts, and figures on third world countries.

Paxton, John. *The Statesman's Year-Book World Gazetteer.* New York: St. Martin's Press, 1991. Details on places of world importance as well as definitions of geographic terms.

Rand McNally Quick Reference World Atlas. Chicago: Rand McNally, 1995. Includes city and country maps of the world.

TEST 5: ART AND ARCHITECTURE

Berenson, Bernard. *Italian Painters of the Renaissance.* New York: Cornell University Press, 1990. Illustrated volume of biographical information on painters from Cimabue to Tiepolo.

Brown, Milton. *American Art.* New Jersey: Prentice Hall Professional Technical Reference, 1990. Description and reproductions of American art.

Encyclopedia of World Art. New York: McGraw-Hill, 1965. Sixteen-volume compendium of art of the world.

Kleiner, Fred, ed. *Gardner's Art through the Ages.* New

York: Wadsworth Publishing Co., 2000. An informative survey of art from prehistory through the present.

Newhall, Beaumont. *The History of Photography.* New York: Museum of Modern Art, 1982. Illustrated volume of the works of photographers.

Roud, Richard, ed. *Cinema: A Critical Dictionary.* New York: The Viking Press, 1980. A two-volume book of articles on the great filmmakers, illustrated with stills from movies.

Trachenberg, Marvin, and Hyman, Isabelle. *Architecture from Prehistory to Post-Modernism.* New York: Pearson, 2001. A study of architecture with over 1,000 illustrations.

TEST 6: MUSIC

Abraham, Gerald, ed. *The New Oxford History of Music.* Oxford: Oxford University Press, 1974. A ten-volume history of world music from ancient to modern times.

Ammer, Christine. *The Harper Dictionary of Music.* New York: Harper Resource, 1991. Entries on terms, composers, works, and instruments.

Arnold, Denis, ed. *The New Oxford Companion to Music.* Oxford: Oxford University Press, 1983. A two-volume reference guide of 6,600 articles on composers, works, instruments, history, and terms.

Kinkle, Roger. *The Complete Encyclopedia of Popular Music and Jazz.* New Rochelle, NY: Crown Publishing, 1982. A four-volume guide to musicals, songs, performers, recordings, and broadcasts from 1900 to the 1970s.

May, Elizabeth, ed. *Musics of Many Cultures*. Berkeley, CA: University of California Press, 1980. Descriptions of music from China, India, Japan, Bali, Australia, Africa, South America, and other places.

Osborne, Charles. *The Dictionary of the Opera*. New York: Welcome Rain, 2001. Includes over 2,000 entries on composers, singers, conductors, and librettists.

Schonberg, Harold C. *Lives of the Great Composers*. New York: W. W. Norton, 1997. Biographical details of composers from Monteverdi to Schoenberg.

TEST 7: MYTH AND RELIGION

Achtemeier, Paul J., ed. *Harper's Bible Dictionary*. San Francisco: Harper & Row, 1996. Entries on all important names, places, and subjects in the Bible.

Bulfinch, Thomas. *Bulfinch's Mythology*. New York: Quiet Vision Publishing, 1999. The texts of well-known myths and legends by a nineteenth-century expert.

Burland, Cottie. *Mythology of the Americas*. London: The Hamlyn Publishing Group, 1970. The myths of North American Indians; Eskimos; Mexican, Central American, and South American Indians.

Graves, Robert. *The Greek Myths*. Harmondsworth, England: Carcanet Press Ltd., 2001. A two-volume collection of myths from the creation through Odysseus' homecoming.

Livingstone, Elizabeth, ed. *Concise Oxford Dictionary of the Christian Church*. Oxford: Oxford University Press, 2000. Emphasis on the Bible and the history of the Christian church.

Werblowsky, R. J. Zwei, ed. *The Encyclopedia of the*

Jewish Religion. New York: Lambda Publishers, Inc., 1990. A comprehensive volume on all aspects of the Jewish tradition.

TEST 8: QUOTES, PHRASES, AND APHORISMS

Auden, W. H. *The Viking Book of Aphorisms.* New York: Barnes & Noble Books, 1988. Pithy quotes and sayings covering many topics.

Bartlett, John. *Bartlett's Familiar Quotations.* Boston: Little, Brown, and Company, 2002. The well-known book of world quotations.

Mieder, Wolfgang, ed. *The Prentice-Hall Encyclopedia of World Proverbs.* Englewood Cliffs, NJ: Fine Communications, 1996. The sources of proverbs from many languages and cultures.

The Oxford Dictionary of Quotations. Oxford: Oxford University Press, Inc., 1999. Quotes from around the world and their sources.

TEST 9: AMERICAN LITERATURE

Barksdale, Richard. *Black Writers of America.* New York: Prentice Hall Professional Technical Reference, 1990. An anthology of black literature from the eighteenth century to the present.

Baym, Nina, ed. *The Norton Anthology of American Literature.* New York: W. W. Norton and Co., March 2003. A two-volume collection of works by American writers such as Walt Whitman, Henry Thoreau, Mark Twain, Henry James, William Faulkner, and others.

Bloom, Harold, ed. *American Fiction,* 1914–1945. New

York: Chelsea House Publishers, 1996. Essays by scholars on writers from World War I to World War II.

Bordman, Gerald. *The Oxford Companion to American Theatre*. New York: Oxford University Press, 1992. Includes 3,000 entries on productions, playwrights, trends, and movements in American theater.

Elliott, Emory, ed. *The Columbia Literary History of the United States*. New York: Columbia University Press, 1991. A one-volume survey of American literary history by eminent critics.

Ellman, Richard, ed. *The New Oxford Book of American Verse*. New York: Oxford University Press, 1976. A collection of 300 years of American poetry.

Faust, Langdon L. *American Women Writers*. New York: Frederick Ungar, 1988. A two-volume reference work of biographies and criticism of works from colonial times to the present.

Hart, James, ed. *The Oxford Companion to American Literature*. Oxford: Oxford University Press, 1995. A compact volume of 2,000 entries on authors, works, and movements.

Herzberg, Max J., ed. *Reader's Encyclopedia of American Literature*. New York: Harper Collins Children's Books, 1962. A comprehensive reference book with information on authors, titles, characters, and literary movements.

TEST 10: WORLD LITERATURE

Allison, Alexander W., ed. *The Norton Anthology of Poetry*. New York: W. W. Norton and Co., 1996. An anthology of poetry in the English language, from Chaucer to the present.

Bain, Carl E., ed. *The Norton Introduction to Literature*. New York: W. W. Norton and Co., 1995. Uses literature to discuss plot, character, genre, theme, tone, figurative language, and more.

Benét, William Rose. *Benét's Reader's Encyclopedia*. New York: HarperCollins, 1996. Includes articles on authors, characters, places, works, and movements.

Drabble, Margaret, ed. *The Oxford Companion to English Literature*. Oxford: Oxford University Press, 2000. Information on English-language authors and their works.

Garland, Henry, and Garland, Mary. *The Oxford Companion to German Literature*. Oxford: Oxford University Press, 1997. Discusses German literature by authors such as Goethe, Kleist, and Mann.

Gilbert, Sandra M., ed. *The Norton Anthology of Literature by Women*. New York: W. W. Norton and Co., 1996. Includes works by Mary Wollstonecraft, Jane Austen, the Brontës, Emily Dickinson, Flannery O'Connor, and others.

Lang, D. M., and Dudley, D. R., eds. *The Penguin Companion to Classical, Oriental, and African Literature*. New York: McGraw-Hill, 1969. Information on literature from Greece, Rome, Byzantium, Japan, China, Africa, and other places.

Russell, Bertrand. *A History of Western Philosophy*. New York: Simon & Schuster, 1976. An overview of philosophers from Plato through Rousseau and Locke to the moderns.

TEST 11: LIFE SCIENCE

Gamlin, Linda, ed. *The Evolution of Life*. Oxford: Oxford University Press, 1990. Clear text on how life evolved, including photographs and diagrams.

Holmes, Sandra. *Henderson's Dictionary of Biological Terms*. New York: Halsted Press, 1989. Definitions of terms used in botany, biology, anatomy, physiology, and more.

McFarland, David, ed. *The Oxford Companion to Animal Behavior*. Oxford: Oxford University Press, 1982. An explanation of animal behavior, arranged alphabetically.

Lewis, Richard J. *Hawley's Condensed Chemical Dictionary*. New York: John Wiley and Sons, Inc., 2002. An up-to-date dictionary of industrial chemicals, terms, processes, and reactions.

Whitfield, Philip, ed. *Macmillan Illustrated Animal Encyclopedia*. New York: Macmillan, 1984. An illustrated encyclopedia of thousands of animals and their conservation status, habits, and habitats.

TEST 12: PHYSICAL SCIENCE

Asimov, Isaac. *Asimov's Biographical Encyclopedia of Science and Technology*. Garden City, NY: Doubleday, 1982. 1,510 biographies of scientists from ancient times to the present, arranged chronologically.

Longman Illustrated Dictionary of Astronomy and Astronautics. Beirut: York Press, 1987. Basic principles of astronomy and astronautics are defined.

Menzel, Donald H. and F. Petersons. *A Field Guide to the Stars and Planets*. Boston: Houghton Mifflin, 1983.

Includes maps, charts, and descriptions of the stars and planets.

Parkinson, Claire. *Breakthroughs: A Chronology of Great Achievements in Science and Mathematics 1200–1930.* Boston: Macmillan Pub. Company Inc., 1985. A description of discoveries and theories from 1200 to 1930.

Rickard, Teresa. *Barnes & Noble Thesaurus of Physics.* New York: Harper Collins Publishing, 1983. Discusses concepts of atomic physics, mechanics, and energy.

Rinsberger, Boyce. *How the World Works: A Guide to Science's Greatest Discoveries.* New York: William Morrow, 1987. Alphabetical listings of terms, concepts, and scientists.

Whitten, D. G. A. *The Penguin Dictionary of Geology.* Harmondsworth, England: Penguin Books, 1986. Definitions of geological terms.

TEST 13: TECHNOLOGY

Bisacre, Michael, ed. *Illustrated Encyclopedia of Technology.* New York: Exeter Books, 1984. Includes consumer, building, transport, military, and space technology.

Desmond, Kevin. *A Timetable of Inventions and Discoveries.* New York: M. Evans, 1986. A chronological list of inventions with over 4,000 entries.

Douglas-Young, John. *Illustrated Encyclopedic Dictionary of Electronics.* Englewood Cliffs, NJ: Prentice-Hall, 1987. Illustrated dictionary with charts, tables, and information on how things work.

Godman, Arthur, ed. *Barnes & Noble Thesaurus of Science and Technology.* New York: Harper & Row,

1985. Entries on physical science, technology, and biological science.

Rand McNally Encyclopedia of Transportation. Chicago: Rand McNally, 1976. Covers all aspects of land, sea, and air transport.

The Way Things Work. New York: Simon & Schuster, 1971. A two-volume encyclopedia of technology with over 300 explanations of how things work.

TEST 14: MATHEMATICS AND ECONOMICS

Clough, Shepard B. *European Economic History.* New York: McGraw-Hill, 1975. Economic history from the ancient world to the present.

Currier, Chet. *The Investor's Encyclopedia.* New York: Franklin Watts, 1987. Reviews 66 savings and investment vehicles.

Downes, John, and Goodman, Jordan Elliot. *Barron's Finance and Investment Handbook.* New York: Barrons, 1998. An explanation of terms, annual reports, tax laws, and stock listings.

Gellert, W., ed. *The VNR Concise Encyclopedia of Mathematics.* New York: John Wiley and Sons, 1988. From traditional elementary math to contemporary mathematics, using examples.

Nelson, Charles R. *The Investor's Guide to Economic Indicators.* New York: John Wiley & Sons, 1989. Explanation of leading indicators, consumer price index, GNP, and other terms and their impacts.

Pearce, David W., ed. *The MIT Dictionary of Modern Economics.* Cambridge, MA: The MIT Press, 1992. 2,650 entries on economic theory, practice, concepts, and economists.

Rachlin, Harvey, ed. *The Money Encyclopedia*. New York: Harper Collins Publishing, 1984. A description of terms and concepts concerning money.

Rosenberg, Jerry M. *Dictionary of Banking and Finance*. New York: John Wiley & Sons, 1982. 10,000 terms defined.

Silk, Leonard. *Economics in Plain English*. New York: Simon & Schuster, 1986. An easy-to-follow guide to the basic concepts of economics.

West, Beverly. *The Prentice-Hall Encyclopedia of Mathematics*. Englewood Cliffs, NJ: Prentice-Hall, 1991. Information from algebra to zero, with puzzles, formulas, and tables.

PHOTO CREDITS

Page 125: Great Wall © Dallas and John Heaton/CORBIS; Page 126: *David* by Michelangelo © Michael S. Yamashita/ CORBIS; Page 127: Haida House with Frontal Pole, Negative No. 39991, Copy by Julius Kirschner, Courtesy Dept. Library Services, © American Museum of Natural History; Page 128: Colosseum in Rome © Vittoriano Rastelli/CORBIS; Page 129: Statue of *Venus de Milo* © Bettmann/CORBIS; Page 130: Façade of St. Peter's Basilica © CORBIS; Page 131: Detail of Third Gold Coffin of Tutankhamen © Gianni Dagli Orti/CORBIS; Page 132: Medieval Illustration from 15th Century Manuscript © Historical Picture Archive/CORBIS; Page 133: *Arrangement in Grey and Black No 1: The Artist's Mother* by James Abbott McNeill Whistler © Francis G. Mayer/CORBIS; Page 134: Exterior View of Daigoji Pagoda © Archive Icongrafico, S.A./CORBIS; Page 135: Detail of Hands from Creation by Adam by Michelangelo Buonarroti © World Films Enterprise/CORBIS; Page 136: *The Annunciation* by Fra Angelico © Archivo Iconografico, S.A./CORBIS; Page 137: *Pears and Peaches* by Paul Cézanne © The Barnes Foundation, Merion Station, Pennsylvania/CORBIS; Page 138: Façade of the Cathedral of Notre Dame © CORBIS; Page 139: Golden Gate Bridge © CORBIS; Page 140: Exterior of Taj Mahal and Reflecting Pool © CORBIS; Page 142: *The Thinker* by Auguste Rodin © Bettmann/CORBIS; Page 143: *Mona Lisa* by Leonardo da Vinci © Gianni Dagli Orti/CORBIS; Page 144: Stone Circle at Stonehenge © Bob Krist/CORBIS; Page 145: A Chokwe Mask, Mwana Pwo © Christie's Images/CORBIS; Page 146: *Selfportrait Before His Easel* Attributed to Vincent van Gogh © Francis G. Mayer/ CORBIS; Page 148: *Fields and Streams* by Thomas Doughty © Francis G. Mayer/CORBIS; Page 149: Dome of the U.S. Capitol © Alan Schein Photography/CORBIS.